A B...
A PROMISING NEW START

With expert readings and forecasts, you can chart a course to romance, adventure, good health, or career opportunities while gaining valuable insight into yourself and others. Offering a daily outlook for 18 full months, this fascinating guide shows you:

- The important dates in your life
- What to expect from an astrological reading
- How the stars can help you stay healthy and fit And more!

Let this sound advice guide you through a year of heavenly possibilities—for today and for every day of 2008!

SYDNEY OMARR'S® DAY-BY-DAY ASTROLOGICAL GUIDE FOR

ARIES—March 21–April 19
TAURUS—April 20–May 20
GEMINI—May 21–June 20
CANCER—June 21–July 22
LEO—July 23–August 22
VIRGO—August 23–September 22
LIBRA—September 23–October 22
SCORPIO—October 23–November 21
SAGITTARIUS—November 22–December 21
CAPRICORN—December 22–January 19
AQUARIUS—January 20–February 18
PISCES—February 19–March 20

IN 2008

SYDNEY OMARR'S®

DAY-BY-DAY ASTROLOGICAL GUIDE FOR

GEMINI

MAY 21–JUNE 20

2008

By Trish MacGregor
with Carol Tonsing

A SIGNET BOOK

SIGNET
Published by New American Library, a division of
Penguin Group (USA) Inc., 375 Hudson Street,
New York, New York 10014, USA
Penguin Group (Canada), 90 Eglinton Avenue East, Suite 700, Toronto,
Ontario M4P 2Y3, Canada (a division of Pearson Penguin Canada Inc.)
Penguin Books Ltd., 80 Strand, London WC2R 0RL, England
Penguin Ireland, 25 St. Stephen's Green, Dublin 2,
Ireland (a division of Penguin Books Ltd.)
Penguin Group (Australia), 250 Camberwell Road, Camberwell, Victoria 3124,
Australia (a division of Pearson Australia Group Pty. Ltd.)
Penguin Books India Pvt. Ltd., 11 Community Centre, Panchsheel Park,
New Delhi - 110 017, India
Penguin Group (NZ), 67 Apollo Drive, Rosedale, North Shore,
Auckland 1311, New Zealand (a division of Pearson New Zealand Ltd.)
Penguin Books (South Africa) (Pty.) Ltd., 24 Sturdee Avenue,
Rosebank, Johannesburg 2196, South Africa

Penguin Books Ltd., Registered Offices:
80 Strand, London WC2R 0RL, England

First published by Signet, an imprint of New American Library,
a division of Penguin Group (USA) Inc.

First Printing, June 2007
10 9 8 7 6 5 4 3 2 1

CONTENTS

INTRODUCTION

Put Astrology in Your Life

This year marks a time of transition as our personal universe opens up with possibilities we never imagined. Thanks to the Internet, we have a command-control center from which we can travel the globe at warp speed. We can meet friends and lovers in cyberspace, gather information from remote sources in moments, and manage the details of our daily lives online. But, as the saying goes, the more things change, the more they stay the same. In our personal lives, we are still searching for the same things that have always made life worth living: love, meaningful work, and fulfilling personal relationships.

Astrology is an age-old tool that can guide us in our search, one that works as well today as it has for several millennia. It can be a support system, career coach, and guide through difficult times. It can help you find your own strengths or assess your marketable talents to land the perfect job. Like links in the Internet, astrological clues can speed you from where you are now to where you'd like to be. But just like many of the newest high-tech laptops, there's a learning curve before you can use it to best advantage. It will take some practice and familiarity to operate effectively in your life. Fortunately a little knowledge can get you up and running quickly.

In this year's guide, we give you basic information to help you get hands-on with astrology. We tell you what you need to know about your sun sign and how to decipher the mysterious symbols on a horoscope chart. Then you can look up other planets in your horoscope to find out how each contributes to your total personality.

Many readers are fascinated by astrology's insights into

relationships. This leap year, find out who you're most likely to get along with and why, then how to attract the right sign. You'll see the celebrity combinations with your sign that made romantic history—and some that didn't.

Whether it's wealth-building advice, fashion tips, or help finding the perfect gift for a hard-to-please relative, astrology has something to say. Astrology can even guide you to the best place to take your vacation. For those who like to surf the Web, we recommend astrology-savvy sites where you can get your chart calculated free. Connecting with other astrology fans is a breeze with the reputable conferences, clubs, and even an accredited college that we list.

There are so many ways to put astrology into your life. Redecorating your home? Follow your sun sign's colors and styles to create the perfect environment. Share your birthday with a celebrity. Design a fitness program according to your sign's preferences.

So here are the year's picks and predictions, along with eighteen months of on-target daily horoscopes to make 2008 your best year ever.

CHAPTER 1

It's A Year of Change: What This Means for You

Astrologers judge the trends of a year by following the slow-moving planets, from Jupiter through Pluto. A change in sign indicates a new cycle, with new emphasis. The farthest planets (Uranus, Neptune, and Pluto), which stay in a sign for at least seven years, cause a very significant change in the atmosphere when they change signs. Shifts in Jupiter, which changes every year, and Saturn, which changes every two years, are more obvious in current events and daily lives. Jupiter generally brings a fortunate, expansive emphasis to its new sign, while Saturn's two-year cycle is a reality check, bringing tests of maturity, discipline, and responsibility.

Does Pluto Still Count?

At this writing, astronomers have demoted tiny Pluto from being a full-fledged planet to a dwarf planet, outranked by its celestial siblings. However, astrologers have been tracking its influence since Pluto was discovered in 1930 and have witnessed that this minuscule celestial body has a powerful effect on both a personal and a global level. So Pluto, which moves into the sign of Capricorn this year, will still be called a planet by astrologers and will be given just as much importance as before.

3

Capricorn Is the Sign to Watch

This year, we will be moving from a fire-sign emphasis to an earth-sign emphasis as Jupiter, Saturn, and Pluto all take up residence in earth signs. Until January 2008, Pluto had been emphasizing everything associated with Sagittarius to prepare us philosphically and spiriturally for things to come. Perhaps the most pervasive sign of Pluto in Sagittarius over the past few years has been globalization in all its forms, re-forming boundaries, creating new forms of travel, interacting with exotic cultures and religions as never before.

As it passed through truth-telling Sagittarius, Pluto shifted our emphasis away from acquiring wealth to a quest for the meaning of it all, as upward strivers discover that money and power are not enough and religious extremists assert themselves. We search the cosmos for something to believe in when many lies and scandals are exposed to public view, exposing leaders in the corporate, political, and religious domains. When ideals and idols are shattered, it becomes time to reevaluate our goals and ask ourselves what is really important in our lives.

Sagittarius is the sign of linking everything together; therefore, the trend has been to find ways to interconnect on spiritual, philosophical, and intellectual levels. The spiritual emphasis of Pluto in Sagittarius has filtered down to our home lives, as religion—and religious controversy—has entered local communities. Vast church complexes are being built to combine religious activities with sports centers, health clubs, malls, and theme parks. Religious education and book publishing have expanded as well.

Sagittarius is known for love of animals, especially horses. It's no surprise that horse racing has become popular again and that America has never been more pet happy. Look for extremes related to animal welfare, such as vegetarianism as a lifestyle. As habitats are destroyed, the care, feeding, and control of wild animals will become a larger issue, especially when deer, bears, and coyotes invade our backyard.

The Sagittarius love of the outdoors combined with

4

Pluto's power has already promoted extreme sports, especially those that require strong legs, like rock climbing, trekking, or snowboarding. Expect the trend toward more adventurous travel to continue, as well as fitness or sports-oriented vacations. Exotic hiking trips to unexplored territories, mountain-climbing expeditions, spa vacations, and sports-associated resorts are part of this trend.

Publishing, which is associated with Sagittarius, has been transformed by global conglomerates and the Internet. It is fascinating that the online bookstore Amazon.com took the Sagittarius-influenced name of the fierce female tribe of archer warriors.

Capricorn Brings Us Down to Earth

This year, both Pluto and Jupiter will meet in Capricorn, which marks a major shift in emphasis to Capricorn-related themes. Until 2024, Pluto will exert its influence in this practical, building, healing earth sign. Capricorn relates to structures, institutions, order, mountains and mountain countries, mineral rights, and issues involving the elderly and growing older—all of which will be emphasized in the coming years. It is the sign of established order, corporations, big business—all of which will be accented. Possibly, it will fall to business structures to create a new sense of order in the world.

Starting this year, you should feel the rumblings of change in the Capricorn area of your horoscope and in the world at large. The last time Pluto was in Capricorn was the years up to and during the American Revolutionary War. Therefore this should be an important time on the United States political scene, as well as a reflection of the aging and maturing of American society in general. Both the rise and fall of the Ottoman Empire happened under Pluto in Capricorn.

Jupiter in Capricorn

During the year that Jupiter remains in a sign, the fields associated with that sign are the ones that arouse excitement and enthusiasm, usually providing excellent opportunities for expansion, fame, and fortune.

One place we notice the Jupiter influence is in fashion, which should veer away from the flamboyance and sexuality of recent years to a more conservative look. Capricorn is concerned with quality, status, and prestige, and should elevate our collective taste level.

Those born under Capricorn should have many opportunities during the year. However, the key is to keep your feet on the ground. The flip side of Jupiter is that there are no limits. You can expand off the planet under a Jupiter transit, which is why the planet is often called the Gateway to Heaven. If something is going to burst (such as an artery) or overextend or go over the top in some way, it could happen under a supposedly lucky Jupiter transit. So beware.

Those born under Cancer may find their best opportunities working with partners this year, as Jupiter will be transiting their seventh house of relationships.

Saturn in Virgo: The Maturing of the Baby Boomers, Reforms in Care and Maintenance

Saturn, the planet of limitation, testing, and restriction, is now transiting Virgo. This is a time when Virgo issues—health care and maintenance and moral standards and controls—will come to the fore. For the next two years, we will be adjusting the structures of our lives, making changes so that we can function at an optimal efficient level. We'll be challenged with a reality check in areas where we have been too optimistic or expansive.

Continuing Trends

Uranus and Neptune continue to do a kind of astrological dance called a mutual reception. This is a supportive relationship where Uranus is in Pisces, the sign ruled by Neptune, while Neptune is in Aquarius, the sign ruled by Uranus. When this dance is over in 2011, it is likely that we will be living under very different political and social circumstances.

Uranus in Pisces

Uranus, known as the Great Awakener, tends to cause both upheaval and innovation in the sign it transits. During previous episodes of Uranus in Pisces, great religions and spiritual movements have come into being, most recently Mormonism and Christian Fundamentalism. In its most positive mode, Pisces promotes imagination and creativity, the art of illusion in theater and film, the inspiration of great artists. A water sign, Pisces is naturally associated with all things liquid—oceans, oil, alcohol—and with those creatures that live in the water—fish, the fishing industry, fish habitats, and fish farming. Currently there is a great debate going on about overfishing, contamination of fish, and fish farming. The underdog, the enslaved, and the disenfranchised should also benefit from Uranus in Pisces.

Since Uranus is a disruptive influence that aims to challenge the status quo, the forces of nature that manifest will most likely be in the Pisces area: oçeans, seas, and rivers. We have seen unprecedented rainy seasons, floods, mud slides, and disastrous hurricanes. Note that 2005's devastating Hurricane Katrina hit an area known for both the oil and fishing industries.

Pisces is associated with the prenatal phase of life, which is related to regenerative medicine. The controversy over embryonic stem cell research should continue to be debated. Petroleum issues, both in the oil-producing countries and offshore oil drilling, will come to a head. Uranus in

7

Pisces suggests that development of new hydroelectric sources may provide the power we need to continue our current power-thirsty lifestyle.

As in previous eras, there should continue to be a flourishing of the arts. We are seeing many new artistic forms developing now, such as computer-created actors and special effects. The sky's the limit on this influence.

Those who have problems with Uranus are those who resist change, so the key is to embrace the future.

Neptune in Aquarius

Neptune is a planet of imagination and creativity, but also of deception and illusion. Neptune is associated with hospitals, which have been the subject of much controversy. On the positive side, hospitals are acquiring cutting-edge technology. The atmosphere of many hospitals is already changing from the intimidating and sterile environment of the past to that of a health-promoting spa. Alternative therapies, such as massage, diet counseling, and aromatherapy, are becoming commonplace, which expresses this Neptune trend. New procedures in plastic surgery, also a Neptune glamour field, and anti-aging therapies are restoring the illusion of youth.

However, issues involving the expense and quality of health care and the evolving relationship between doctors, drug companies, and HMOs reflect a darker side of this trend.

What About the New Planets?

Our solar system is very crowded; astronomers continue to discover new objects circling the sun. In addition to the familiar planets, there are dwarf planets, comets, cometoids, asteroids, and strange icy bodies in the Kuiper Belt beyond Neptune. The newest object at this writing is a planetlike orb slightly larger than Pluto, discovered in 2005, which was tentatively named Xena, after the TV series heroine. Recently this dwarf planet was christened with a permanent name by its dicoverer, Dr. Michael E. Brown of the California Institute of Technology. He dubbed the new planet Eris, after a goddess of discord and strife. In mythology, Eris was a troublemaker who made men think their opinions were right and others wrong. What an appropriate name for a planet discovered during a time of discord in the Middle East and elsewhere! Eris has a companion moon named Dysnomia for her daughter, described as a demon spirit of lawlessness. With mythological associations like these, we wonder what the effect of this mother-daughter duo will be. Once Eris's orbit is established, astrologers will track the impact of this planet on our horoscopes. Eris takes about 560 years to orbit the sun, which means its emphasis in a given astrological sign will affect several generations.

CHAPTER 2

Put Time on Your Side

"Do not squander time, for that is the stuff that life is made of," said Benjamin Franklin, our practical Founding Father. Yet many times your best-laid plans run amuck, your schedule is upset by sudden events, or your projects stall. On the other hand, there are days when projects get done effortlessly, people respond to you favorably, and perhaps you have some extra sex appeal.

Astrology offers many explanations why this might happen. For instance, when mischievous Mercury creates havoc with communications, it's time to back up your vital computer files, read between the lines of contracts, and be extra patient with coworkers. When Venus passes through your sign you've got extra sex appeal, time to try a knockout new outfit or hairstyle, and the nerve to ask someone you'd like to know better to dinner. Venus timing can also help you charm clients with a stunning sales pitch or make an offer they won't refuse.

In this chapter, you will learn how to manage your time by working with natural astrological cycles. You can find your best times to do specific projects as well as which times to avoid them. You will also learn how to read the moods of the moon and make them work for you. Use the information in this chapter and the planet tables in this book and also use the moon sign listings in your daily forecasts.

Here are the happenings to note on your agenda:

- Dates of your sun sign (high-energy period)
- The month previous to your sun sign (low-energy period)

- Dates of planets in your sign this year
- Full and new moons (Pay special attention when these fall in your sun sign!)
- Eclipses
- Moon in your sun sign every month, as well as moon in the opposite sign (listed in daily forecast)
- Mercury retrogrades
- Other retrograde periods

Your High-Power Time

Every birthday starts off a new cycle of solar energy for you. You should feel a new surge of vitality as the powerful sun enters your sign. This is the time when predominant energies are most favorable to you. So go for it! Start new projects, make your big moves (especially when the new moon is in your sign, doubling your charisma). You'll get the recognition you deserve now, when everyone is attuned to your sun sign. Look in the tables in this book to see if other planets will also be passing through your sun sign at this time. Venus (love, beauty), Mars (energy, drive), and Mercury (communication, mental sharpness) reinforce the sun and give an extra boost to your life in the areas they affect. Venus will rev up your social and love life, making you seem especially attractive. Mars amplifies your energy and drive. Mercury fuels your brainpower and helps you communicate. Jupiter signals an especially lucky period of expansion.

There are two downtimes related to the sun. During the month before your birthday period, when you are winding up your annual cycle, you could be feeling especially vulnerable and depleted. So at that time get extra rest, watch your diet, and take it easy. Don't overstress yourself. Use this time to gear up for a big "push" when the sun enters your sign.

Another downtime is when the sun is in a sign opposite your sun sign (six months from your birthday). That's when the prevailing energies are very different from yours. You may feel at odds with the world. You'll have to work harder for recognition because people are not on your wavelength. However, this could be a good time to work on a team, in cooperation with others, or behind the scenes.

Plan Your Day with the Moon

The moon is a powerful tool to divine the mood of the moment. You can work with the moon in two ways. Plan by the *sign* the moon is in; plan by the *phase* of the moon. The sign will tell you the kind of activities that suit the moon's mood. The phase will tell you the best time to start or finish a certain activity.

Working with the phases of the moon is as easy as looking up at the night sky. During the new moon, when both the sun and moon are in the same sign, begin new ventures—especially activities that are favored by that sign. Then you'll utilize the powerful energies pulling you in the same direction. You'll be focused outward, toward action, and in a doing mode. Postpone breaking off, terminating, deliberating, or reflecting—activities that require introspection and passive work. These are better suited to a later moon phase.

Get your project under way during the first quarter. Then go public at the full moon, a time of high intensity, when feelings come out into the open. This is your time to shine—to express yourself. Be aware, however, that because pressures are being released, other people will also be letting off steam. Since confrontations are possible, take advantage of this time either to air grievances or to avoid arguments.

About three days after the full moon comes the disseminating phase, a time when the energy of the cycle begins to wind down. From the last quarter of the moon to the next new moon, it's a time to cut off unproductive relationships, do serious thinking, and focus on inward-directed activities.

You'll feel some new and full moons more strongly than others, especially those new moons that fall in your sun sign and full moons in your opposite sign. Because that full moon happens at your low-energy time of year, it is likely to be an especially stressful time in a relationship, when any hidden problems or unexpressed emotions could surface.

Full and New Moons in 2008

All dates are calculated for eastern standard time and eastern daylight time.

New Moon—January 8 in Capricorn
Full Moon—January 22 in Leo

New Moon—February 6 in Aquarius (solar eclipse)
Full Moon—February 20 in Virgo (lunar eclipse)

New Moon—March 7 in Pisces
Full Moon—March 21 in Libra

New Moon—April 5 in Aries
Full Moon—April 20 in Scorpio

New Moon—May 5 in Taurus
Full Moon—May 19 in Scorpio (second full moon in Scorpio)

New Moon—June 3 in Gemini
Full Moon—June 18 in Sagittarius

New Moon—July 2 in Cancer
Full Moon—July 18 in Capricorn

New Moon—August 1 in Leo (solar eclipse)
Full Moon—August 16 in Aquarius (lunar eclipse)
New Moon—August 30 in Virgo

Full Moon—September 15 in Pisces
New Moon—September 29 in Libra

Full Moon—October 14 in Aries

New Moon—October 28 in Scorpio

Full Moon—November 13 in Taurus
New Moon—November 27 in Sagittarius

New Moon—December 12 in Gemini
Full Moon—December 27 in Capricorn

How to Schedule Activities by the Moon Sign

To forecast the daily emotional "weather," to determine your monthly high and low days, or to synchronize your activities with the cycles of the moon, take note of the moon sign under your daily forecast at the end of the book. Here are some of the activities favored and the moods you are likely to encounter under each moon sign.

Moon in Aries: Get Moving!

The new moon in Aries is an ideal time to start new projects. Everyone is pushy, raring to go, rather impatient, and short-tempered. Leave details and follow-up for later. Competitive sports or martial arts are great ways to let off steam. Quiet types could use some assertiveness, but it's a great day for dynamos. Be careful not to step on too many toes.

Moon in Taurus: Lay the Foundations for Success

Do solid, methodical tasks like follow-through or backup work. Make investments, buy real estate, do appraisals, do some hard bargaining. Attend to your property. Get out in the country or spend some time in your garden. Enjoy creature comforts, music, a good dinner, sensual lovemaking. Forget starting a diet—this is a day when you'll feel self-indulgent.

14

Moon in Gemini: Communicate

Talk means action today. Telephone, write letters, fax! Make new contacts, stay in touch with steady customers. You can juggle lots of tasks today. It's a great time for mental activity of any kind. Don't try to pin people down—they, too, are feeling restless. Keep it light. Flirtations and socializing are good. Watch gossip—and don't give away secrets.

Moon in Cancer: Pay Attention to Loved Ones

This is a moody, sensitive, emotional time. People respond to personal attention, to mothering. Stay at home, have a family dinner, call your mother. Nostalgia, memories, and psychic powers are heightened. You'll want to hang on to people and things (don't clean out your closets now). You could have shrewd insights into what others really need and want. Pay attention to dreams, intuition, and gut reactions.

Moon in Leo: Be Confident

Everybody is in a much more confident, warm, generous mood. It's a good day to ask for a raise, show what you can do, dress like a star. People will respond to flattery, enjoy a bit of drama and theater. You may be extravagant, treat yourself royally, and show off a bit—but don't break the bank! Be careful you don't promise more than you can deliver.

Moon in Virgo: Be Practical

Do practical down-to-earth chores. Review your budget, make repairs, be an efficiency expert. Not a day to ask for a raise. Tend to personal care and maintenance. Have a health checkup, go on a diet, buy vitamins or health food. Make your home spotless. Take care of details and piled-up chores. Reorganize your work and life so they run more smoothly and efficiently. Save money. Be prepared for others to be in a critical, faultfinding mood.

Moon in Libra: Be Diplomatic

Attend to legal matters. Negotiate contracts. Arbitrate. Do things with your favorite partner. Socialize. Be romantic. Buy a special gift, a beautiful object. Decorate yourself or your surroundings. Buy new clothes. Throw a party. Have an elegant, romantic evening. Smooth over any ruffled feathers. Avoid confrontations. Stick to civilized discussions.

Moon in Scorpio: Solve Problems

This is a day to do things with passion. You'll have excellent concentration and focus. Try not to get too intense emotionally. Avoid sharp exchanges with loved ones. Others may tend to go to extremes, get jealous, overreact. Great for troubleshooting, problem solving, research, scientific work—and making love. Pay attention to those psychic vibes.

Moon in Sagittarius: Sell and Motivate

A great time for travel, philosophical discussions, setting long-range career goals. Work out, do sports, buy athletic equipment. Others will be feeling upbeat, exuberant, and adventurous. Risk taking is favored. You may feel like taking a gamble, betting on the horses, visiting a local casino, buying a lottery ticket. Teaching, writing, and spiritual activities also get the green light. Relax outdoors. Take care of animals.

Moon in Capricorn: Get Organized

You can accomplish a lot now, so get on the ball! Attend to business. Issues concerning your basic responsibilities, duties, family, and elderly parents could crop up. You'll be expected to deliver on promises. Weed out the deadwood from your life. Get a dental checkup. Not a good day for gambling or taking risks.

Moon in Aquarius: Join the Group

A great day for doing things with groups—clubs, meetings, outings, politics, parties. Campaign for your candidate. Work for a worthy cause. Deal with larger issues that affect humanity—the environment and metaphysical questions. Buy a computer or electronic gadget. Watch TV. Wear something outrageous. Try something you've never done before. Present an original idea. Don't stick to a rigid schedule—go with the flow. Take a class in meditation, mind control, yoga.

Moon in Pisces: Be Creative

This can be a very creative day, so let your imagination work overtime. Film, theater, music, ballet could inspire you. Spend some time alone, resting and reflecting, reading or writing poetry. Daydreams can also be profitable. Help those less fortunate. Lend a listening ear to someone who may be feeling blue. Don't overindulge in self-pity or escapism, however. People are especially vulnerable to substance abuse now. Turn your thoughts to romance and someone special.

Retrogrades: When the Planets Seem to Backstep

All the planets, except for the sun and moon, have times when they appear to move backward—or retrograde—as it seems from our point of view on earth. At these times, planets do not work as they normally do. So it's best to "take a break" from that planet's energies in our life and to do some work on an inner level.

Mercury Retrograde: The Key Is in "Re"

Mercury goes retrograde most often, and its effects can be especially irritating. When it reaches a short distance ahead of the sun several times a year, it seems to move backward from our point of view. Astrologers often compare retrograde motion to the optical illusion that occurs when we ride on a train that passes another train traveling at a different speed—the second train appears to be moving in reverse.

What this means to you is that the Mercury-ruled areas of your life—analytical thought processes, communications, scheduling—are subject to all kinds of confusion. Be prepared. Communications equipment can break down. Schedules may be changed on short notice. People are late for appointments or don't show up at all. Traffic is terrible. Major purchases malfunction, don't work out, or get delivered in the wrong color. Letters don't arrive or are delivered to the wrong address. Employees will make errors that have to be corrected later. Contracts don't work out or must be renegotiated.

Since most of us can't put our lives on "hold" during Mercury retrogrades, we should learn to tame the trickster and make it work for us. The key is in the prefix *re-*. This is the time to go back over things in your life, *re*flect on what you've done during the previous months. Now you can get deeper insights, spot errors you've missed. So take time to *re*view and *re*evaluate what has happened. *Re*st and *re*ward yourself—it's a good time to take a vacation, especially if you *re*visit a favorite place. *Re*organize your work and finish up projects that are backed up. Clean out your desk and closets. Throw away what you can't *re*cycle. If you must sign contracts or agreements, do so with a contingency clause that lets you *re*evaluate the terms later.

Postpone major purchases or commitments for the time being. Don't get married (unless you're *re*marrying the same person). Try not to *re*ly on other people keeping appointments, contracts, or agreements to the letter; have several alternatives. Double-check and *re*ad between the lines.

18

Don't buy anything connected with communications or transportation (if you must, be sure to cover yourself).

Mercury retrograding through your sun sign will intensify its effect on your life.

If Mercury was retrograde when you were born, you may be one of the lucky people who don't suffer the frustrations of this period. If so, your mind probably works in a very intuitive, insightful way.

The sign in which Mercury is retrograding can give you an idea of what's in store—as well as the sun signs that will be especially challenged.

Mercury Retrogrades in 2008

Mercury has three retrograde periods, which fall in the air signs (Aquarius, Gemini, Libra) this year. This means it will be especially important to watch all activities which involve mental processes and communication.

January 28 to February 18 in Aquarius
May 26 to June 19 in Gemini
September 24 to October 15 in Libra

Venus Retrograde: Relationships Move Backward

Retrograding Venus can cause your relationships to take a backward step, or it can make you extravagant and impractical. Shopping till you drop and buying what you cannot afford are problems at this time. It's *not* a good time to redecorate—you'll hate the color of the walls later. Postpone getting a new hairstyle. Try not to fall in love either. But if you wish to make amends in an already troubled relationship, make peaceful overtures at this time.

Venus Retrogrades in 2008

There are no Venus retrograde periods in 2008.

Use the Go Power of Mars

Mars shows how and when to get where you want to go. Timing your moves with Mars on your side can give you a big push. On the other hand, pushing Mars the wrong way can guarantee that you'll run into frustrations in every corner. Your best times to forge ahead are during the weeks when Mars is traveling through your sun sign or your Mars sign (look these up in the tables in this book). Also consider times when Mars is in a compatible sign (fire with air signs, or earth with water signs). You'll be sure to have planetary power on your side.

Mars Retrogrades in 2008

Mars is retrograde in Gemini until January 30, 2008.

When Other Planets Retrograde

The slower-moving planets stay retrograde for months at a time (Jupiter, Saturn, Neptune, Uranus, and Pluto).

When Saturn is retrograde, it's an uphill battle with self-discipline. You may not be in the mood for work. You may feel more like hanging out at the beach than getting things done.

Neptune retrograde promotes a dreamy escapism from reality, when you may feel you're in a fog (Pisces will feel this, especially).

Uranus retrograde may mean setbacks in areas where there have been sudden changes, when you may be forced to regroup or reevaluate the situation.

Pluto retrograde is a time to work on establishing proportion and balance in areas where there have been recent dramatic transformations.

When the planets move forward again, there's a shift in the atmosphere. Activities connected with each planet start moving ahead, plans that were stalled get rolling. Make a special note of those days on your calendar and proceed accordingly.

Other Retrogrades in 2008

The five slower-moving planets all go retrograde in 2008.

Jupiter retrogrades from May 9 to September 7 in Capricorn.

Saturn retrogrades from December 19, 2007, until May 2, 2008, in Virgo. It turns retrograde again on December 31.

Uranus retrogrades from June 26 to November 27 in Pisces.

Neptune retrogrades from May 26 to November 1 in Aquarius.

Pluto turns retrograde from April 2 in Capricorn, then returns to Sagittarius on June 13. It turns direct in Sagittarius on September 8 and reenters Capricorn on November 26.

CHAPTER 3

Planetary Shake-Ups This Year

When the planetary weather is stormy, it's best to be prepared. Fortunately we can predict certain times when there are more likely to be shake-ups in your world, such as eclipses and Saturn transits, two events that could slow you down or make you change direction. With some basic astrological knowledge, you can find out where these events are likely to impact your life and what to expect when they happen.

Eclipses Clear the Air

Eclipses can bring on milestones in your life, if they aspect a key point in your horoscope. In general, they shake up the status quo, bringing hidden areas out into the open. During this time, problems you've been avoiding or have brushed aside can surface to demand your attention. A good coping strategy is to accept whatever comes up as a challenge that could make a positive difference in your life. And don't forget the power of your sense of humor. If you can laugh at something, you'll never be afraid of it.

What Is the Best Thing to Do During an Eclipse?

When the natural rhythms of the sun and moon are disturbed, it's best to postpone important activities. Be sure to mark eclipse days on your calendar, especially if the eclipse falls in your birth sign. This year, those born under Aquarius, Leo, and Virgo should take special note of the feelings that arise. With lunar eclipses, some possibilities could be a break from attachments or the healing of an illness or substance abuse, which had been triggered by the subconscious. The temporary event could be a healing time, when you gain perspective. During solar eclipses, when you might be in a highly subjective state, pay attention to the hidden subconscious patterns that surface, the emotional truth that is revealed at this time.

The effect of the eclipse can reverberate for some time, often months after the event. But it is especially important to stay cool and make no major moves during the period known as the shadow of the eclipse, which begins about a week before and lasts until at least three days after the eclipse. After three days, the daily rhythms should return to normal, and you can proceed with business as usual.

This Year's Eclipse Dates

February 6: Solar eclipse in Aquarius
February 20: Lunar eclipse in Virgo
August 1: Solar eclipse in Leo
August 16: Lunar eclipse in Aquarius

Saturn Gives You a Reality Check

When Saturn hits a critical point in your horoscope, you can count on an experience that will make you slow up, pull back, and reexamine your life. It is a call to eliminate what is not working, to shape up, to set priorities, to examine the boundaries and structures in your life (or lack of them) and set new ones. During this process, you may feel restricted, frustrated, or inhibited—not a fun time, but one that will serve you well in the long run. You may need to take on more responsibilities that will test your limits.

By the end of its twenty-eight-year trip around the zodiac, Saturn will have tested you in all areas of your life. The major tests happen in seven-year cycles, when Saturn passes over the angles of your chart, which means your rising sign, the top of your chart or midheaven, your descendant, and the nadir or bottom of your chart. This is when the real life-changing experiences happen. But you are also in for a testing period whenever Saturn passes a planet in your chart or stresses that planet from a distance. It is useful to check your planetary positions with the timetable of Saturn or prepare in advance, or at least to brace yourself.

When Saturn returns to its location at the time of your birth, at approximately age twenty-eight, you'll have your first Saturn return. At this time, a person usually takes stock or settles down to find his mission in life and assume full adult duties and responsibilities.

Another way Saturn helps us is to reveal the karmic lessons from previous lives and give us the chance to overcome them. So look at Saturn's challenges as much-needed opportunities for self-improvement.

Outwitting the Planets

Second-guessing Saturn and the eclipses this year is easy if you have a copy of your horoscope calculated by a computer. This enables you to pinpoint the area of your life that will be affected. However, you can make an educated guess, by setting up a rough diagram on your own. If you'd like to find out which area of your life this year's Saturn change is most likely to affect, follow these easy steps.

First, you must know the time of day you were born and look up your rising sign listed on the tables in this book (see chapter 7). Set up an estimated horoscope by drawing a circle, then dividing it into four parts by making a cross directly through the center. Continue to divide each of the parts into thirds, as if you were dividing a cake, until you have twelve slices. Write your rising sign on the middle left-hand slice, which would be the nine o'clock point, if you were looking at your watch. Then write the following signs on the dividing line of each slice, working counterclockwise, until you have listed all twelve signs of the zodiac.

You should now have a basic diagram of your horoscope

chart (minus the planets, of course). Starting with your rising-sign slice, number each portion consecutively, again working counterclockwise.

Since this year's eclipses will fall in Aquarius, Leo, and Virgo, find the number of these slices, or houses, on the chart and read the following descriptions for the kinds of issues that are likely to be emphasized. Saturn is now traveling through Virgo, so check this house in your chart for Saturn-related events.

If an eclipse or Saturn falls in your FIRST HOUSE:

Events cause you to examine the ways you are acting independently and push you to become more visible, to assert yourself. This is a time when you feel compelled to make your own decisions. You may want to change your physical appearance, body image, or style of dress in some way. Under affliction, there might be illness or physical harm.

If an eclipse or Saturn falls in your SECOND HOUSE:

This is the place where you consider all matters of security. You consolidate your resources, earn money, acquire property, and decide what you value and what you want to own. On a deeper level, this house reveals your sense of self-worth.

If an eclipse or Saturn falls in your THIRD HOUSE:

Here you reach out to others, express your ideas, and explore different courses of action. You may feel especially restless or have confrontations with neighbors or siblings. In your search for more knowledge, you may decide to improve your skills, get more education, or sign up for a course that interests you. Local transportation, especially your car, might be affected by an eclipse here.

If an eclipse or Saturn falls in your FOURTH HOUSE:

Here is where you put down roots and establish a base. You'll consider what home really means to you. Issues involving parents, the physical setup or location of your home, and your immediate family demand your attention. You may be especially concerned with parenting or relationships with your own mother. You may consider moving your home to a new location or leaving home.

If an eclipse or Saturn falls in your FIFTH HOUSE:

Here is where you express yourself, either through your personal talents or through procreating children. You are interested in making your special talents visible. This is also the house of love affairs and the romantic aspect of life, where you flirt, have fun, and enjoy the excitement of love. Hobbies and crafts fall in this area.

If an eclipse or Saturn falls in your SIXTH HOUSE:

How well are you doing your job? This is your maintenance department, where you take care of your health, organize your life, and set up a daily routine. It is also the place where you perfect your skills and add polish to your life. The chores you do every day, the skills you learn, and the techniques you use fall here. If something doesn't work in your life, an eclipse is sure to bring this to light. If you've been neglecting your health, diet, and fitness, you'll probably pay the consequences during an eclipse. Or you may be faced with work that requires much routine organization and steady effort, rather than creative ability. Or you may be required to perform services for others.

If an eclipse or Saturn falls in your SEVENTH HOUSE:

This is the area of committed relationships, of those which involve legal agreements, of working in a close relationship with another. Here you'll be dealing with how you relate, what you'll be willing to give up for the sake of a marriage or partnership. Eclipses here can put extra pressure on a relationship and, if it's not working, precipitate a breakup. Lawsuits and open enemies also reside here.

If an eclipse or Saturn falls in your EIGHTH HOUSE:

This area is concerned with power and control. Consider what you are willing to give up in order that something might happen. Power struggles, intense relationships, and desires to penetrate deeper mysteries belong here. Debts, loans, financial matters that involve another party, and wheeling and dealing also come into focus. So does sex, where you surrender your individual power to create a new life together. Matters involving birth and death are also involved here.

If an eclipse or Saturn falls in your NINTH HOUSE:

Here is where you look at the big picture. You'll seek information that helps you find meaning in life: higher education, religion, travel, global issues. Eclipses here can push you to get out of your rut, to explore something you've never done before, and to expand your horizons.

If an eclipse or Saturn falls in your TENTH HOUSE:

This is the high-profile point in your chart. Here is where you consider how society looks at you and your position in the outside world. You'll be concerned about whether you receive proper credit for your work and if you're recognized by higher-ups. Promotions, raises, and other forms of recognition can be given or denied. If you have worked hard, Saturn can give you well-deserved rewards here. Either your standing in your career or in your community can be challenged, or you'll be publicly acknowledged for achieving a goal. An eclipse here can make you famous or burst your balloon if you've been too ambitious or neglecting other areas of your life.

If an eclipse or Saturn falls in your ELEVENTH HOUSE:

Your relationship with groups of people comes under scrutiny during an eclipse: whom you are identified with, whom you socialize with, and how well you are accepted by other members of your team. Activities of clubs and political parties, networking, and other social interactions become important. You'll be concerned about what other people think.

If an eclipse or Saturn falls in your TWELFTH HOUSE:

This is the time when the focus turns to your inner life. An especially favorable eclipse here might bring you great insight and inspiration. On the other hand, events may happen that cause you to retreat from public life. Here is where we go to be alone or to work in retreats, hospitals, or religious institutions, or to explore psychotherapy. Here is where you deliver selfless service, through charitable acts. Good aspects from an eclipse could promote an ability to go with the flow or to rise above the competition to find an inner, almost mystical strength that enables you to connect with the deepest needs of others.

CHAPTER 4

Blame It on Moon Glow: The Moon's Effect on Emotions

In some astrological systems, the moon sign is considered just as important as the sun sign. It adds many levels of meaning to a horoscope, because it reveals how a person reacts to life's problems, what makes the person feel comfortable, secure, romantic. The moon reveals secrets like what you really care about. It's the emotional factor in the horoscope, representing the receptive, reflective, female, nurturing self. It also reflects who you were nurtured by—the mother or mother figure in your chart. In a man's chart, the moon position describes his receptive, emotional, yin side, as well as the woman in his life who will have the deepest effect, usually his mother. (Venus reveals the kind of woman who will attract him physically.)

The moon is more at home in some signs than others. It rules maternal Cancer and is exalted in Taurus—both comforting, home-loving signs where the natural emotional energies of the moon are easily and productively expressed. But when the moon is in the opposite signs—Capricorn and Scorpio—it leaves the comfortable nest and deals with emotional issues of power and achievement in the outside world. Those of you with the moon in these signs are likely to find your emotional role more challenging in life.

Since detailed moon tables are too extensive for this book, check through the following listing to find the moon sign that feels most familiar.

Moon in Aries

This placement makes you both independent and ardent. An idealist, you tend to fall in and out of love easily. You love a challenge but could cool once your quarry is captured. Your emotional reactions are fast and fiery, quickly expressed and quickly forgotten. You may not think before expressing your feelings. It's not easy to hide how you feel. Channeling all your emotional energy could be one of your big challenges.

Moon in Taurus

A sentimental soul, you are very fond of the good life, and you gravitate toward solid, secure relationships. You like displays of affection and creature comforts—all the tangible trappings of a cozy, safe, calm atmosphere. You are sensual and steady emotionally, but very stubborn, possessive, and determined. You can't be pushed, and you tend to dislike changes. You should make an effort to broaden your horizons and to take a risk sometimes. You may become very attached to your home turf. You may also be a collector of objects that are meaningful to you.

Moon in Gemini

You crave mental stimulation and variety in life, which you usually get through either an ever-varied social life, the excitement of flirtation and/or multiple professional involvements. You may marry more than once and have a rather chaotic emotional life due to your difficulty with commitment and settling down, as well as your need to be constantly on the go. (Be sure to find a partner who is as outgoing as you are.) You will have to learn at some point to focus your energies because you tend to be somewhat fragmented—to do two things at once, to have two homes or even two lovers. If you can find a creative way to express your many-faceted nature, you'll be ahead of the game.

Moon in Cancer

This is the most powerful lunar position, which is sure to make a deep imprint on your character. Your needs are very much associated with your reaction to the needs of others. You are very sensitive, caring, and self-protective, though some of you may mask this with a hard shell, like the moon-sensitive crab. This placement also gives an excellent memory, keen intuition, and an uncanny ability to perceive the needs of others. All of the lunar phases will affect you, especially full moons and eclipses, so you would do well to mark them on your calendar. Because you're happiest at home, you may work at home or turn your office into a second home, where you can nurture and comfort people. (You may tend to mother the world.) With natural psychic, intuitive ability, you might be drawn to occult work in some way. Or you may get professionally involved with providing food and shelter to others.

Moon in Leo

This warm, passionate moon takes everything to heart. You are attracted to all that is noble, generous, and aristocratic in life (and may be a bit of a snob). You have an innate ability to take command emotionally, but you do need strong support, loyalty, and loud applause from those you love. You are possessive of your loved ones and your turf and will roar if anyone threatens to take over your territory.

Moon in Virgo

You are rather cool until you decide if others measure up. But once someone or something meets your ideal standards, you hold up your end of the arrangement perfectly. You may, in fact, drive yourself too hard to attain some notion of perfection. Try to be a bit easier on yourself and others. Don't always act the censor! You love to be the teacher and are drawn to situations where you can change others for the better, but sometimes you must learn to accept others for what they are—enjoy what you have!

Moon in Libra

Like other air-sign moons, you think before you feel. Therefore, you may not immediately recognize the emotional needs of others. However, you are relationship oriented and may find it difficult to be alone or to do things alone. After you have learned emotional balance by leaning on yourself first, you can have excellent partnerships. It is best for you to avoid extremes, which set your scales swinging and can make your love life precarious. You thrive in a rather conservative, traditional, romantic relationship, where you receive attention and flattery—but not possessiveness—from your partner. You'll be your most charming in an elegant, harmonious atmosphere.

Moon in Scorpio

This is a moon that enjoys and responds to intense, passionate feelings. You may go to extremes and have a very dramatic emotional life, full of ardor, suspicion, jealousy, and obsession. It would be much healthier to channel your need for power and control into meaningful work. This is a good position for anyone in the fields of medicine, police work, research, the occult, psychoanalysis, or intuitive work, because life-and-death situations don't faze you. However, you do take personal disappointments very hard.

Moon in Sagittarius

You take life's ups and downs with good humor and the proverbial grain of salt. You'll love 'em and leave 'em—take off on a great adventure at a moment's notice. Born free could be your slogan. Attracted by the exotic, you have wanderlust mentally and physically. You may be too much in search of new mental and spiritual stimulation to ever settle down.

Moon in Capricorn

Are you ever accused of being too cool and calculating? You have an earthy side, but you take prestige and position very seriously. Your strong drive to succeed extends to your romantic life, where you will be devoted to improving your lifestyle, rising to the top. A structured situation where you can advance methodically makes you feel wonderfully secure. You may be attracted to someone older or very much younger or from a different social world. It may be difficult to look at the lighter side of emotional relationships. Though this moon is placed in the sign of its detriment, the good news is that you tend to be very dutiful and responsible to those you care for.

Moon in Aquarius

You are a people collector with many friends of all backgrounds. You are happiest surrounded by people and may feel uneasy when left alone. Though you usually stay friends with lovers, intense emotions and demanding one-on-one relationships turn you off. You don't like anything to be too rigid or scheduled. Though tolerant and understanding, you can be emotionally unpredictable and may opt for an unconventional love life. With plenty of space, you will be able to sustain relationships with liberal, freedom-loving types.

Moon in Pisces

You are very responsive and empathetic to others, especially if they have problems or are the underdog. (Be on guard against attracting too many people with sob stories.) You'll be happiest if you can express your creative imagination in the arts or in the spiritual or healing professions. Because you may tend to escape in fantasies or overreact to the moods of others, you need an emotional anchor to help you keep a firm foothold in reality. Steer clear of too much escapism (especially in alcohol) or reclusiveness. Places near water soothe your moods. Working in a field that gives you emotional variety will also help you be productive.

CHAPTER 5

Hands-On Astrology for Beginners

After you learn all about your zodiac sign (and those of your friends), you may be ready to delve more deeply into astrology. This chapter can get you up and running. It's a quick owner's manual, your fast track to getting hands-on with astrology. You'll learn the difference between a sign and a constellation (they're not the same). And what happens in a house. You'll be able to define a sign and figure out why astrologers say what they do about each one. When you look at your astrological chart, you'll have a good idea of what's going on in each portion of the horoscope. Here's your key to understanding the basic principles of this fascinating, but often confusing subject.

Signs and Constellations: What's the Difference?

Most readers know their signs, but many often confuse them with constellations. Signs are actually a type of celestial real estate, located on the zodiac, an imaginary 360-degree belt circling the earth. This belt is divided into twelve equal thirty-degree portions, which are the signs. There's a lot of confusion about the difference between the signs and the constellations of the zodiac. The latter are patterns of stars that originally marked the twelve divisions, like signposts. Though a sign is named after the constellation that once marked the same area, the constellations are no longer in the same place relative to the earth that they were many centuries ago. Over hundreds of years, the earth's orbit has shifted, so that from our point of view here on earth, the constellations seem to have moved. However, the signs remain in place. (Most Western astrology uses the twelve-equal-part division of the zodiac, though there are some other methods of astrology that still use the constellations instead of the signs.)

Most people think of themselves in terms of their sun sign. A sun sign refers to the sign the sun is orbiting through at a given moment (from our point of view here on earth). For instance, "I'm an Aries" means that the sun was passing through Aries when that person was born. However, there are nine other planets (plus asteroids, fixed stars, and sensitive points) that also form our total astrological personality, and some or many of these will be located in other signs. No one is completely Aries, with all astrological components in one sign! (Please note that, in astrology, the sun and moon are usually referred to as planets, though of course they're not.) Pluto is also still called a planet by astrologers.

As we mentioned before, the sun signs are places on the zodiac. They do not do anything (the planets are the doers). However, they are associated with many things, depending on their location.

How We Define the Signs

The definitions of the signs evolved systematically from four components that interrelate. These four different criteria are a sign's element: its quality, its polarity or sex, and its order in the progression of the zodiac. All these factors work together to tell us what the sign is like.

The system is magically mathematical. The number 12—as in the twelve signs of the zodiac—is divisible by 4, by 3, and by 2. There are four elements, three qualities, and two polarities, which follow each other in sequence around the zodiac.

The four elements (earth, air, fire, and water) are the building blocks of astrology. The use of an element to describe a sign probably dates from man's first attempts to categorize what he saw. Ancient sages believed that all things were composed of combinations of these basic elements—earth, air, fire, and water. This included the human character, which was fiery/choleric, earthy/melancholy, airy/sanguine, or watery/phlegmatic. The elements also correspond to our emotional (water), physical (earth), mental (air) and spiritual (fire) natures. The energies of each of the elements were then observed to be related to the time of year when the sun was passing through a certain segment of the zodiac.

Those born with the sun in fire signs—Aries, Leo, Sagittarius—embody the characteristic of that element. Optimism, warmth, hot tempers, enthusiasm, and spirit are typical of these signs. Taurus, Virgo, and Capricorn are earthy—more grounded, physical, materialistic, organized and deliberate than fire-sign people. Air-sign people— Gemini, Libra, and Aquarius—are mentally oriented communicators. Water signs—Cancer, Scorpio, and Pisces—are emotional, sensitive, and creative.

Think of what each element does to the others. Water puts out fire or evaporates under heat. Air fans the flames or blows them out. Earth smothers fire, drifts and erodes with too much wind, becomes mud or fertile soil with water. Those are often perfect analogies for the relationships between people of different sun-sign elements. This astro-chemistry was one of the first ways man described his relationships. Fortunately, no one is entirely air or fire. We all have a bit, or a lot, of each element in our horoscopes. It is this unique mix that defines each astrological personality.

Within each element, there are three qualities that describe types of behavior associated with the sign. Those of cardinal signs are activists, go-getters. These four signs— Aries, Cancer, Libra, and Capricorn—begin each season. Fixed signs, which happen in the middle of the season, are associated with builders, stabilizers. You'll find that sun signs Taurus, Leo, Scorpio, and Aquarius are usually gifted with concentration, stamina, and focus. Mutable signs— Gemini, Virgo, Sagittarius, and Pisces—fall at the end of each season and thus are considered catalysts for change. People born under mutable signs are flexible, adaptable.

The polarity of a sign is either its positive or negative charge. It can be masculine, active, positive, and yang like air or fire signs. Or feminine, reactive, negative, and yin like the water and earth signs.

Finally, we consider the sign's place in the order of the zodiac. This is vital to the balance of all the forces and the transmission of energy moving through the signs. You may have noticed that your sign is quite different from your neighboring sign on either side. Yet each seems to grow out of its predecessor like links in a chain and transmits a synthesis of energy gathered along the chain to the following sign, beginning with the fire-powered, active, positive charge of Aries.

How the Signs Add Up

SIGN	ELEMENT	QUALITY	POLARITY	PLACE
Aries	fire	cardinal	masculine	first
Taurus	earth	fixed	feminine	second
Gemini	air	mutable	masculine	third
Cancer	water	cardinal	feminine	fourth
Leo	fire	fixed	masculine	fifth
Virgo	earth	mutable	feminine	sixth
Libra	air	cardinal	masculine	seventh
Scorpio	water	fixed	feminine	eighth
Sagittarius	fire	mutable	masculine	ninth
Capricorn	earth	cardinal	feminine	tenth
Aquarius	air	fixed	masculine	eleventh
Pisces	water	mutable	feminine	twelfth

Your Sign's Special Planet

Each sign has a ruling planet that is most compatible with its energies. Mars adds its fiery assertive characteristics to Aries. The sensual beauty and comfort-loving side of Venus rules Taurus, whereas the idealistic side of Venus rules Libra. Quick-moving Mercury rules two mutable signs, Gemini and Virgo. Its mental agility belongs to Gemini while its analytical, critical side is best expressed in Virgo. The changeable emotional moon is associated with Cancer, while the outgoing Leo personality is ruled by the sun. Scorpio originally shared Mars, but when Pluto was discovered in this century, its powerful magnetic energies were deemed more suitable to the intense vibrations of the fixed water sign Scorpio. Though Pluto has, as of this writing, been downgraded, it is still considered by astrologers to be a powerful force in the horoscope. Disciplined Capricorn is ruled by Saturn, and expansive Sagittarius by Jupiter. Unpredictable Aquarius is ruled by Uranus and creative, imaginative Pisces by Neptune. In a horoscope, if a planet is placed in the sign it rules, it is sure to be especially powerful.

The Layout of a Horoscope Chart

A horoscope chart is a map of the heavens at a given moment in time. It looks like a wheel divided with twelve spokes. In between each of the spokes is a section called a house.

Each house deals with a different area of life and is influenced by a special sign and a planet. Astrologers look at the house to tell in what area of life an event is happening or about to happen.

The house is governed by the sign passing over the spoke (or cusp of the house) at that particular moment. Though the first house is naturally associated with Aries and Mars, it would also have an additional Capricorn influence if that sign was passing over the house cusp at the time the chart was cast. The sequence of the houses starts with the first house located at the left center spoke (or the number 9 position, if you were reading a clock). The houses are then read counterclockwise around the chart, with the fourth house at the bottom of the chart, and the tenth house at the top or twelve o'clock position.

Where do the planets belong? Around the horoscope, planets are placed within the houses according to their location at the time of the chart. That is why it is so important to have an accurate time; with no specific time, the planets have no specific location in the houses and one cannot determine which area of life they will apply to. Since the signs move across the houses as the earth turns, planets in a house will naturally intensify the importance of that house. The house that contains the sun is naturally one of the most prominent.

The First House: Home of Aries and Mars

The sign passing over the first house at the time of your birth is known as your *ascendant,* or *rising sign.* The first house is the house of "firsts"—the first impression you make, how you initiate matters, the image you choose to project. This is where you advertise yourself, where you project your personality. Planets that fall here will intensify the way you come across to others.

The Second House: Home of Taurus and Venus

This house is where you experience the material world—what you value. Here are your attitudes about money, possessions, finances, whatever belongs to you, and what you own, as well as your earning and spending capacity. On a deeper level, this house reveals your sense of self-worth, the inner values that draw wealth in various forms.

The Third House: Home of Gemini and Mercury

This house describes how you communicate with others, how you reach out to others nearby, and how you interact with the immediate environment. It shows how your thinking process works and the way you express your thoughts. Are you articulate or tongue-tied? Can you think on your feet? This house also shows your first relationships, your experiences with brothers and sisters, and how you deal with people close to you such as your neighbors or pals. It's where you take short trips, write letters, or use the telephone. It shows how your mind works in terms of left-brain logical and analytical functions.

The Fourth House: Home of Cancer and the Moon

The fourth house shows the foundation of life, the psychological underpinnings. At the bottom of the chart, this house shows how you are nurtured and made to feel secure—your roots! It shows your early home environment and the circumstances at the end of your life (your final "home") as well as the place you call home now. Astrologers look here for information about the parental nurturers in your life.

The Fifth House: Home of Leo and the Sun

The fifth house is where the creative potential develops. Here you express yourself and procreate in the sense that children are outgrowths of your creative ability. But this house most represents your inner childlike self who delights in play. If your inner security has been established by the time you reach this house, you are now free to have fun, romance, and love affairs and to give of yourself. This is also the place astrologers look for playful love affairs, flirtations, and brief romantic encounters (rather than long-term commitments).

The Sixth House: Home of Virgo and Mercury

The sixth house has been called the "care and maintenance" department. This house shows how you take care of your body and organize yourself to perform efficiently in the world. Here is where you get things done, look after others, and fulfill service duties such as taking care of pets. Here is what you do to survive on a day-to-day basis. The sixth house demands order in your life; otherwise there would be chaos. This house is your "job" (as opposed to your career, which is the domain of the tenth house), your diet, and your health and fitness regimens.

The Seventh House: Home of Libra and Venus

This house shows your attitude toward partners and those with whom you enter into commitments, contracts, or agreements. Here is the way you relate to others, as well as your close, intimate, one-on-one relationships (including open enemies—those you "face off" with). Open hostilities, lawsuits, divorces, and marriages happen here. If the first house represents the "I," the seventh or opposite house is the "not-I"—the complementary partner you attract by the way you come across. If you are having trouble with partnerships, consider what you are attracting by the energies of your first and seventh houses.

The Eighth House: Home of Scorpio and Pluto (also Mars)

The eighth house refers to how you merge with something or someone, and how you handle power and control. This is one of the most mysterious and powerful houses, where your energy transforms itself from "I" to "we." As you give up power and control by uniting with something or someone, two kinds of energies merge and become something greater, leading to a regeneration of the self on a higher level. Here are your attitudes toward sex, shared resources, taxes (what you share with the government). Because this house involves what belongs to others, you face issues of control and power struggles, or undergo a deep psychological transformation as you bond with another. Here you transcend yourself with dreams, drugs, and occult or psychic experiences that reflect the collective unconscious.

The Ninth House: Home of Sagittarius and Jupiter

The ninth house shows your search for wisdom and higher knowledge—your belief system. As the third house represents the "lower mind," its opposite on the wheel, the ninth house, is the "higher mind"—the abstract, intuitive, spiritual mind that asks "big" questions like "Why are we here?" After the third house has explored what was close at hand, the ninth stretches out to broaden you mentally with higher education and travel. Here you stretch spiritually with religious activity. Since you are concerned with how everything is related, you tend to push boundaries, take risks. Here is where you express your ideas in a book or thesis, where you pontificate, philosophize, or preach.

The Tenth House: Home of Capricorn and Saturn

The tenth house is associated with your public life and high-profile activities. Located directly overhead at the "high noon" position on the horoscope wheel, this is the most "visible" house in the chart, the one where the world sees you. It deals with your career (but not your routine "job") and your reputation. Here is where you go public, take on responsibilities (as opposed to the fourth house, where you stay home). This will affect the career you choose and your "public relations." This house is also associated with your father figure or the main authority figure in your life.

The Eleventh House: Home of Aquarius and Uranus

The eleventh house is where you extend yourself to a group, a goal, or a belief system. This house is where you define what you really want, the kinds of friends you have, your political affiliations, and the kind of groups you identify with as an equal. Here is where you become concerned with "what other people think" or where you rebel against social conventions. Here is where you could become a socially conscious humanitarian or a partygoing social butterfly. It's where you look to others to stimulate you and discover your kinship to the rest of humanity. The sign on this house can help you understand what you gain and lose from friendships.

The Twelfth House: Home of Pisces and Neptune

Old-fashioned astrologers used to put a rather negative spin on this house, calling it the house of self-undoing. When we undo ourselves, we surrender control, boundaries, limits, and rules. The twelfth house is where the boundaries between yourself and others become blurred and you become selfless. But instead of being self-undoing, the twelfth house can be a place of great creativity and talent. It is the place where you can tap into the collective unconscious, where your imagination is limitless.

In your trip around the zodiac, you've gone from the I of self-assertion in the first house to the final house, which symbolizes the dissolution that happens before rebirth. The twelfth house is where accumulated experiences are processed in the unconscious. Spiritually oriented astrologers look to this house for evidence of past lives and karma. Places where we go for solitude or to do spiritual or reparatory work belong here, such as retreats, religious institutions, or hospitals. Here is also where we withdraw from society voluntarily or involuntarily or are put in prison because of antisocial activity. Selfless giving through charitable acts is part of this house, as is dependence on charity.

In your daily life, the twelfth house reveals your deepest intimacies, your best-kept secrets, especially those you hide from yourself and keep repressed deep in the unconscious. It is where we surrender a sense of a separate self to a deep feeling of wholeness, such as selfless service in religion or any activity that involves merging with the greater whole. Many sports stars have important planets in the twelfth house that enable them to play in the zone, finding an inner, almost mystical, strength that transcends their limits.

Who's Home in Your Houses?

Houses are stronger or weaker depending on how many planets are inhabiting them. If there are many planets in a given house, it follows that the activities of that house will be especially important in your life. If the planet that rules the house is also located there, this too adds power to the house.

CHAPTER 6

Getting to Know All Your Planets

When you know a person's sun sign, you already know some very useful generic qualities about that person. But when you know the placement of all ten planets, that person becomes an astrological individual, with a unique horoscope. The horoscope chart lights up with colorations from many different signs and planets. Therefore, you'll have a much more accurate profile, and with the full planetary picture of the horoscope, you'll be more capable of predicting how that individual will act in a given situation.

The planets are the actors of the chart, each representing a basic force in life. The sign and house where the planet is located represent how and where this force will manifest. The importance of a planet in your horoscope depends on its position. A planet that's close to your rising sign will be highlighted in your chart. If two or more planets are grouped together in one sign, they usually operate like a team, playing off each other rather than expressing their energy singularly. A lone planet that stands far away from the others is usually outstanding and often calls the shots.

The sign of each planet also has a powerful influence. In some signs, the planetary energies are very much at home and can easily express themselves. In others, the planet has to work harder and is slightly out of sorts. The sign that most corresponds to the energies of a planet is said to be ruled by that planet and obviously is the best place for it to be. The next best place is in a sign where it is exalted, or especially harmonious. On the other hand, there are places in the horoscope where a planet has to work harder to play its role, such as the sign opposite a planet's rulership, which embodies the opposite area of life, and the sign opposite its exaltation. However, a planet that must work harder can actually be more complete, because it must stretch itself to meet the challenges of living in a more difficult sign. Like world leaders who've had to struggle for greatness, this planet may actually develop great strength and character.

Here's a list of the best places for each planet to be. Note that, as new planets were discovered, they replaced the traditional rulers of signs which best complemented their energies.

ARIES—Mars
TAURUS—Venus, in its most sensual form
GEMINI—Mercury, in its communicative role
CANCER—the moon
LEO—the sun
VIRGO—also Mercury, this time in its more critical capacity
LIBRA—also Venus, in its more aesthetic, judgmental form
SCORPIO—Pluto, replacing Mars, the sign's original ruler
SAGITTARIUS—Jupiter
CAPRICORN—Saturn
AQUARIUS—Uranus, replacing Saturn, its original ruler
PISCES—Neptune, replacing Jupiter, its original ruler

A person who has many planets in exalted signs is lucky indeed, for here is where the planet can accomplish the most and be its most influential and creative.

SUN—exalted in Aries, where its energy creates action
MOON—exalted in Taurus, where instincts and reactions operate on a highly creative level
MERCURY—exalted in Aquarius, where it can reach analytical heights
VENUS—exalted in Pisces, a sign whose sensitivity encourages love and creativity
MARS—exalted in Capricorn, a sign that puts energy to work productively
JUPITER—exalted in Cancer, where it encourages nurturing and growth

45

SATURN—at home in Libra, where it steadies the scales of justice and promotes balanced, responsible judgment

URANUS—powerful in Scorpio, where it promotes transformation

NEPTUNE—especially favored in Cancer, where it gains the security to transcend to a higher state

PLUTO—exalted in Pisces, where it dissolves the old cycle to make way for transition to the new

The Personal Planets: Mercury, Venus, and Mars

These planets work in your immediate personal life.

Mercury affects how you communicate and how your mental processes work. Are you a quick study who grasps information rapidly? Or do you learn more slowly and thoroughly? How is your concentration? Can you express yourself easily? Are you a good writer? All these questions can be answered by your Mercury placement.

Venus shows what you react to. What turns you on? What appeals to you aesthetically? Are you charming to others? Are you attractive to look at? Your taste, your refinement, your sense of balance and proportion are all Venus-ruled.

Mars is your outgoing energy, your drive and ambition. Do you reach out for new adventures? Are you assertive? Are you motivated? Self-confident? Hot-tempered? How you channel your energy and drive is revealed by your Mars placement.

Mercury Shows How Your Mind Works

Mercury shows how you think and speak, how logical you are. Since it stays close to the sun, read the description for Mercury in your sun sign, then the sign preceding and following it. Then decide which reflects the way you think.

Mercury in Aries

Your mind is very active and assertive. It approaches a plan aggressively. You never hesitate to say what you think, never shy away from a battle. In fact, you may relish a verbal confrontation. Tact is not your strong point, so you may have to learn not to trip over your tongue.

Mercury in Taurus

This is a cautious Mercury. Though you may be a slow learner, you have good concentration and mental stamina. You want to make your ideas really happen. You'll attack a problem methodically and consider every angle thoroughly, never jumping to conclusions. You'll stick with a subject until you master it.

Mercury in Gemini

You are a wonderful communicator with great facility for expressing yourself both verbally and in writing. You love gathering all kinds of information. You probably finish other people's sentences, and express yourself with eloquent hand gestures. You can talk to anybody anytime . . . and probably have phone and e-mail bills to prove it. You read anything from sci-fi to Shakespeare, and might need an extra room just for your book collection. Though you learn fast, you may lack focus and discipline. Watch a tendency to jump from subject to subject.

Mercury in Cancer

You rely on intuition more than logic. Your mental processes are usually colored by your emotions, so you may seem shy or hesitant to voice your opinions. However, this placement gives you the advantage of great imagination and empathy in the way you communicate with others.

Mercury in Leo

You are enthusiastic and very dramatic in the way you express yourself. You like to hold the attention of groups, and could be a great public speaker. Your mind thinks big, so you prefer to deal with the overall picture rather than with the details.

Mercury in Virgo

This is one of the best places for Mercury. It should give you critical ability, attention to details, and thorough analysis. Your mind focuses on the practical side of things. This type of thinking is very well suited to being a teacher or editor.

Mercury in Libra

You're either a born diplomat who smoothes over ruffled feathers or a talented debater. Many lawyers have this placement. However, since you're forever weighing the pros and cons of a situation, you may vacillate when making decisions.

Mercury in Scorpio

This is an investigative mind that stops at nothing to get the answers. You may have a sarcastic, stinging wit or a gift for the cutting remark. There's always a grain of truth to your verbal sallies, thanks to your penetrating insight.

Mercury in Sagittarius

You are a supersalesman with a tendency to expound. Though you are very broad-minded, you can be dogmatic when it comes to telling others what's good for them. You won't hesitate to tell the truth as you see it, so watch a tendency toward tactlessness. On the plus side, you have a great sense of humor. This position of Mercury is often considered by astrologers to be at a disadvantage because

Sagittarius opposes Gemini, the sign Mercury rules, and squares off with Virgo, another Mercury-ruled sign. What often happens is that Mercury in Sagittarius oversteps its bounds and loses sight of the facts in a situation. Do a reality check before making promises you may not be able to deliver.

Mercury in Capricorn

This placement endows good mental discipline. You have a love of learning and a very orderly approach to your subjects. You will patiently plod through the facts and figures until you have mastered the tasks. You grasp structured situations easily, but may be short on creativity.

Mercury in Aquarius

An independent, original thinker, you'll have more cutting-edge ideas than the average person. You will be quick to check out any unusual opportunities. Your opinions are so well-researched and grounded that once your mind is made up, it is difficult to change.

Mercury in Pisces

You have the psychic and intuitive mind of a natural poet. Learn to make use of your creative imagination. You may think in terms of helping others, but check a tendency to be vague and forgetful of details.

Venus Relates

Venus shows where you receive pleasure, what you love to do. Find your Venus placement from the charts at the end of this chapter by looking for the year of your birth in the left-hand column. Then follow the line of that year across the page until you reach the time period of your birthday. The sign heading that column will be your Venus. If you were born on a day when Venus was changing signs, check the signs preceding or following that day to determine if that sign feels more like your Venus nature.

Venus in Aries

You can't stand to be bored, confined, or ordered around. But a good challenge, maybe even a rousing row, turns you on. Confess—don't you pick a fight now and then just to get someone stirred up? You're attracted by the chase, not the catch, which could cause some problems in your love life if the object of your affection becomes too attainable. You like to wear red, and you can spot a trend before anyone else.

Venus in Taurus

All your senses work in high gear. You love to be surrounded by glorious tastes, smells, textures, sounds, and visuals. Austerity is not for you! Neither is being rushed. You like time to enjoy your pleasures. Soothing surroundings with plenty of creature comforts are your cup of tea. You like to feel secure in your nest, with no sudden jolts or surprises. You like familiar objects—in fact, you may hate to let anything or anyone go.

Venus in Gemini

You are a lively, sparkling personality who thrives in a situation that affords a constant variety and a frequent change of scenery. A varied social life is important to you, with plenty of stimulation and a chance to engage in some light flirtation. Commitment may be difficult, because playing the field is so much fun.

Venus in Cancer

An atmosphere where you feel protected, coddled, and mothered is best for you. You love to be surrounded by children in a cozy, homelike situation. You are attracted to those who are tender and nurturing, who make you feel secure and well provided for. You may be quite secretive about your emotional life, or attracted to clandestine relationships.

Venus in Leo

First-class attention in large doses turns you on, and so does the glitter of real gold and the flash of mirrors. You like to feel like a star at all times, surrounded by your admiring audience. The side effect is that you may be attracted to flatterers and tinsel, while the real gold requires some digging.

Venus in Virgo

Everything neatly in its place? On the surface, you are attracted to an atmosphere where everything is in perfect order, but underneath are some basic, earthy urges. You are attracted to those who appeal to your need to teach, to be of service, or to play out a Pygmalion fantasy. You are at your best when you are busy doing something useful.

Venus in Libra

Elegance and harmony are your key words. You can't abide an atmosphere of contention. Your taste tends toward the classic, with light harmonies of color—nothing clashing, trendy, or outrageous. You love doing things with a partner, and should be careful to pick one who is decisive but patient enough to let you weigh the pros and cons. And steer clear of argumentative types!

Venus in Scorpio

Hidden mysteries intrigue you. In fact, anything that is too open and aboveboard is a bit of a bore. You surely have a stack of whodunits by the bed, along with an erotic magazine or two. You like to solve puzzles, and may also be fascinated with the occult, crime, or scientific research. Intense, all-or-nothing situations add spice to your life, and you love to ferret out the secrets of others. But you could get burned by your flair for living dangerously. The color black, spicy food, dark wood furniture, and heady perfume all get you in the right mood.

Venus in Sagittarius

If you are not actually a world traveler, your surroundings are sure to reflect your love of faraway places. You like a casual outdoor atmosphere and a dog or two to pet. There should be plenty of room for athletic equipment and suitcases. You're attracted to kindred souls who love to travel and who share your freedom-loving philosophy of life. Athletics and spiritual or New Age pursuits could be other interests.

Venus in Capricorn

No fly-by-night relationships for you! You want substance in life, and you are attracted to whatever will help you get where you are going. Status objects turn you on. And so do those who have a serious, responsible, businesslike approach as well as those who remind you of a beloved parent. It is characteristic of this placement to be attracted to someone of a different generation. Antiques, traditional clothing, and dignified behavior are becoming to you.

Venus in Aquarius

This Venus wants to make friends, to be "cool." You like to be in a group, particularly one pushing a worthy cause. You feel quite at home surrounded by people, and could even court fame. Yet all the while you remain detached from any intense commitment. Original ideas and unpredictable people fascinate you. You don't like everything to be planned out in advance, preferring spontaneity and delightful surprises.

Venus in Pisces

This Venus loves to give of yourself, and you find plenty of takers. Stray animals and people appeal to your heart and your pocketbook, but be careful to look at their motives realistically once in a while. You are extremely vulnerable to sob stories of all kinds. Fantasy, the arts (especially film, dance, and theater), and psychic or spiritual activities also speak to you.

Mars Creates Action

Mars is the mover and shaker in your life. It shows how you pursue your goals, whether you have energy to burn or proceed at a slow, steady pace. It will also show how you get angry. Do you explode or do a slow burn or hold everything inside, then get revenge later?

To find your Mars, turn to the charts on pages 88–97. Then find your birth year in the left-hand column and trace the line across horizontally until you come to the column headed by the month of your birth. There you will find an abbreviation of your Mars sign. If the description of your Mars sign doesn't ring true, read the description of the signs preceding and following it. You may have been born on a day when Mars was changing signs, in which case your Mars might be in the adjacent sign.

Mars in Aries

In the sign it rules, Mars shows its brilliant fiery nature. You have an explosive temper and can be quite impatient. On the other hand, you have tremendous courage, energy, and drive. You'll let nothing stand in your way as you race to be first! Obstacles are met head-on and broken through by force. However, those that require patience and persistence can have you exploding in rage. You're a great starter, but not necessarily around for the finish.

Mars in Taurus

Slow, steady, concentrated energy gives you staying power to last until the finish line. You have great stamina, and you never give up. Your tactic is to wear away obstacles with your persistence. Often you come out a winner because you've had the patience to hang in there. When angered, you do a slow burn.

Mars in Gemini

You can't sit still for long. This Mars craves variety. You often have two or more things going on at once—it's all an amusing game to you. Your life can get very complicated, but that only adds spice and stimulation. What drives you into a nervous, hyper state? Boredom, sameness, routine, and confinement. You can do wonderful things with your hands, and you have a way with words.

Mars in Cancer

You rarely attack head-on. Instead, you'll keep things to yourself, make plans in secret, and always cover your actions. This might be interpreted by some as manipulative, but you are only being self-protective. You get furious when anyone knows too much about you. But you do like to know all about others. Your mothering and feeding instincts can be put to good use if you work in the food, hotel, or child-care business. You may have to overcome your fragile sense of security, which prompts you not to take risks and to get physically upset when criticized. Don't take things so personally!

Mars in Leo

You have a very dominant personality that takes center stage. Modesty is not one of your traits, nor is taking a backseat. You prefer giving the orders, and have been known to make a dramatic scene if they are not obeyed.

Properly used, this Mars confers leadership ability, endurance, and courage.

Mars in Virgo

You are the faultfinder of the zodiac. You notice every detail. Mistakes of any kind make you very nervous. You may worry, even if everything is going smoothly. You may not express your anger directly, but you sure can nag. You have definite likes and dislikes, and you are sure you can do the job better than anyone else. You are certainly more industrious and detail-oriented than other signs. Your Mars energy is often most positively expressed in some kind of teaching role.

Mars in Libra

This Mars will have a passion for beauty, justice, and art. Generally, you will avoid confrontations at all costs. You prefer to spend your energy finding diplomatic solutions or weighing pros and cons. Your other techniques are passive aggression or exercising your well-known charm to get people to do what you want.

Mars in Scorpio

This is a powerful placement, so intense that it demands careful channeling into worthwhile activities. Otherwise, you could become obsessed with your sexuality or might use your need for power and control to manipulate others. You are strong-willed, shrewd, and very private about your affairs, and you'll usually have a secret agenda behind your actions. Your great stamina, focus, and discipline would be excellent assets for careers in the military or medical fields, especially research or surgery. When angry, you don't get mad—you get even!

Mars in Sagittarius

This expansive Mars often propels people into sales, travel, athletics, or philosophy. Your energies function well when you are on the move. You have a hot temper, and are inclined to say what you think before you consider the consequences. You shoot for high goals—and talk endlessly about them—but you may be weak on groundwork. This Mars needs a solid foundation. Watch a tendency to take unnecessary risks.

Mars in Capricorn

This is an ambitious Mars with an excellent sense of timing. You have an eye for those who can be of use to you, and you may dismiss people ruthlessly when you're angry, but you drive yourself hard and deliver full value. This is a good placement for an executive. You'll aim for status and a high material position in life, and you'll keep climbing despite the odds. A great Mars to have!

Mars in Aquarius

This is the most rebellious Mars. You seem to have a drive to assert yourself against the status quo. You may enjoy provoking people, shocking them out of traditional views. Or this placement could express itself in an offbeat sex life. Somehow you often find yourself in unconventional situations. You enjoy being a leader of an active group, which pursues forward-looking studies, politics, or goals.

Mars in Pisces

This Mars is a good actor who knows just how to appeal to the sympathies of others. You create and project wonderful fantasies, or you use your sensitive antennae to crusade for those less fortunate. You get what you want through creating a veil of illusion and glamour. This is a good Mars for someone in the creative and imaginative fields—a dancer, performer, photographer, actor. Many famous film stars have this placement. Watch a tendency to manipulate by making others feel sorry for you.

Jupiter Expands Your Life

This big, bright, swirling mass of gases is associated with abundance, prosperity, and the kind of windfall you get without too much hard work. You're optimistic under Jupiter's influence, when anything seems possible. You'll travel, expand your mind with higher education, and publish to share your knowledge widely. On the other hand, Jupiter's influence is neither discriminating nor disciplined. It represents the principle of growth without judgment, and therefore could result in extravagance, weight gain, laziness, and carelessness, if not kept in check.

Be sure to look up your Jupiter in the tables in this book. When the current position of Jupiter is favorable, you may get that lucky break. This is a great time to try new things, take risks, travel, or get more education. Opportunities seem to open up easily, so take advantage of them.

Once a year, Jupiter changes signs. That means you are due for an expansive time every twelve years, when Jupiter travels through your sun sign. You'll also have up periods every four years, when Jupiter is in the same element as your sun sign.

Jupiter in Aries

You are the soul of enthusiasm and optimism. Your luckiest times are when you are getting started on an exciting project or selling an idea that you really believe in. You may have to watch a tendency to be arrogant with those who do not share your enthusiasm. You follow your impulses, often ignoring budget or other commonsense limitations. To produce real, solid benefits, you'll need patience and follow-through wherever this Jupiter falls in your horoscope.

Jupiter in Taurus

You'll spend on beautiful material things, especially those that come from nature—items made of rare woods, natural fabrics, or precious gems, for instance. You can't have too much comfort or too many sensual pleasures. Watch a tendency to overindulge in good food, or to overpamper yourself with nothing but the best. Spartan living is not for you! You may be especially lucky in matters of real estate.

Jupiter in Gemini

You are the great talker of the zodiac, and you may be a great writer, too. But restlessness could be your weak point. You jump around, talk too much, and could be a jack-of-all-trades. Keeping a secret is especially difficult, so you'll have to watch a tendency to spill the beans. Since you love to be at the center of a beehive of activity, you'll have a vibrant social life. Your best opportunities will come through your talent for language—speaking, writing, communicating, and selling.

Jupiter in Cancer

You are luckiest in situations where you can find emotional closeness or deal with basic security needs such as food, nurturing, or shelter. You may be a great collector. Or you may simply love to accumulate things—you are the one who stashes things away for a rainy day. You probably have a very good memory and love children. In fact, you may have many children to care for. The food, hotel, child-care, and shipping businesses hold good opportunities for you.

Jupiter in Leo

You are a natural showman who loves to live in a larger-than-life way. Yours is a personality full of color that always finds its way into the limelight. You can't have too much attention or applause. Showbiz is a natural place for you, and so is any area where you can play to a crowd.

Exercising your flair for drama, your natural playfulness, and your romantic nature brings you good fortune. But watch a tendency to be overly extravagant or to monopolize center stage.

Jupiter in Virgo

You actually love those minute details others find boring. To you, they make all the difference between the perfect and the ordinary. You are the fine craftsman who spots every flaw. You expand your awareness by finding the most efficient methods and by being of service to others. Many of you will be drawn to medical or teaching fields. You'll also have luck in publishing, crafts, nutrition, and service professions. Watch out for a tendency to overwork.

Jupiter in Libra

This is an other-directed Jupiter that develops best with a partner. The stimulation of others helps you grow. You are also most comfortable in harmonious, beautiful situations and you work well with artistic people. You have a great sense of fair play and an ability to evaluate the pros and cons of a situation. You usually prefer to play the role of diplomat rather than adversary.

Jupiter in Scorpio

You love the feeling of power and control, of taking things to their limit. You can't resist a mystery. Your shrewd, penetrating mind sees right through to the heart of most situations and people. You have luck in work that provides for solutions to matters of life and death. You may be drawn to undercover work, behind-the-scenes intrigue, psychotherapy, the occult, and sex-related ventures. Your challenge will be to develop a sense of moderation and tolerance for other beliefs. You may have luck in handling other people's money—insurance, taxes, and inheritance can bring you a windfall.

Jupiter in Sagittarius

Independent, outgoing, and idealistic, you'll shoot for the stars. This Jupiter compels you to travel far and wide, both physically and mentally, via higher education. You may have luck while traveling in an exotic place. You also have luck with outdoor ventures, exercise, and animals, particularly horses. Since you tend to be very open about your opinions, watch a tendency to be tactless and to exaggerate. Instead, use your wonderful sense of humor to make your point.

Jupiter in Capricorn

Jupiter is much more restrained in Capricorn, the sign of rules and authority. Here, Jupiter can make you overwork and heighten any ambition or sense of duty you may have. You'll expand in areas that advance your position, putting you farther up the social or corporate ladder. You are lucky working within the establishment in a very structured situation where you can show off your ability to organize and reap rewards for your hard work.

Jupiter in Aquarius

This is another freedom-loving Jupiter, with great tolerance and originality. You are at your best when you are working for a humanitarian cause and in the company of many supporters. This is a good Jupiter for a political career. You'll relate to all kinds of people on all social levels. You have an abundance of original ideas, but you are best off away from routine and any situation that imposes rigid rules. You need mental stimulation!

Jupiter in Pisces

You are a giver whose feelings and pocketbook are easily touched by others, so choose your companions with care. You could be the original sucker for a hard-luck story. Better find a worthy hospital or a charity that will appreciate your selfless support. You have a great creative imagination. You may attract good fortune in fields related to oil, perfume, pharmaceuticals, petroleum, dance, footwear, and alcohol. But beware of overindulgence in alcohol—focus on a creative outlet instead.

Saturn Puts on the Brakes

Jupiter speeds you up with *lucky breaks* and quick energy. Then along comes Saturn to slow you down with the *disciplinary brakes*. Saturn has unfairly been called a malefic planet, one of the bad guys of the zodiac. On the contrary, Saturn is one of our best friends, the kind who tells you what you need to hear even if it's not good news. Under a Saturn transit, we grow up, take responsibility for our lives, and emerge from whatever test this planet has in store as far wiser, more capable and mature human beings. It is when we are under pressure that we grow stronger.

When Saturn hits a critical point in your horoscope, you can count on an experience that will make you slow up, pull back, and reexamine your life. It is a call to eliminate what is not working and to shape up. By the end of its twenty-eight-year trip around the zodiac, Saturn will have tested you in all areas of your life. The major tests happen in seven-year cycles, when Saturn passes over the angles of your chart—your rising sign, the top of your chart or midheaven, your descendant, and the nadir, or bottom, of your chart. This is when the real life-changing experiences happen. But you are also in for a testing period whenever Saturn passes a planet in your chart or stresses that planet from a distance. Therefore, it is useful to check your planetary positions with the timetable of Saturn to prepare in advance, or at least to brace yourself.

When Saturn returns to its location at the time of your birth, at approximately age twenty-eight, you'll have your first Saturn return. At this time, a person usually takes stock or settles down to find his mission in life and assumes full adult duties and responsibilities.

Another way Saturn helps us is to reveal the karmic lessons from previous lives and give us the chance to overcome them. So look at Saturn's challenges as much-needed opportunities for self-improvement. Under a Jupiter influence, you'll have more fun, but Saturn gives you solid, long-lasting results.

Look up your natal Saturn in the tables in this book for clues on where you need work.

Saturn in Aries

Saturn here puts the brakes on Aries' natural drive and enthusiasm. There is often an angry side to this placement. You don't let anyone push you around, and you know what's best for yourself. Following orders is not your strong point, and neither is diplomacy. You tend to be quick to go on the offensive in relationships, attacking first, before anyone attacks you. Because no one quite lives up to your standards, you often wind up doing everything yourself. You'll have to learn to cooperate and tone down self-centeredness. Both Pat Buchanan and Saddam Hussein have this Saturn.

Saturn in Taurus

A big issue is getting control of the cash flow. There will be lean periods that can be frightening, but you have the patience and endurance to stick them out and the methodical drive to prosper in the end. Learn to take a philosophical attitude, like Ben Franklin, who also had this placement and who said, "A penny saved is a penny earned."

Saturn in Gemini

You are a serious student of life, but you may have difficulty communicating or sharing your knowledge. You may be shy, speak slowly, or have fears about communicating, like Eleanor Roosevelt. You dwell in the realms of science, theory, or abstract analysis—even when you are dealing with the emotions, like Sigmund Freud, who also had this placement.

Saturn in Cancer

Your tests come with establishing a secure emotional base. In doing so, you may have to deal with some very basic fears centering on your early home environment. Most of your Saturn tests will have emotional roots in those early childhood experiences. You may have difficulty remaining objective in terms of what you try to achieve. So it will be especially important for you to deal with negative feelings such as guilt, paranoia, jealousy, resentment, and suspicion. Galileo and Michelangelo also navigated these murky waters.

Saturn in Leo

This is an authoritarian Saturn—a strict, demanding parent who may deny the pleasure principle in your zeal to see that rules are followed. Though you may feel guilty about taking the spotlight, you are very ambitious and loyal. You have to watch a tendency toward rigidity, also toward overwork and holding back affection. Joseph Kennedy and Billy Graham share this placement.

Saturn in Virgo

This is a cautious, exacting Saturn. You are intensely hard on yourself. Most of all, you give yourself the roughest time with your constant worries about every little detail, often making yourself sick. You may have difficulties setting priorities and getting the job done. Your tests will come in learning tolerance and understanding of others. Charles de Gaulle, Mae West, and Nathaniel Hawthorne had this meticulous Saturn.

Saturn in Libra

Saturn is exalted here, which makes this planet an ally. You may choose very serious, older partners in life, perhaps stemming from a fear of dependency. You need to learn to stand solidly on your own before you commit to another.

You are extremely cautious as you deliberate every involvement—with good reason. It is best that you find an occupation that makes good use of your sense of duty and honor. Steer clear of fly-by-night situations. Both Khrushchev and Mao Tse-tung had this placement.

Saturn in Scorpio

You have great staying power. This Saturn tests you in situations involving the control of others. You may feel drawn to some kind of intrigue or undercover work, like J. Edgar Hoover. Or there may be an air of mystery surrounding your life and death, like Marilyn Monroe and Robert Kennedy, who both had this placement. There are lessons to be learned from your sexual involvements. Often sex is used for manipulation or is somehow out of the ordinary. The Roman emperor Caligula and the transsexual Christine Jorgensen are extreme cases.

Saturn in Sagittarius

Your challenges and lessons will come from tests of your spiritual and philosophical values, as happened to Martin Luther King and Gandhi. You are high-minded and sincere with this reflective, moral placement. Uncompromising in your ethical standards, you could become a benevolent despot.

Saturn in Capricorn

With the help of Saturn at maximum strength, your judgment will improve with age. And like Spencer Tracy's screen image, you'll be the gray-haired hero with a strong sense of responsibility. You advance in life slowly but steadily, always with a strong hand at the helm and an eye for the advantageous situation. Like Pat Robertson, you're likely to stand for conservative values. Negatively, you may be a loner, prone to periods of melancholy.

Saturn in Aquarius

Your tests come from relationships with groups. Do you care too much about what others think? Do you feel like an outsider, like Greta Garbo? You may fear being different from others and therefore slight your own unique, forward-looking gifts. Or like Lord Byron and Howard Hughes, you may take the opposite tack and rebel in the extreme. You can apply discipline to accomplish great humanitarian goals, as Albert Schweitzer did.

Saturn in Pisces

Your fear of the unknown and the irrational may lead you to the safety and protection of an institution. You may go on the run like Jesse James, who had this placement, to avoid looking too deeply inside. Or you might go in the opposite, more positive direction and develop a disciplined psychoanalytic approach, which puts you more in control of your feelings. Some of you will take refuge in work with hospitals, charities, or religious institutions. Queen Victoria, who had this placement, symbolized an era when institutions of all kinds were sustained. Discipline applied to artistic work, especially poetry and dance, or to spiritual work, such as yoga or meditation, might be helpful.

How Uranus, Neptune, and Pluto Influence a Whole Generation

These three planets remain in signs such a long time that a whole generation bears the imprint of the sign. Mass movements, great sweeping changes, fads that characterize a generation, even the issues of the conflicts and wars of the time are influenced by these "outer three" planets. When one of those distant planets changes signs, there is a definite shift in the atmosphere, the feeling of the end of an era.

Since these planets are so far away from the sun—too distant to be seen by the naked eye—they pick up signals from the universe at large. These planetary receivers literally link the sun with distant energies, and then perform a similar function in your horoscope by linking your central character with intuitive, spiritual, transformative forces from the cosmos. Each planet has a special domain, and will reflect this in the area of your chart where it falls.

Uranus Is the Surprise Ingredient

Uranus is the unexpected ingredient that sets you and your generation apart. There is nothing ordinary about this quirky green planet that seems to be traveling on its side, surrounded by a swarm of moons. Is it any wonder that astrologers assigned it to Aquarius, the most eccentric and gregarious sign? Uranus seems to wend its way around the sun, marching to its own tune.

Significantly, Uranus follows Saturn, the planet of limitations and structures. Often we get caught up in the structures we have created to give ourselves a sense of security. However, if we lose contact with our spiritual roots, then Uranus is likely to jolt us out of our comfortable rut and wake us up.

Uranus energy is electrical, happening in sudden flashes. It is not influenced by karma or past events, nor does it regard tradition, sex, or sentiment. The Uranus key words are surprise and awakening. Suddenly, there's that flash of inspiration, that bright idea, that totally new approach to revolutionize whatever scheme you were undertaking. A Uranus event takes you by surprise; it happens from out of the blue, for better or for worse. The Uranus place in your life is where you awaken and become your own person, leaving the structures of Saturn behind. And it is probably the most unconventional place in your chart.

Look up the sign of Uranus at the time of your birth and see where you follow your own tune.

Uranus in Aries

Birth Dates:
    March 31, 1927–November 4, 1927

January 13, 1928–June 6, 1934
October 10, 1934–March 28, 1935

Your generation is original, creative, pioneering. It developed the computer, the airplane, and the cyclotron. You let nothing hold you back from exploring the unknown, and you have a powerful mixture of fire and electricity behind you. Women of your generation were among the first to be liberated. You were the unforgettable style setters. You have a surprise in store for everyone. Like Yoko Ono, Grace Kelly, and Jacqueline Onassis, your life may be jolted by sudden and violent changes.

Uranus in Taurus

Birth Dates:
June 6, 1934–October 10, 1934
March 28, 1935–August 7, 1941
October 5, 1941–May 15, 1942

The great territorial shake-ups of World War II began during your generation. You are independent, probably self-employed or would like to be. You have original ideas about making money, and you brace yourself for sudden changes of fortune. This Uranus can cause shake-ups, particularly in finances, but it can also make you a born entrepreneur, like Martha Stewart.

Uranus in Gemini

Birth Dates:
August 7, 1941–October 5, 1941
May 15, 1942–August 30, 1948
November 12, 1948–June 10, 1949

You were the first children to be influenced by television. Now, in your adult years, your generation stocks up on answering machines, cell phones, computers, and fax machines—any new way you can communicate. You have an inquiring mind, but your interests may be rather short-lived. This Uranus can be easily fragmented if there is no structure and focus.

Uranus in Cancer

Birth Dates:
  August 30, 1948–November 12, 1948
  June 10, 1949–August 24, 1955
  January 28, 1956–June 10, 1956

This generation came at a time when divorce was becoming commonplace, so your home image is unconventional. You may have an unusual relationship with your parents; you may have come from a broken home or an unconventional one. You'll have unorthodox ideas about parenting, intimacy, food, and shelter. You may also be interested in dreams, psychic phenomena, and memory work.

Uranus in Leo

Birth Dates:
  August 24, 1955–January 28, 1956
  June 10, 1956–November 1, 1961
  January 10, 1962–August 10, 1962

This generation understood how to use electronic media. Many of your group are now leaders in the high-tech industries, and you also understand how to use the new media to promote yourself. Like Isadora Duncan, you may have a very eccentric kind of charisma and a life that is sparked by unusual love affairs. Your children, too, may have traits that are out of the ordinary. Where this planet falls in your chart, you'll have a love of freedom, be a bit of an egomaniac, and show the full force of your personality in a unique way, like tennis great Martina Navratilova.

Uranus in Virgo

Birth Dates:
  November 1, 1961–January 10, 1962
  August 10, 1962–September 28, 1968
  May 20, 1969–June 24, 1969

You'll have highly individual work methods. Many of you will be finding newer, more practical ways to use computers. Like Einstein, who had this placement, you'll break the rules brilliantly. Your generation came at a time of student rebellions, the civil rights movement, and the general acceptance of health foods. Chances are, you're concerned about pollution and cleaning up the environment. You may also be involved with nontraditional healing methods.

Uranus in Libra

Birth Dates:
  September 28, 1968–May 20, 1969
  June 24, 1969–November 21, 1974
  May 1, 1975–September 8, 1975
Your generation will be always changing partners. Born during the era of women's liberation, you may have come from a broken home and may have no clear image of what a marriage entails. There will be many sudden splits and experiments before you settle down. Your generation will be much involved in legal and political reforms and in changing artistic and fashion looks.

Uranus in Scorpio

Birth Dates:
  November 21, 1974–May 1, 1975
  September 8, 1975–February 17, 1981
  March 20, 1981–November 16, 1981
Interest in transformation, meditation, and life after death signaled the beginning of New Age consciousness. Your generation recognizes no boundaries, no limits, and no external controls. You'll have new attitudes toward death and dying, psychic phenomena, and the occult. Like Mae West and Casanova, you'll shock 'em sexually, too.

Uranus in Sagittarius

Birth Dates:
  February 17, 1981–March 20, 1981
  November 16, 1981–February 15, 1988
  May 27, 1988–December 2, 1988
Could this generation be the first to travel in outer

space? An earlier generation with this placement included Charles Lindbergh and a time when the first zeppelins and the Wright Brothers were conquering the skies. Uranus here forecasts great discoveries, mind expansion, and long-distance travel. Like Galileo and Martin Luther, those born in these years will generate new theories about the cosmos and mankind's relation to it.

Uranus in Capricorn

Birth Dates:
  December 20, 1904–January 30, 1912
  September 4, 1912–November 12, 1912
  February 15, 1988–May 27, 1988
  December 2, 1988–April 1, 1995
  June 9, 1995–January 12, 1996
This generation, now growing up, will challenge traditions with the help of electronic gadgets. In these years, we got organized with the help of technology put to practical use. The Internet was born following the great economic boom of the 1990s. Great leaders who were movers and shakers of history, like Julius Caesar and Henry VIII, were born under this placement.

Uranus in Aquarius

Birth Dates:
  January 30, 1912–September 4, 1912
  November 12, 1912–April 1, 1919
  August 16, 1919–January 22, 1920
  April 1, 1995–June 9, 1995
  January 12, 1996–March 10, 2003
  September 15, 2003–December 30, 2003
Uranus in Aquarius is the strongest placement for this planet. Recently we've had the opportunity to witness the full force of its power of innovation, as well as its sudden wake-up calls and insistence on humanitarian values. This was a time of high-tech development, when home computers became as ubiquitous as television. It was a time of globalization, of surprise attacks (9/11), and underdevel-

oped countries demanding attention. The last generation with this placement produced great innovative minds such as Leonard Bernstein and Orson Welles. The next will become another radical breakthrough generation, much concerned with global issues that involve all humanity.

Uranus in Pisces

Birth Dates:
   April 1, 1919–August 16, 1919
   January 22, 1920–March 31, 1927
   November 4, 1927–January 12, 1928
   March 10, 2003–September 15, 2003
   December 20, 2003–May 28, 2010

Uranus is now in Pisces, ushering in a new generation. In the past century, Uranus in Pisces focused attention on the rise of electronic entertainment—radio and the cinema—and the secretiveness of Prohibition. This produced a generation of idealists exemplified by Judy Garland's theme "Somewhere over the Rainbow." Uranus in Pisces also hints at stealth activities, at hospital and prison reform, at high-tech drugs and medical experiments, at shake-ups and reforms in the Pisces-ruled petroleum industry, offshore drilling in new and unusual locations. Issues regarding the water and oil supply, water-related storm damage (Hurricane Katrina), sudden hurricanes, and floods demand our attention.

Neptune Is the Magic Solvent

Neptune is often maligned as the planet of illusions that dissolves reality, enabling you to escape the material world. Under Neptune's influence, you see what you want to see. But Neptune also encourages you to create. It embodies glamour, subtlety, mystery, and mysticism, and it governs anything that takes you beyond the mundane world, including out-of-body experiences.

Neptune acts to transcend your ordinary perceptions to take you to another level, where you experience either confusion or ecstasy. Its force can pull you off course only if you allow this to happen. Those who use Neptune wisely can translate their daydreams into poetry, theater, design, or inspired moves in the business world, avoiding the tricky "con artist" side of this planet.

Find your Neptune listed below.

Neptune in Cancer

Birth Dates:
> July 19, 1901–December 25, 1901
> May 21, 1902–September 23, 1914
> December 14, 1914–July 19, 1915
> March 19, 1916–May 2, 1916

Dreams of the homeland, idealistic patriotism, and glamorization of the nurturing assets of women characterized this time. You who were born here have unusual psychic ability and deep insights into basic needs of others.

Neptune in Leo

Birth Dates:
> September 23, 1914–December 14, 1914
> July 19, 1915–March 19, 1916
> May 2, 1916–September 21, 1928
> February 19, 1929–July 24, 1929

Neptune in Leo brought us the glamour and high living of the 1920s and the big spenders of that time. The Neptune temptations of gambling, seduction, theater, and lavish entertaining distracted from the realities of the age. Those born in that generation also made great advances in the arts.

Neptune in Virgo

Birth Dates:
> September 21, 1928–February 19, 1929
> July 24, 1929–October 3, 1942
> April 17, 1943–August 2, 1943

Neptune in Virgo encompassed the 1930s, the Great Depression, and the beginning of World War II, when a new order was born. There was a time of facing "what doesn't work." Many were unemployed and found solace at the movies, watching the great Virgo star Greta Garbo or the escapist dance films of Busby Berkeley. New public services were born. Those with Neptune in Virgo later spread the gospel of health and fitness. This generation's devotion to spending hours at the office inspired the term *workaholic*.

Neptune in Libra

Birth Dates:
   October 3, 1942–April 17, 1943
   August 2, 1943–December 24, 1955
   March 12, 1956–October 19, 1956
   June 15, 1957–August 6, 1957

This was the time of World War II and the postwar period, when the world regained balance and returned to relative stability. Neptune in Libra was the romantic generation who would later be concerned with relating. As this generation matured, there was a new trend toward marriage and commitment. Racial and sexual equality became important issues, as they redesigned traditional roles to suit modern times.

Neptune in Scorpio

Birth Dates:
   December 24, 1955–March 12, 1956
   October 19, 1956–June 15, 1957
   August 6, 1957–January 4, 1970
   May 3, 1970–November 6, 1970

Neptune in Scorpio brought in a generation that would become interested in transformative power. Born in an era that glamorized sex, drugs, rock and roll, and Eastern religion, they matured in a more sobering time of AIDS, cocaine abuse, and New Age spirituality. As they evolve, they will become active in healing the planet from the results of the abuse of power.

Neptune in Sagittarius

Birth Dates:
   January 4, 1970–May 3, 1970
   November 6, 1970–January 19, 1984
   June 23, 1984–November 21, 1984

Neptune in Sagittarius was the time when space and astronaut travel became a reality. The Neptune influence glamorized new approaches to mysticism, religion, and mind expansion. This generation will take a new approach to spiritual life, with emphasis on visions, mysticism, and clairvoyance.

Neptune in Capricorn

Birth Dates:
   January 19, 1984–June 23, 1984
   November 21, 1984–January 29, 1998

Neptune in Capricorn brought a time when delusions about material power were glamorized in the mid–1980s and 1990s. There was a boom in the stock market, and the Internet era spawned young tycoons who later lost it all. It was also a time when the psychic and occult worlds spawned a new category of business enterprise, and sold services on television.

Neptune in Aquarius

Birth Dates:
   January 29, 1998–April 4, 2011

This should continue to be a time of breakthroughs. Here the creative influence of Neptune reaches a universal audience. This is a time of dissolving barriers, of globalization—when we truly become one world. During this transit of high-tech Aquarius, new kinds of entertainment media reach across cultural differences. However, the transit of Neptune has also raised boundary issues between cultures, especially in Middle Eastern countries with Neptune-ruled oil fields. As Neptune raises issues of social and political structures not being as solid as they seem, this could continue to produce rebellion and chaos in the environment. However, by using imagination (Neptune) in partnership with a global view (Aquarius) we could reach creative solutions.

Those born with this placement should be true citizens of the world with a remarkable creative ability to transcend social and cultural barriers.

Pluto Can Transform You

Though Pluto is a tiny, mysterious body in space, its influence is great. When Pluto zaps a strategic point in your horoscope, your life changes dramatically.

Little Pluto is the power behind the scenes; it affects you at deep levels of consciousness, causing events to come to the surface that will transform you and your generation. Nothing escapes, or is sacred, with this probing planet. Its purpose is to wipe out the past so something new can happen.

The Pluto place in your horoscope is where you have invisible power (Mars governs the visible power), where you can transform, heal, and affect the unconscious needs of the masses. Pluto tells lots about how your generation projects power, what makes it seem cool to others. And when Pluto changes signs, there is a whole new concept of what's cool. Pluto's strange elliptical orbit occasionally runs inside the orbit of neighboring Neptune. Because of its eccentric path, the length of time Pluto stays in any given sign can vary from thirteen to thirty-two years. It covered only seven signs in the last century.

Pluto in Gemini

Birth Dates:
   Late 1800s–May 26, 1914
   This was a time of mass suggestion and breakthroughs in communications, a time when many brilliant writers such as Ernest Hemingway and F. Scott Fitzgerald were born. Henry Miller, D. H. Lawrence, and James Joyce scandalized society by using explicit sexual images and language

in their literature. "Muckraking" journalists exposed corruption. Pluto-ruled Scorpio President Theodore Roosevelt said, "Speak softly, but carry a big stick." This generation had an intense need to communicate and made major breakthroughs in knowledge. A compulsive restlessness and a thirst for a variety of experiences characterized many of this generation.

Pluto in Cancer

Birth Dates:
    May 26, 1914–June 14, 1939
    Dictators and mass media arose to wield emotional power over the masses. Women's rights was a popular issue. Deep sentimental feelings, acquisitiveness, and possessiveness characterized these times and people. Most of the great stars of the Hollywood era that embodied the American image were born during this period: Grace Kelly, Esther Williams, Frank Sinatra, Lana Turner, to name a few.

Pluto in Leo

Birth Dates:
    June 14, 1939–August, 19, 1957
    The performing arts played on the emotions of the masses. Mick Jagger, John Lennon, and rock and roll were born at this time. So were "baby boomers" like Bill and Hillary Clinton. Those born here tend to be self-centered, powerful, and boisterous. This generation does its own thing, for better or for worse.

Pluto in Virgo

Birth Dates:
    August 19, 1957–October 5, 1971
    April 17, 1972–July 30, 1972
    This is the "yuppie" generation that sparked a mass movement toward fitness, health, and career. It is a much more sober, serious, driven generation than the fun-loving Pluto in Leo. During this time, machines were invented to

process detail work efficiently. Inventions took a practical turn with answering machines, fax machines, car phones, and home office equipment—all making the workplace far more efficient.

Pluto in Libra

Birth Dates:
October 5, 1971–April 17, 1972
July 30, 1972–November 5, 1983
May 18, 1984–August 27, 1984

A mellower generation, people born at this time are concerned with partnerships, working together, and finding diplomatic solutions to problems. Marriage is important to this generation, and they will define it by combining traditional values with equal partnership. This was a time of women's liberation, gay rights, ERA, and legal battles over abortion, all of which transformed our ideas about relationships.

Pluto in Scorpio

Birth Dates:
November 5, 1983–May 18, 1984
August 27, 1984–January 17, 1995

Pluto was in the sign it rules for a comparatively short period of time. However, this was a time of record achievements, destructive sexually transmitted diseases, nuclear power controversies, and explosive political issues. Pluto destroys in order to create new understanding—the phoenix rising from the ashes—which should be some consolation for those of you who felt Pluto's force before 1995. Sexual shockers were par for the course during these intense years when black clothing, transvestites, body piercing, tattoos, and sexually explicit advertising pushed the boundaries of good taste.

Pluto in Sagittarius

Birth Dates:
January 17, 1995–April 20, 1995

November 10, 1995–January 26, 2008

During the most recent Pluto transit, we were pushed to expand our horizons, to find deeper spiritual meaning in life. Pluto's opposition with Saturn in 2001 brought an enormous conflict between traditional societies and the forces of change. It signals a time when religious convictions exerted more power in our political life as well.

Since Sagittarius is associated with travel, Pluto, the planet of extremes, made space travel a reality for some wealthy adventurers, who paid for the privilege of travel on space shuttles.

New dimensions in electronic publishing, concern with animal rights and the environment, and an increasing emphasis on extreme forms of religion are other signs of these times. Charismatic religious leaders asserted themselves and questions of the boundaries between church and state arose. There were also sexual scandals associated with the church. Because this period ends this year, hopefully we will have developed far-reaching philosphies to elevate our lives with a new sense of purpose.

Pluto in Capricorn

Birth Dates:
January 25, 2008–June 13, 2008
November 26, 2008–January 20, 2024

Since Pluto in Jupiter-ruled Sagittarius signaled a time of expansion and globalization, Pluto's entry into Saturn-ruled Capricorn this year will signal a time of adjustment, of facing reality and limitations, then finding pragmatic solutions. It will be a time when a new structure is imposed, when we become concerned with what actually works. Because Capricorn is associated with corporations and also with responsibility and duty, look for dramatic changes in business practices, hopefully with more attention paid to ethical and social responsibility as well as the bottom line. Big business will have enormous power during this transit, perhaps handling what governments have been unable to accomplish. There will be an emphasis on trimming down, perhaps a new belt-tightening regime. And since Capricorn is the sign of Father Time, there will be a new emphasis on the aging of the population. The generation born now is sure to be a more practical and realistic one than that of their older Pluto-in-Sagittarius siblings.

VENUS SIGNS 1901–2008

	Aries	Taurus	Gemini	Cancer	Leo	Virgo
1901	3/29–4/22	4/22–5/17	5/17–6/10	6/10–7/5	7/5–7/29	7/29–8/23
1902	5/7–6/3	6/3–6/30	6/30–7/25	7/25–8/19	8/19–9/13	9/13–10/7
1903	2/28–3/24	3/24–4/18	4/18–5/13	5/13–6/9	6/9–7/7	7/7–8/17
						9/6–11/8
1904	3/13–5/7	5/7–6/1	6/1–6/25	6/25–7/19	7/19–8/13	8/13–9/6
1905	2/3–3/6	3/6–4/9	7/8–8/6	8/6–9/1	9/1–9/27	9/27–10/21
	4/9–5/28	5/28–7/8				
1906	3/1–4/7	4/7–5/2	5/2–5/26	5/26–6/20	6/20–7/16	7/16–8/11
1907	4/27–5/22	5/22–6/16	6/16–7/11	7/11–8/4	8/4–8/29	8/29–9/22
1908	2/14–3/10	3/10–4/5	4/5–5/5	5/5–9/8	9/8–10/8	10/8–11/3
1909	3/29–4/22	4/22–5/16	5/16–6/10	6/10–7/4	7/4–7/29	7/29–8/23
1910	5/7–6/3	6/4–6/29	6/30–7/24	7/25–8/18	8/19–9/12	9/13–10/6
1911	2/28–3/23	3/24–4/17	4/18–5/12	5/13–6/8	6/9–7/7	7/8–11/18
1912	4/13–5/6	5/7–5/31	6/1–6/24	6/24–7/18	7/19–8/12	8/13–9/5
1913	2/3–3/6	3/7–5/1	7/8–8/5	8/6–8/31	9/1–9/26	9/27–10/20
	5/2–5/30	5/31–7/7				
1914	3/14–4/6	4/7–5/1	5/2–5/25	5/26–6/19	6/20–7/15	7/16–8/10
1915	4/27–5/21	5/22–6/15	6/16–7/10	7/11–8/3	8/4–8/28	8/29–9/21
1916	2/14–3/9	3/10–4/5	4/6–5/5	5/6–9/8	9/9–10/7	10/8–11/2
1917	3/29–4/21	4/22–5/15	5/16–6/9	6/10–7/3	7/4–7/28	7/29–8/21
1918	5/7–6/2	6/3–6/28	6/29–7/24	7/25–8/18	8/19–9/11	9/12–10/5
1919	2/27–3/22	3/23–4/16	4/17–5/12	5/13–6/7	6/8–7/7	7/8–11/8
1920	4/12–5/6	5/7–5/30	5/31–6/23	6/24–7/18	7/19–8/11	8/12–9/4
1921	2/3–3/6	3/7–4/25	7/8–8/5	8/6–8/31	9/1–9/25	9/26–10/20
	4/26–6/1	6/2–7/7				
1922	3/13–4/6	4/7–4/30	5/1–5/25	5/26–6/19	6/20–7/14	7/15–8/9
1923	4/27–5/21	5/22–6/14	6/15–7/9	7/10–8/3	8/4–8/27	8/28–9/20
1924	2/13–3/8	3/9–4/4	4/5–5/5	5/6–9/8	9/9–10/7	10/8–11/12
1925	3/28–4/20	4/21–5/15	5/16–6/8	6/9–7/3	7/4–7/27	7/28–8/21

Libra	Scorpio	Sagittarius	Capricorn	Aquarius	Pisces
8/23–9/17	9/17–10/12	10/12–1/16	1/16–2/9 11/7–12/5	2/9–3/5 12/5–1/11	3/5–3/29
10/7–10/31	10/31–11/24	11/24–12/18	12/18–1/11	2/6–4/4	1/11–2/6 4/4–5/7
8/17–9/6 11/8–12/9	12/9–1/5			1/11–2/4	2/4–2/28
9/6–9/30	9/30–10/25	1/5–1/30 10/25–11/18	1/30–2/24 11/18–12/13	2/24–3/19 12/13–1/7	3/19–4/13
10/21–11/14	11/14–12/8	12/8–1/1/06			1/7–2/3
8/11–9/7	9/7–10/9 12/15–12/25	10/9–12/15 12/25–2/6	1/1–1/25	1/25–2/18	2/18–3/14
9/22–10/16	10/16–11/9	11/9–12/3	2/6–3/6 12/3–12/27	3/6–4/2 12/27–1/20	4/2–4/27
11/3–11/28	11/28–12/22	12/22–1/15			1/20–2/4
8/23–9/17	9/17–10/12	10/12–11/17	1/15–2/9 11/17–12/5	2/9–3/5 12/5–1/15	3/5–3/29
10/7–10/30	10/31–11/23	11/24–12/17	12/18–12/31	1/1–1/15 1/29–4/4	1/16–1/28 4/5–5/6
11/19–12/8	12/9–12/31		1/1–1/10	1/11–2/2	2/3–2/27
9/6–9/30	1/1–1/4 10/1–10/24	1/5–1/29 10/25–11/17	1/30–2/23 11/18–12/12	2/24–3/18 12/13–12/31	3/19–4/12
10/21–11/13	11/14–12/7	12/8–12/31		1/1–1/6	1/7–2/2
8/11–9/6	9/7–10/9 12/6–12/30	10/10–12/5 12/31	1/1–1/24	1/25–2/17	2/18–3/13
9/22–10/15	10/16–11/8	1/1–2/6 11/9–12/2	2/7–3/6 12/3–12/26	3/7–4/1 12/27–12/31	4/2–4/26
11/3–11/27	11/28–12/21	12/22–12/31		1/1–1/19	1/20–2/13
8/22–9/16	9/17–10/11	1/1–1/14 10/12–11/6	1/15–2/7 11/7–12/5	2/8–3/4 12/6–12/31	3/5–3/28
10/6–10/29	10/30–11/22	11/23–12/16	12/17–12/31	1/1–4/5	4/6–5/6
11/9–12/8	12/9–12/31		1/1–1/9	1/10–2/2	2/3–2/26
9/5–9/30	1/1–1/3 9/31–10/23	1/4–1/28 10/24–11/17	1/29–2/22 11/18–12/11	2/23–3/18 12/12–12/31	3/19–4/11
10/21–11/13	11/14–12/7	12/8–12/31		1/1–1/6	1/7–2/2
8/10–9/6	9/7–10/10 11/29–12/31	10/11–11/28	1/1–1/24	1/25–2/16	2/17–3/12
9/21–10/14	1/1 10/15–11/7	1/2–2/6 11/8–12/1	2/7–3/5 12/2–12/25	3/6–3/31 12/26–12/31	4/1–4/26
11/13–11/26	11/27–12/21	12/22–12/31		1/1–1/19	1/20–2/12
8/22–9/15	9/16–10/11	1/1–1/14 10/12–11/6	1/15–2/7 11/7–12/5	2/8–3/3 12/6–12/31	3/4–3/27

VENUS SIGNS 1901–2008

	Aries	Taurus	Gemini	Cancer	Leo	Virgo
1926	5/7–6/2	6/3–6/28	6/29–7/23	7/24–8/17	8/18–9/11	9/12–10/5
1927	2/27–3/22	3/23–4/16	4/17–5/11	5/12–6/7	6/8–7/7	7/8–11/9
1928	4/12–5/5	5/6–5/29	5/30–6/23	6/24–7/17	7/18–8/11	8/12–9/4
1929	2/3–3/7	3/8–4/19	7/8–8/4	8/5–8/30	8/31–9/25	9/26–10/19
	4/20–6/2	6/3–7/7				
1930	3/13–4/5	4/6–4/30	5/1–5/24	5/25–6/18	6/19–7/14	7/15–8/9
1931	4/26–5/20	5/21–6/13	6/14–7/8	7/9–8/2	8/3–8/26	8/27–9/19
1932	2/12–3/8	3/9–4/3	4/4–5/5	5/6–7/12	9/9–10/6	10/7–11/1
			7/13–7/27	7/28–9/8		
1933	3/27–4/19	4/20–5/28	5/29–6/8	6/9–7/2	7/3–7/26	7/27–8/20
1934	5/6–6/1	6/2–6/27	6/28–7/22	7/23–8/16	8/17–9/10	9/11–10/4
1935	2/26–3/21	3/22–4/15	4/16–5/10	5/11–6/6	6/7–7/6	7/7–11/8
1936	4/11–5/4	5/5–5/28	5/29–6/22	6/23–7/16	7/17–8/10	8/11–9/4
1937	2/2–3/8	3/9–4/13	7/7–8/3	8/4–8/29	8/30–9/24	9/25–10/18
	4/14–6/3	6/4–7/6				
1938	3/12–4/4	4/5–4/28	4/29–5/23	5/24–6/18	6/19–7/13	7/14–8/8
1939	4/25–5/19	5/20–6/13	6/14–7/8	7/9–8/1	8/2–8/25	8/26–9/19
1940	2/12–3/7	3/8–4/3	4/4–5/5	5/6–7/4	9/9–10/5	10/6–10/31
			7/5–7/31	8/1–9/8		
1941	3/27–4/19	4/20–5/13	5/14–6/6	6/7–7/1	7/2–7/26	7/27–8/20
1942	5/6–6/1	6/2–6/26	6/27–7/22	7/23–8/16	8/17–9/9	9/10–10/3
1943	2/25–3/20	3/21–4/14	4/15–5/10	5/11–6/6	6/7–7/6	7/7–11/8
1944	4/10–5/3	5/4–5/28	5/29–6/21	6/22–7/16	7/17–8/9	8/10–9/2
1945	2/2–3/10	3/11–4/6	7/7–8/3	8/4–8/29	8/30–9/23	9/24–10/18
	4/7–6/3	6/4–7/6				
1946	3/11–4/4	4/5–4/28	4/29–5/23	5/24–6/17	6/18–7/12	7/13–8/8
1947	4/25–5/19	5/20–6/12	6/13–7/7	7/8–8/1	8/2–8/25	8/26–9/18
1948	2/11–3/7	3/8–4/3	4/4–5/6	5/7–6/28	9/8–10/5	10/6–10/31
			6/29–8/2	8/3–9/7		
1949	3/26–4/19	4/20–5/13	5/14–6/6	6/7–6/30	7/1–7/25	7/26–8/19
1950	5/5–5/31	6/1–6/26	6/27–7/21	7/22–8/15	8/16–9/9	9/10–10/3
1951	2/25–3/21	3/22–4/15	4/16–5/10	5/11–6/6	6/7–7/7	7/8–11/9

Libra	Scorpio	Sagittarius	Capricorn	Aquarius	Pisces
10/6–10/29	10/30–11/22	11/23–12/16	12/17–12/31	1/1–4/5	4/6–5/6
11/10–12/8	12/9–12/31	1/1–1/7	1/8	1/9–2/1	2/2–2/26
9/5–9/28	1/1–1/3	1/4–1/28	1/29–2/22	2/23–3/17	3/18–4/11
	9/29–10/23	10/24–11/16	11/17–12/11	12/12–12/31	
10/20–11/12	11/13–12/6	12/7–12/30	12/31	1/1–1/5	1/6–2/2
8/10–9/6	9/7–10/11	10/12–11/21	1/1–1/23	1/24–2/16	2/17–3/12
	11/22–12/31				
9/20–10/13	1/1–1/3	1/4–2/6	2/7–3/4	3/5–3/31	4/1–4/25
	10/14–11/6	11/7–11/30	12/1–12/24	12/25–12/31	
11/2–11/25	11/26–12/20	12/21–12/31		1/1–1/18	1/19–2/11
8/21–9/14	9/15–10/10	1/1–1/13	1/14–2/6	2/7–3/2	3/3–3/26
		10/11–11/5	11/6–12/4	12/5–12/31	
10/5–10/28	10/29–11/21	11/22–12/15	12/16–12/31	1/1–4/5	4/6–5/5
11/9–12/7	12/8–12/31		1/1–1/7	1/8–1/31	2/1–2/25
9/5–9/27	1/1–1/2	1/3–1/27	1/28–2/21	2/22–3/16	3/17–4/10
	9/28–10/22	10/23–11/15	11/16–12/10	12/11–12/31	
10/19–11/11	11/12–12/5	12/6–12/29	12/30–12/31	1/1–1/5	1/6–2/1
8/9–9/6	9/7–10/13	10/14–11/14	1/1–1/22	1/23–2/15	2/16–3/11
	11/15–12/31				
9/20–10/13	1/1–1/3	1/4–2/5	2/6–3/4	3/5–3/30	3/31–4/24
	10/14–11/6	11/7–11/30	12/1–12/24	12/25–12/31	
11/1–11/25	11/26–12/19	12/20–12/31		1/1–1/18	1/19–2/11
8/21–9/14	9/15–10/9	1/1–1/12	1/13–2/5	2/6–3/1	3/2–3/26
		10/10–11/5	11/6–12/4	12/5–12/31	
10/4–10/27	10/28–11/20	11/21–12/14	12/15–12/31	1/1–4/5	4/6–5/5
11/9–12/7	12/8–12/31		1/1–1/7	1/8–1/31	2/1–2/24
9/3–9/27	1/1–1/2	1/3–1/27	1/28–2/20	2/21–3/16	3/17–4/9
	9/28–10/21	10/22–11/15	11/16–12/10	12/11–12/31	
10/19–11/11	11/12–12/5	12/6–12/29	12/30–12/31	1/1–1/4	1/5–2/1
8/9–9/6	9/7–10/15	10/16–11/7	1/1–1/21	1/22–2/14	2/15–3/10
	11/8–12/31				
9/19–10/12	1/1–1/4	1/5–2/5	2/6–3/4	3/5–3/29	3/30–4/24
	10/13–11/5	11/6–11/29	11/30–12/23	12/24–12/31	
11/1–11/25	11/26–12/19	12/20–12/31		1/1–1/17	1/18–2/10
8/20–9/14	9/15–10/9	1/1–1/12	1/13–2/5	2/6–3/1	3/2–3/25
		10/10–11/5	11/6–12/5	12/6–12/31	
10/4–10/27	10/28–11/20	11/21–12/13	12/14–12/31	1/1–4/5	4/6–5/4
11/10–12/7	12/8–12/31		1/1–1/7	1/8–1/31	2/1–2/24

VENUS SIGNS 1901–2008

	Aries	Taurus	Gemini	Cancer	Leo	Virgo
1952	4/10–5/4	5/5–5/28	5/29–6/21	6/22–7/16	7/17–8/9	8/10–9/3
1953	2/2–3/3	3/4–3/31	7/8–8/3	8/4–8/29	8/30–9/24	9/25–10/18
	4/1–6/5	6/6–7/7				
1954	3/12–4/4	4/5–4/28	4/29–5/23	5/24–6/17	6/18–7/13	7/14–8/8
1955	4/25–5/19	5/20–6/13	6/14–7/7	7/8–8/1	8/2–8/25	8/26–9/18
1956	2/12–3/7	3/8–4/4	4/5–5/7	5/8–6/23	9/9–10/5	10/6–10/31
			6/24–8/4	8/5–9/8		
1957	3/26–4/19	4/20–5/13	5/14–6/6	6/7–7/1	7/2–7/26	7/27–8/19
1958	5/6–5/31	6/1–6/26	6/27–7/22	7/23–8/15	8/16–9/9	9/10–10/3
1959	2/25–3/20	3/21–4/14	4/15–5/10	5/11–6/6	6/7–7/8	7/9–9/20
					9/21–9/24	9/25–11/9
1960	4/10–5/3	5/4–5/28	5/29–6/21	6/22–7/15	7/16–8/9	8/10–9/2
1961	2/3–6/5	6/6–7/7	7/8–8/3	8/4–8/29	8/30–9/23	9/24–10/17
1962	3/11–4/3	4/4–4/28	4/29–5/22	5/23–6/17	6/18–7/12	7/13–8/8
1963	4/24–5/18	5/19–6/12	6/13–7/7	7/8–7/31	8/1–8/25	8/26–9/18
1964	2/11–3/7	3/8–4/4	4/5–5/9	5/10–6/17	9/9–10/5	10/6–10/31
			6/18–8/5	8/6–9/8		
1965	3/26–4/18	4/19–5/12	5/13–6/6	6/7–6/30	7/1–7/25	7/26–8/19
1966	5/6–5/31	6/1–6/26	6/27–7/21	7/22–8/15	8/16–9/8	9/9–10/2
1967	2/24–3/20	3/21–4/14	4/15–5/10	5/11–6/6	6/7–7/8	7/9–9/9
					9/10–10/1	10/2–11/9
1968	4/9–5/3	5/4–5/27	5/28–6/20	6/21–7/15	7/16–8/8	8/9–9/2
1969	2/3–6/6	6/7–7/6	7/7–8/3	8/4–8/28	8/29–9/22	9/23–10/17
1970	3/11–4/3	4/4–4/27	4/28–5/22	5/23–6/16	6/17–7/12	7/13–8/8
1971	4/24–5/18	5/19–6/12	6/13–7/6	7/7–7/31	8/1–8/24	8/25–9/17
1972	2/11–3/7	3/8–4/3	4/4–5/10	5/11–6/11		
			6/12–8/6	8/7–9/8	9/9–10/5	10/6–10/30
1973	3/25–4/18	4/18–5/12	5/13–6/5	6/6–6/29	7/1–7/25	7/26–8/19
1974	5/5–5/31	6/1–6/25	6/26–7/21	7/22–8/14	8/15–9/8	9/9–10/2
1975	2/24–3/20	3/21–4/13	4/14–5/9	5/10–6/6	6/7–7/9	7/10–9/2
					9/3–10/4	10/5–11/9

Libra	Scorpio	Sagittarius	Capricorn	Aquarius	Pisces
9/4–9/27	1/1–1/2	1/3–1/27	1/28–2/20	2/21–3/16	3/17–4/9
	9/28–10/21	10/22–11/15	11/16–12/10	12/11–12/31	
10/19–11/11	11/12–12/5	12/6–12/29	12/30–12/31	1/1–1/5	1/6–2/1
8/9–9/6	9/7–10/22	10/23–10/27	1/1–1/22	1/23–2/15	2/16–3/11
	10/28–12/31				
9/19–10/13	1/1–1/6	1/7–2/5	2/6–3/4	3/5–3/30	3/31–4/24
	10/14–11/5	11/6–11/30	12/1–12/24	12/25–12/31	
11/1–11/25	11/26–12/19	12/20–12/31		1/1–1/17	1/18–2/11
8/20–9/14	9/15–10/9	1/1–1/12	1/13–2/5	2/6–3/1	3/2–3/25
		10/10–11/5	11/6–12/6	12/7–12/31	
10/4–10/27	10/28–11/20	11/21–12/14	12/15–12/31	1/1–4/6	4/7–5/5
11/10–12/7	12/8–12/31		1/1–1/7	1/8–1/31	2/1–2/24
9/3–9/26	1/1–1/2	1/3–1/27	1/28–2/20	2/21–3/15	3/16–4/9
	9/27–10/21	10/22–11/15	11/16–12/10	12/11–12/31	
10/18–11/11	11/12–12/4	12/5–12/28	12/29–12/31	1/1–1/5	1/6–2/2
8/9–9/6	9/7–12/31		1/1–1/21	1/22–2/14	2/15–3/10
9/19–10/12	1/1–1/6	1/7–2/5	2/6–3/4	3/5–3/29	3/30–4/23
	10/13–11/5	11/6–11/29	11/30–12/23	12/24–12/31	
11/1–11/24	11/25–12/19	12/20–12/31		1/1–1/16	1/17–2/10
8/20–9/13	9/14–10/9	1/1–1/12	1/13–2/5	2/6–3/1	3/2–3/25
		10/10–11/5	11/6–12/7	12/8–12/31	
10/3–10/26	10/27–11/19	11/20–12/13	2/7–2/25	1/1–2/6	4/7–5/5
			12/14–12/31	2/26–4/6	
11/10–12/7	12/8–12/31		1/1–1/6	1/7–1/30	1/31–2/23
9/3–9/26	1/1	1/2–1/26	1/27–2/20	2/21–3/15	3/16–4/8
	9/27–10/21	10/22–11/14	11/15–12/9	12/10–12/31	
10/18–11/10	11/11–12/4	12/5–12/28	12/29–12/31	1/1–1/4	1/5–2/2
8/9–9/7	9/8–12/31		1/1–1/21	1/22–2/14	2/15–3/10
9/18–10/11	1/1–1/7	1/8–2/5	2/6–3/4	3/5–3/29	3/30–4/23
	10/12–11/5	11/6–11/29	11/30–12/23	12/24–12/31	
10/31–11/24	11/25–12/18	12/19–12/31		1/1–1/16	1/17–2/10
8/20–9/13	9/14–10/8	1/1–1/12	1/13–2/4	2/5–2/28	3/1–3/24
		10/9–11/5	11/6–12/7	12/8–12/31	
10/3–10/26	10/27–11/19	11/20–12/13	12/14–12/31	3/1–4/6	4/7–5/4
			1/30–2/28	1/1–1/29	
11/10–12/7	12/8–12/31		1/1–1/6	1/7–1/30	1/31–2/23

VENUS SIGNS 1901–2008

	Aries	Taurus	Gemini	Cancer	Leo	Virgo
1976	4/8–5/2	5/2–5/27	5/27–6/20	6/20–7/14	7/14–8/8	8/8–9/1
1977	2/2–6/6	6/6–7/6	7/6–8/2	8/2–8/28	8/28–9/22	9/22–10/17
1978	3/9–4/2	4/2–4/27	4/27–5/22	5/22–6/16	6/16–7/12	7/12–8/6
1979	4/23–5/18	5/18–6/11	6/11–7/6	7/6–7/30	7/30–8/24	8/24–9/17
1980	2/9–3/6	3/6–4/3	4/3–5/12	5/12–6/5	9/7–10/4	10/4–10/30
			6/5–8/6	8/6–9/7		
1981	3/24–4/17	4/17–5/11	5/11–6/5	6/5–6/29	6/29–7/24	7/24–8/18
1982	5/4–5/30	5/30–6/25	6/25–7/20	7/20–8/14	8/14–9/7	9/7–10/2
1983	2/22–3/19	3/19–4/13	4/13–5/9	5/9–6/6	6/6–7/10	7/10–8/27
					8/27–10/5	10/5–11/9
1984	4/7–5/2	5/2–5/26	5/26–6/20	6/20–7/14	7/14–8/7	8/7–9/1
1985	2/2–6/6	6/7–7/6	7/6–8/2	8/2–8/28	8/28–9/22	9/22–10/16
1986	3/9–4/2	4/2–4/26	4/26–5/21	5/21–6/15	6/15–7/11	7/11–8/7
1987	4/22–5/17	5/17–6/11	6/11–7/5	7/5–7/30	7/30–8/23	8/23–9/16
1988	2/9–3/6	3/6–4/3	4/3–5/17	5/17–5/27	9/7–10/4	10/4–10/29
			5/27–8/6	8/28–9/22	9/22–10/16	
1989	3/23–4/16	4/16–5/11	5/11–6/4	6/4–6/29	6/29–7/24	7/24–8/18
1990	5/4–5/30	5/30–6/25	6/25–7/20	7/20–8/13	8/13–9/7	9/7–10/1
1991	2/22–3/18	3/18–4/13	4/13–5/9	5/9–6/6	6/6–7/11	7/11–8/21
					8/21–10/6	10/6–11/9
1992	4/7–5/1	5/1–5/26	5/26–6/19	6/19–7/13	7/13–8/7	8/7–8/31
1993	2/2–6/6	6/6–7/6	7/6–8/1	8/1–8/27	8/27–9/21	9/21–10/16
1994	3/8–4/1	4/1–4/26	4/26–5/21	5/21–6/15	6/15–7/11	7/11–8/7
1995	4/22–5/16	5/16–6/10	6/10–7/5	7/5–7/29	7/29–8/23	8/23–9/16
1996	2/9–3/6	3/6–4/3	4/3–8/7	8/7–9/7	9/7–10/4	10/4–10/29
1997	3/23–4/16	4/16–5/10	5/10–6/4	6/4–6/28	6/28–7/23	7/23–8/17
1998	5/3–5/29	5/29–6/24	6/24–7/19	7/19–8/13	8/13–9/6	9/6–9/30
1999	2/21–3/18	3/18–4/12	4/12–5/8	5/8–6/5	6/5–7/12	7/12–8/15
					8/15–10/7	10/7–11/9
2000	4/6–5/1	5/1–5/25	5/25–6/13	6/13–7/13	7/13–8/6	8/6–8/31
2001	2/2–6/6	6/6–7/5	7/5–8/1	8/1–8/26	8/26–9/20	9/20–10/15
2002	3/7–4/1	4/1–4/25	4/25–5/20	5/20–6/14	6/14–7/10	7/10–8/7
2003	4/21–5/16	5/16–6/9	6/9–7/4	7/4–7/29	7/29–8/22	8/22–9/15
2004	2/8–3/5	3/5–4/3	4/3–8/7	8/7–9/6	9/6–10/3	10/3–10/28
2005	3/22–4/15	4/15–5/10	5/10–6/3	6/3–6/28	6/28–7/23	7/23–8/17
2006	5/3–5/29	5/29–6/24	6/24–7/19	7/19–8/12	8/12–9/6	9/6–9/30
2007	2/21–3/16	3/17–4/10	4/11–5/7	5/8–6/4	6/5–7/13	7/14–8/7
					8/8–10/6	10/7–11/7
2008	4/6–4/30	5/1–5/24	5/25–6/17	6/18–7/11	7/12–8/4	8/5–8/29

Libra	Scorpio	Sagittarius	Capricorn	Aquarius	Pisces
9/1–9/26	9/26–10/20	1/1–1/26	1/26–2/19	2/19–3/15	3/15–4/8
10/17–11/10	11/10–12/4	12/4–12/27	12/27–1/20/78		1/4–2/2
8/6–9/7	9/7–1/7			1/20–2/13	2/13–3/9
9/17–10/11	10/11–11/4	1/7–2/5	2/5–3/3	3/3–3/29	3/29–4/23
		11/4–11/28	11/28–12/22	12/22–1/16/80	
10/30–11/24	11/24–12/18	12/18–1/11/81			1/16–2/9
8/18–9/12	9/12–10/9	10/9–11/5	1/11–2/4	2/4–2/28	2/28–3/24
			11/5–12/8	12/8–1/23/82	
10/2–10/26	10/26–11/18	11/18–12/12	1/23–3/2	3/2–4/6	4/6–5/4
			12/12–1/5/83		
11/9–12/6	12/6–1/1/84			1/5–1/29	1/29–2/22
9/1–9/25	9/25–10/20	1/1–1/25	1/25–2/19	2/19–3/14	3/14–4/7
		10/20–11/13	11/13–12/9	12/10–1/4	
10/16–11/9	11/9–12/3	12/3–12/27	12/28–1/19		1/4–2/2
8/7–9/7	9/7–1/7			1/20–2/13	2/13–3/9
9/16–10/10	10/10–11/3	1/7–2/5	2/5–3/3	3/3–3/28	3/28–4/22
		11/3–11/28	11/28–12/22	12/22–1/15	
10/29–11/23	11/23–12/17	12/17–1/10			1/15–2/9
8/18–9/12	9/12–10/8	10/8–11/5	1/10–2/3	2/3–2/27	2/27–3/23
			11/5–12/10	12/10–1/16/90	
10/1–10/25	10/25–11/18	11/18–12/12	1/16–3/3	3/3–4/6	4/6–5/4
			12/12–1/5		
11/9–12/6	12/6–12/31	12/31–1/25/92		1/5–1/29	1/29–2/22
8/31–9/25	9/25–10/19	10/19–11/13	1/25–2/18	2/18–3/13	3/13–4/7
			11/13–12/8	12/8–1/3/93	
10/16–11/9	11/9–12/2	12/2–12/26	12/26–1/19		1/3–2/2
8/7–9/7	9/7–1/7			1/19–2/12	2/12–3/8
9/16–10/10	10/10–11/13	1/7–2/4	2/4–3/2	3/2–3/28	3/28–4/22
		11/3–11/27	11/27–12/21	12/21–1/15	
10/29–11/23	11/23–12/17	12/17–1/10/97			1/15–2/9
8/17–9/12	9/12–10/8	10/8–11/5	1/10–2/3	2/3–2/27	2/27–3/23
			11/5–12/12	12/12–1/9	
9/30–10/24	10/24–11/17	11/17–12/11	1/9–3/4	3/4–4/6	4/6–5/3
11/9–12/5	12/5–12/31	12/31–1/24		1/4–1/28	1/28–2/21
8/31–9/24	9/24–10/19	10/19–11/13	1/24–2/18	2/18–3/12	3/13–4/6
			11/13–12/8	12/8	
10/15–11/8	11/8–12/2	12/2–12/26	12/26/01–1/18/02	12/8/00–1/3/01	1/3–2/2
8/7–9/7	9/7–1/7/03		12/26/01–1/18	1/18–2/11	2/11–3/7
9/15–10/9	10/9–11/2	1/7–2/4	2/4–3/2	3/2–3/27	3/27–4/21
		11/2–11/26	11/26–12/21	12/21–1/14/04	
10/28–11/22	11/22–12/16	12/16–1/9/05		1/1–1/14	1/14–2/8
8/17–9/11	9/11–10/8	10/8–11/15	1/9–2/2	2/2–2/26	2/26–3/22
			11/5–12/15	12/15–1/1/06	
9/30–10/24	10/24–11/17	11/17–12/11	1/1–3/5	3/5–4/6	4/6–5/3
11/8–12/4	12/5–12/29	12/30–1/24/08		1/3–1/26	1/27–2/20
8/30–9/22	9/23–10/17	10/18–11/11	1/24–2/16	2/17–3/11	3/12–4/5
			11/12–12/6	12/7–1/2/09	

87

How to Use the Mars, Jupiter, and Saturn Tables

Find the year of your birth on the left side of each column. The dates when the planet entered each sign are listed on the right side of each column. (Signs are abbreviated to three letters.) Your birthday should fall on or between each date listed, and your planetary placement should correspond to the earlier sign of that period.

All planet changes are calculated for the Greenwich Mean Time zone.

MARS SIGNS 1901–2008

Year	Mon	Day	Sign		Year	Mon	Day	Sign
1901	MAR	1	Leo			OCT	1	Vir
	MAY	11	Vir			NOV	20	Lib
	JUL	13	Lib		1905	JAN	13	Scp
	AUG	31	Scp			AUG	21	Sag
	OCT	14	Sag			OCT	8	Cap
	NOV	24	Cap			NOV	18	Aqu
1902	JAN	1	Aqu			DEC	27	Pic
	FEB	8	Pic		1906	FEB	4	Ari
	MAR	19	Ari			MAR	17	Tau
	APR	27	Tau			APR	28	Gem
	JUN	7	Gem			JUN	11	Can
	JUL	20	Can			JUL	27	Leo
	SEP	4	Leo			SEP	12	Vir
	OCT	23	Vir			OCT	30	Lib
	DEC	20	Lib			DEC	17	Scp
1903	APR	19	Vir		1907	FEB	5	Sag
	MAY	30	Lib			APR	1	Cap
	AUG	6	Scp			OCT	13	Aqu
	SEP	22	Sag			NOV	29	Pic
	NOV	3	Cap		1908	JAN	11	Ari
	DEC	12	Aqu			FEB	23	Tau
1904	JAN	19	Pic			APR	7	Gem
	FEB	27	Ari			MAY	22	Can
	APR	6	Tau			JUL	8	Leo
	MAY	18	Gem			AUG	24	Vir
	JUN	30	Can			OCT	10	Lib
	AUG	15	Leo			NOV	25	Scp

1909	JAN	10	Sag		MAR	9	Pic
	FEB	24	Cap		APR	16	Ari
	APR	9	Aqu		MAY	26	Tau
	MAY	25	Pic		JUL	6	Gem
	JUL	21	Ari		AUG	19	Can
	SEP	26	Pic		OCT	7	Leo
	NOV	20	Ari	1916	MAY	28	Vir
1910	JAN	23	Tau		JUL	23	Lib
	MAR	14	Gem		SEP	8	Scp
	MAY	1	Can		OCT	22	Sag
	JUN	19	Leo		DEC	1	Cap
	AUG	6	Vir	1917	JAN	9	Aqu
	SEP	22	Lib		FEB	16	Pic
	NOV	6	Scp		MAR	26	Ari
	DEC	20	Sag		MAY	4	Tau
1911	JAN	31	Cap		JUN	14	Gem
	MAR	14	Aqu		JUL	28	Can
	APR	23	Pic		SEP	12	Leo
	JUN	2	Ari		NOV	2	Vir
	JUL	15	Tau	1918	JAN	11	Lib
	SEP	5	Gem		FEB	25	Vir
	NOV	30	Tau		JUN	23	Lib
1912	JAN	30	Gem		AUG	17	Scp
	APR	5	Can		OCT	1	Sag
	MAY	28	Leo		NOV	11	Cap
	JUL	17	Vir		DEC	20	Aqu
	SEP	2	Lib	1919	JAN	27	Pic
	OCT	18	Scp		MAR	6	Ari
	NOV	30	Sag		APR	15	Tau
1913	JAN	10	Cap		MAY	26	Gem
	FEB	19	Aqu		JUL	8	Can
	MAR	30	Pic		AUG	23	Leo
	MAY	8	Ari		OCT	10	Vir
	JUN	17	Tau		NOV	30	Lib
	JUL	29	Gem	1920	JAN	31	Scp
	SEP	15	Can		APR	23	Lib
1914	MAY	1	Leo		JUL	10	Scp
	JUN	26	Vir		SEP	4	Sag
	AUG	14	Lib		OCT	18	Cap
	SEP	29	Scp		NOV	27	Aqu
	NOV	11	Sag	1921	JAN	5	Pic
	DEC	22	Cap		FEB	13	Ari
1915	JAN	30	Aqu		MAR	25	Tau

	MAY	6	Gem		OCT	26	Scp
	JUN	18	Can		DEC	8	Sag
	AUG	3	Leo	1928	JAN	19	Cap
	SEP	19	Vir		FEB	28	Aqu
	NOV	6	Lib		APR	7	Pic
	DEC	26	Scp		MAY	16	Ari
1922	FEB	18	Sag		JUN	26	Tau
	SEP	13	Cap		AUG	9	Gem
	OCT	30	Aqu		OCT	3	Can
	DEC	11	Pic		DEC	20	Gem
1923	JAN	21	Ari	1929	MAR	10	Can
	MAR	4	Tau		MAY	13	Leo
	APR	16	Gem		JUL	4	Vir
	MAY	30	Can		AUG	21	Lib
	JUL	16	Leo		OCT	6	Scp
	SEP	1	Vir		NOV	18	Sag
	OCT	18	Lib		DEC	29	Cap
	DEC	4	Scp	1930	FEB	6	Aqu
1924	JAN	19	Sag		MAR	17	Pic
	MAR	6	Cap		APR	24	Ari
	APR	24	Aqu		JUN	3	Tau
	JUN	24	Pic		JUL	14	Gem
	AUG	24	Aqu		AUG	28	Can
	OCT	19	Pic		OCT	20	Leo
	DEC	19	Ari	1931	FEB	16	Can
1925	FEB	5	Tau		MAR	30	Leo
	MAR	24	Gem		JUN	10	Vir
	MAY	9	Can		AUG	1	Lib
	JUN	26	Leo		SEP	17	Scp
	AUG	12	Vir		OCT	30	Sag
	SEP	28	Lib		DEC	10	Cap
	NOV	13	Scp	1932	JAN	18	Aqu
	DEC	28	Sag		FEB	25	Pic
1926	FEB	9	Cap		APR	3	Ari
	MAR	23	Aqu		MAY	12	Tau
	MAY	3	Pic		JUN	22	Gem
	JUN	15	Ari		AUG	4	Can
	AUG	1	Tau		SEP	20	Leo
1927	FEB	22	Gem		NOV	13	Vir
	APR	17	Can	1933	JUL	6	Lib
	JUN	6	Leo		AUG	26	Scp
	JUL	25	Vir		OCT	9	Sag
	SEP	10	Lib		NOV	19	Cap

	DEC	28	Aqu		FEB	17	Tau
1934	FEB	4	Pic		APR	1	Gem
	MAR	14	Ari		MAY	17	Can
	APR	22	Tau		JUL	3	Leo
	JUN	2	Gem		AUG	19	Vir
	JUL	15	Can		OCT	5	Lib
	AUG	30	Leo		NOV	20	Scp
	OCT	18	Vir	1941	JAN	4	Sag
	DEC	11	Lib		FEB	17	Cap
1935	JUL	29	Scp		APR	2	Aqu
	SEP	16	Sag		MAY	16	Pic
	OCT	28	Cap		JUL	2	Ari
	DEC	7	Aqu	1942	JAN	11	Tau
1936	JAN	14	Pic		MAR	7	Gem
	FEB	22	Ari		APR	26	Can
	APR	1	Tau		JUN	14	Leo
	MAY	13	Gem		AUG	1	Vir
	JUN	25	Can		SEP	17	Lib
	AUG	10	Leo		NOV	1	Scp
	SEP	26	Vir		DEC	15	Sag
	NOV	14	Lib	1943	JAN	26	Cap
1937	JAN	5	Scp		MAR	8	Aqu
	MAR	13	Sag		APR	17	Pic
	MAY	14	Scp		MAY	27	Ari
	AUG	8	Sag		JUL	7	Tau
	SEP	30	Cap		AUG	23	Gem
	NOV	11	Aqu	1944	MAR	28	Can
	DEC	21	Pic		MAY	22	Leo
1938	JAN	30	Ari		JUL	12	Vir
	MAR	12	Tau		AUG	29	Lib
	APR	23	Gem		OCT	13	Scp
	JUN	7	Can		NOV	25	Sag
	JUL	22	Leo	1945	JAN	5	Cap
	SEP	7	Vir		FEB	14	Aqu
	OCT	25	Lib		MAR	25	Pic
	DEC	11	Scp		MAY	2	Ari
1939	JAN	29	Sag		JUN	11	Tau
	MAR	21	Cap		JUL	23	Gem
	MAY	25	Aqu		SEP	7	Can
	JUL	21	Cap		NOV	11	Leo
	SEP	24	Aqu		DEC	26	Can
	NOV	19	Pic	1946	APR	22	Leo
1940	JAN	4	Ari		JUN	20	Vir

	AUG	9	Lib		OCT	12	Cap
	SEP	24	Scp		NOV	21	Aqu
	NOV	6	Sag		DEC	30	Pic
	DEC	17	Cap	1953	FEB	8	Ari
1947	JAN	25	Aqu		MAR	20	Tau
	MAR	4	Pic		MAY	1	Gem
	APR	11	Ari		JUN	14	Can
	MAY	21	Tau		JUL	29	Leo
	JUL	1	Gem		SEP	14	Vir
	AUG	13	Can		NOV	1	Lib
	OCT	1	Leo		DEC	20	Scp
	DEC	1	Vir	1954	FEB	9	Sag
1948	FEB	12	Leo		APR	12	Cap
	MAY	18	Vir		JUL	3	Sag
	JUL	17	Lib		AUG	24	Cap
	SEP	3	Scp		OCT	21	Aqu
	OCT	17	Sag		DEC	4	Pic
	NOV	26	Cap	1955	JAN	15	Ari
1949	JAN	4	Aqu		FEB	26	Tau
	FEB	11	Pic		APR	10	Gem
	MAR	21	Ari		MAY	26	Can
	APR	30	Tau		JUL	11	Leo
	JUN	10	Gem		AUG	27	Vir
	JUL	23	Can		OCT	13	Lib
	SEP	7	Leo		NOV	29	Scp
	OCT	27	Vir	1956	JAN	14	Sag
	DEC	26	Lib		FEB	28	Cap
1950	MAR	28	Vir		APR	14	Aqu
	JUN	11	Lib		JUN	3	Pic
	AUG	10	Scp		DEC	6	Ari
	SEP	25	Sag	1957	JAN	28	Tau
	NOV	6	Cap		MAR	17	Gem
	DEC	15	Aqu		MAY	4	Can
1951	JAN	22	Pic		JUN	21	Leo
	MAR	1	Ari		AUG	8	Vir
	APR	10	Tau		SEP	24	Lib
	MAY	21	Gem		NOV	8	Scp
	JUL	3	Can		DEC	23	Sag
	AUG	18	Leo	1958	FEB	3	Cap
	OCT	5	Vir		MAR	17	Aqu
	NOV	24	Lib		APR	27	Pic
1952	JAN	20	Scp		JUN	7	Ari
	AUG	27	Sag		JUL	21	Tau

	SEP	21	Gem		NOV	6	Vir
	OCT	29	Tau	1965	JUN	29	Lib
1959	FEB	10	Gem		AUG	20	Scp
	APR	10	Can		OCT	4	Sag
	JUN	1	Leo		NOV	14	Cap
	JUL	20	Vir		DEC	23	Aqu
	SEP	5	Lib	1966	JAN	30	Pic
	OCT	21	Scp		MAR	9	Ari
	DEC	3	Sag		APR	17	Tau
1960	JAN	14	Cap		MAY	28	Gem
	FEB	23	Aqu		JUL	11	Can
	APR	2	Pic		AUG	25	Leo
	MAY	11	Ari		OCT	12	Vir
	JUN	20	Tau		DEC	4	Lib
	AUG	2	Gem	1967	FEB	12	Scp
	SEP	21	Can		MAR	31	Lib
1961	FEB	5	Gem		JUL	19	Scp
	FEB	7	Can		SEP	10	Sag
	MAY	6	Leo		OCT	23	Cap
	JUN	28	Vir		DEC	1	Aqu
	AUG	17	Lib	1968	JAN	9	Pic
	OCT	1	Scp		FEB	17	Ari
	NOV	13	Sag		MAR	27	Tau
	DEC	24	Cap		MAY	8	Gem
1962	FEB	1	Aqu		JUN	21	Can
	MAR	12	Pic		AUG	5	Leo
	APR	19	Ari		SEP	21	Vir
	MAY	28	Tau		NOV	9	Lib
	JUL	9	Gem		DEC	29	Scp
	AUG	22	Can	1969	FEB	25	Sag
	OCT	11	Leo		SEP	21	Cap
1963	JUN	3	Vir		NOV	4	Aqu
	JUL	27	Lib		DEC	15	Pic
	SEP	12	Scp	1970	JAN	24	Ari
	OCT	25	Sag		MAR	7	Tau
	DEC	5	Cap		APR	18	Gem
1964	JAN	13	Aqu		JUN	2	Can
	FEB	20	Pic		JUL	18	Leo
	MAR	29	Ari		SEP	3	Vir
	MAY	7	Tau		OCT	20	Lib
	JUN	17	Gem		DEC	6	Scp
	JUL	30	Can	1971	JAN	23	Sag
	SEP	15	Leo		MAR	12	Cap

	MAY	3	Aqu		JUN	6	Tau
	NOV	6	Pic		JUL	17	Gem
	DEC	26	Ari		SEP	1	Can
1972	FEB	10	Tau		OCT	26	Leo
	MAR	27	Gem	1978	JAN	26	Can
	MAY	12	Can		APR	10	Leo
	JUN	28	Leo		JUN	14	Vir
	AUG	15	Vir		AUG	4	Lib
	SEP	30	Lib		SEP	19	Scp
	NOV	15	Scp		NOV	2	Sag
	DEC	30	Sag		DEC	12	Cap
1973	FEB	12	Cap	1979	JAN	20	Aqu
	MAR	26	Aqu		FEB	27	Pic
	MAY	8	Pic		APR	7	Ari
	JUN	20	Ari		MAY	16	Tau
	AUG	12	Tau		JUN	26	Gem
	OCT	29	Ari		AUG	8	Can
	DEC	24	Tau		SEP	24	Leo
1974	FEB	27	Gem		NOV	19	Vir
	APR	20	Can	1980	MAR	11	Leo
	JUN	9	Leo		MAY	4	Vir
	JUL	27	Vir		JUL	10	Lib
	SEP	12	Lib		AUG	29	Scp
	OCT	28	Scp		OCT	12	Sag
	DEC	10	Sag		NOV	22	Cap
1975	JAN	21	Cap		DEC	30	Aqu
	MAR	3	Aqu	1981	FEB	6	Pic
	APR	11	Pic		MAR	17	Ari
	MAY	21	Ari		APR	25	Tau
	JUL	1	Tau		JUN	5	Gem
	AUG	14	Gem		JUL	18	Can
	OCT	17	Can		SEP	2	Leo
	NOV	25	Gem		OCT	21	Vir
1976	MAR	18	Can		DEC	16	Lib
	MAY	16	Leo	1982	AUG	3	Scp
	JUL	6	Vir		SEP	20	Sag
	AUG	24	Lib		OCT	31	Cap
	OCT	8	Scp		DEC	10	Aqu
	NOV	20	Sag	1983	JAN	17	Pic
1977	JAN	1	Cap		FEB	25	Ari
	FEB	9	Aqu		APR	5	Tau
	MAR	20	Pic		MAY	16	Gem
	APR	27	Ari		JUN	29	Can

	AUG	13	Leo	1990	JAN	29	Cap
	SEP	30	Vir		MAR	11	Aqu
	NOV	18	Lib		APR	20	Pic
1984	JAN	11	Scp		MAY	31	Ari
	AUG	17	Sag		JUL	12	Tau
	OCT	5	Cap		AUG	31	Gem
	NOV	15	Aqu		DEC	14	Tau
	DEC	25	Pic	1991	JAN	21	Gem
1985	FEB	2	Ari		APR	3	Can
	MAR	15	Tau		MAY	26	Leo
	APR	26	Gem		JUL	15	Vir
	JUN	9	Can		SEP	1	Lib
	JUL	25	Leo		OCT	16	Scp
	SEP	10	Vir		NOV	29	Sag
	OCT	27	Lib	1992	JAN	9	Cap
	DEC	14	Scp		FEB	18	Aqu
1986	FEB	2	Sag		MAR	28	Pic
	MAR	28	Cap		MAY	5	Ari
	OCT	9	Aqu		JUN	14	Tau
	NOV	26	Pic		JUL	26	Gem
1987	JAN	8	Ari		SEP	12	Can
	FEB	20	Tau	1993	APR	27	Leo
	APR	5	Gem		JUN	23	Vir
	MAY	21	Can		AUG	12	Lib
	JUL	6	Leo		SEP	27	Scp
	AUG	22	Vir		NOV	9	Sag
	OCT	8	Lib		DEC	20	Cap
	NOV	24	Scp	1994	JAN	28	Aqu
1988	JAN	8	Sag		MAR	7	Pic
	FEB	22	Cap		APR	14	Ari
	APR	6	Aqu		MAY	23	Tau
	MAY	22	Pic		JUL	3	Gem
	JUL	13	Ari		AUG	16	Can
	OCT	23	Pic		OCT	4	Leo
	NOV	1	Ari		DEC	12	Vir
1989	JAN	19	Tau	1995	JAN	22	Leo
	MAR	11	Gem		MAY	25	Vir
	APR	29	Can		JUL	21	Lib
	JUN	16	Leo		SEP	7	Scp
	AUG	3	Vir		OCT	20	Sag
	SEP	19	Lib		NOV	30	Cap
	NOV	4	Scp	1996	JAN	8	Aqu
	DEC	18	Sag		FEB	15	Pic

Year	Month	Day	Sign		Year	Month	Day	Sign
	MAR	24	Ari			MAR	1	Tau
	MAY	2	Tau			APR	13	Gem
	JUN	12	Gem			MAY	28	Can
	JUL	25	Can			JUL	13	Leo
	SEP	9	Leo			AUG	29	Vir
	OCT	30	Vir			OCT	15	Lib
1997	JAN	3	Lib			DEC	1	Scp
	MAR	8	Vir		2003	JAN	17	Sag
	JUN	19	Lib			MAR	4	Cap
	AUG	14	Scp			APR	21	Aqu
	SEP	28	Sag			JUN	17	Pic
	NOV	9	Cap			DEC	16	Ari
	DEC	18	Aqu		2004	FEB	3	Tau
1998	JAN	25	Pic			MAR	21	Gem
	MAR	4	Ari			MAY	7	Can
	APR	13	Tau			JUN	23	Leo
	MAY	24	Gem			AUG	10	Vir
	JUL	6	Can			SEP	26	Lib
	AUG	20	Leo			NOV	11	Sep
	OCT	7	Vir			DEC	25	Sag
	NOV	27	Lib		2005	FEB	6	Cap
1999	JAN	26	Scp			MAR	20	Aqu
	MAY	5	Lib			MAY	1	Pic
	JUL	5	Scp			JUN	12	Ari
	SEP	2	Sag			JUL	28	Tau
	OCT	17	Cap		2006	FEB	17	Gem
	NOV	26	Aqu			APR	14	Can
2000	JAN	4	Pic			JUN	3	Leo
	FEB	12	Ari			JUL	22	Vir
	MAR	23	Tau			SEP	8	Lib
	MAY	3	Gem			OCT	23	Scp
	JUN	16	Can			DEC	6	Sag
	AUG	1	Leo		2007	JAN	16	Cap
	SEP	17	Vir			FEB	25	Aqu
	NOV	4	Lib			APR	6	Pic
	DEC	23	Scp			MAY	15	Ari
2001	FEB	14	Sag			JUNE	24	Tau
	SEP	8	Cap			AUG	7	Gem
	OCT	27	Aqu			SEP	28	Can
	DEC	8	Pic			DEC	31	Gem*
2002	JAN	18	Ari					

*Repeat means planet is retrograde.

2008	MAR	4	Can		OCT	3	Scp
	MAY	9	Leo		NOV	16	Sag
	JUL	1	Vir		DEC	27	Cap
	AUG	19	Lib				

JUPITER SIGNS 1901–2008

1901	JAN	19	Cap		SEP	11	Pic
1902	FEB	6	Aqu		1928	JAN	23	Ari
1903	FEB	20	Pic			JUN	4	Tau
1904	MAR	1	Ari		1929	JUN	12	Gem
	AUG	8	Tau		1930	JUN	26	Can
	AUG	31	Ari		1931	JUL	17	Leo
1905	MAR	7	Tau		1932	AUG	11	Vir
	JUL	21	Gem		1933	SEP	10	Lib
	DEC	4	Tau		1934	OCT	11	Scp
1906	MAR	9	Gem		1935	NOV	9	Sag
	JUL	30	Can		1936	DEC	2	Cap
1907	AUG	18	Leo		1937	DEC	20	Aqu
1908	SEP	12	Vir		1938	MAY	14	Pic
1909	OCT	11	Lib			JUL	30	Aqu
1910	NOV	11	Scp			DEC	29	Pic
1911	DEC	10	Sag		1939	MAY	11	Ari
1913	JAN	2	Cap			OCT	30	Pic
1914	JAN	21	Aqu			DEC	20	Ari
1915	FEB	4	Pic		1940	MAY	16	Tau
1916	FEB	12	Ari		1941	MAY	26	Gem
	JUN	26	Tau		1942	JUN	10	Can
	OCT	26	Ari		1943	JUN	30	Leo
1917	FEB	12	Tau		1944	JUL	26	Vir
	JUN	29	Gem		1945	AUG	25	Lib
1918	JUL	13	Can		1946	SEP	25	Scp
1919	AUG	2	Leo		1947	OCT	24	Sag
1920	AUG	27	Vir		1948	NOV	15	Cap
1921	SEP	25	Lib		1949	APR	12	Aqu
1922	OCT	26	Scp			JUN	27	Cap
1923	NOV	24	Sag			NOV	30	Aqu
1924	DEC	18	Cap		1950	APR	15	Pic
1926	JAN	6	Aqu			SEP	15	Aqu
1927	JAN	18	Pic			DEC	1	Pic
	JUN	6	Ari		1951	APR	21	Ari

97

1952	APR	28	Tau			AUG	15	Scp
1953	MAY	9	Gem	1971	JAN	14	Sag
1954	MAY	24	Can			JUN	5	Scp
1955	JUN	13	Leo			SEP	11	Sag
	NOV	17	Vir	1972	FEB	6	Cap
1956	JAN	18	Leo			JUL	24	Sag
	JUL	7	Vir			SEP	25	Cap
	DEC	13	Lib	1973	FEB	23	Aqu
1957	FEB	19	Vir	1974	MAR	8	Pic
	AUG	7	Lib	1975	MAR	18	Ari
1958	JAN	13	Scp	1976	MAR	26	Tau
	MAR	20	Lib			AUG	23	Gem
	SEP	7	Scp			OCT	16	Tau
1959	FEB	10	Sag	1977	APR	3	Gem
	APR	24	Scp			AUG	20	Can
	OCT	5	Sag			DEC	30	Gem
1960	MAR	1	Cap	1978	APR	12	Can
	JUN	10	Sag			SEP	5	Leo
	OCT	26	Cap	1979	FEB	28	Can
1961	MAR	15	Aqu			APR	20	Leo
	AUG	12	Cap			SEP	29	Vir
	NOV	4	Aqu	1980	OCT	27	Lib
1962	MAR	25	Pic	1981	NOV	27	Scp
1963	APR	4	Ari	1982	DEC	26	Sag
1964	APR	12	Tau	1984	JAN	19	Cap
1965	APR	22	Gem	1985	FEB	6	Aqu
	SEP	21	Can	1986	FEB	20	Pic
	NOV	17	Gem	1987	MAR	2	Ari
1966	MAY	5	Can	1988	MAR	8	Tau
	SEP	27	Leo			JUL	22	Gem
1967	JAN	16	Can			NOV	30	Tau
	MAY	23	Leo	1989	MAR	11	Gem
	OCT	19	Vir			JUL	30	Can
1968	FEB	27	Leo	1990	AUG	18	Leo
	JUN	15	Vir	1991	SEP	12	Vir
	NOV	15	Lib	1992	OCT	10	Lib
1969	MAR	30	Vir	1993	NOV	10	Scp
	JUL	15	Lib	1994	DEC	9	Sag
	DEC	16	Scp	1996	JAN	3	Cap
1970	APR	30	Lib	1997	JAN	21	Aqu
				1998	FEB	4	Pic

1999	FEB	13	Ari	2003	AUG	27	Vir
	JUN	28	Tau	2004	SEP	24	Lib
	OCT	23	Ari	2005	OCT	26	Scp
2000	FEB	14	Tau	2006	NOV	24	Sag
	JUN	30	Gem	2007	DEC	17	Cap
2001	JUL	14	Can	2008			Cap
2002	AUG	1	Leo				

SATURN SIGNS 1903–2008

1903	JAN	19	Aqu		OCT	18	Pic
1905	APR	13	Pic	1938	JAN	14	Ari
	AUG	17	Aqu	1939	JUL	6	Tau
1906	JAN	8	Pic		SEP	22	Ari
1908	MAR	19	Ari	1940	MAR	20	Tau
1910	MAY	17	Tau	1942	MAY	8	Gem
	DEC	14	Ari	1944	JUN	20	Can
1911	JAN	20	Tau	1946	AUG	2	Leo
1912	JUL	7	Gem	1948	SEP	19	Vir
	NOV	30	Tau	1949	APR	3	Leo
1913	MAR	26	Gem		MAY	29	Vir
1914	AUG	24	Can	1950	NOV	20	Lib
	DEC	7	Gem	1951	MAR	7	Vir
1915	MAY	11	Can		AUG	13	Lib
1916	OCT	17	Leo	1953	OCT	22	Scp
	DEC	7	Can	1956	JAN	12	Sag
1917	JUN	24	Leo		MAY	14	Scp
1919	AUG	12	Vir		OCT	10	Sag
1921	OCT	7	Lib	1959	JAN	5	Cap
1923	DEC	20	Scp	1962	JAN	3	Aqu
1924	APR	6	Lib	1964	MAR	24	Pic
	SEP	13	Scp		SEP	16	Aqu
1926	DEC	2	Sag		DEC	16	Pic
1929	MAR	15	Cap	1967	MAR	3	Ari
	MAY	5	Sag	1969	APR	29	Tau
	NOV	30	Cap	1971	JUN	18	Gem
1932	FEB	24	Aqu	1972	JAN	10	Tau
	AUG	13	Cap		FEB	21	Gem
	NOV	20	Aqu	1973	AUG	1	Can
1935	FEB	14	Pic	1974	JAN	7	Gem
1937	APR	25	Ari		APR	18	Can

1975	SEP	17	Leo	1993	MAY	21	Pic
1976	JAN	14	Can		JUN	30	Aqu
	JUN	5	Leo	1994	JAN	28	Pic
1977	NOV	17	Vir	1996	APR	7	Ari
1978	JAN	5	Leo	1998	JUN	9	Tau
	JUL	26	Vir		OCT	25	Ari
1980	SEP	21	Lib	1999	MAR	1	Tau
1982	NOV	29	Scp	2000	AUG	10	Gem
1983	MAY	6	Lib		OCT	16	Tau
	AUG	24	Scp	2001	APR	21	Gem
1985	NOV	17	Sag	2003	JUN	3	Can
1988	FEB	13	Cap	2005	JUL	16	Leo
	JUN	10	Sag	2007	SEP	2	Vir
	NOV	12	Cap	2008			Vir
1991	FEB	6	Aqu				

CHAPTER 7

The Leader of the Parade: Your Rising Sign

Your rising sign is the degree of the zodiac ascending over the eastern horizon at the time you were born. (That's why it's often called the ascendant.) It is important to know the rising sign, because it determines *where* things happen in the horoscope chart. It marks the first point in the horoscope, the beginning of the first house, one of twelve divisions of the horoscope, each of which represents a different area of life. After the rising sign, the other houses parade around the chart in sequence, with the following sign on the house cusp.

You can learn much about a person by the signs and interactions of the sun, moon, and planets in the horoscope, but you need to know the rising sign to determine where in that person's life an activity will take place. For example, you might know that a person has Mars in Aries, which will describe that person's dynamic, fiery energy. But if you also know that the person has a Capricorn rising sign, this Mars will fall in the fourth house of home and family, so you know where that energy will operate. Without a valid rising sign, the collection of planets have no homes. One would have no idea which area of life would be influenced by a particular planet.

Due to the earth's rotation, the rising sign changes every two hours, which means that even though other babies born later or earlier on the same day in the same hospital as you were will have most planets in the same signs as you, they may not have the same rising sign and their planets may fall in different houses in the chart. For instance, if Mars is in Gemini and your rising sign is Taurus, Mars will most likely be active in the second or financial house of your chart. Someone born later in the day, when the rising sign is Virgo, would have Mars positioned at the top of the chart, energizing the tenth house of career.

Most astrologers insist on knowing the exact time of a client's birth before analyzing a chart. The more accurate your birth time, the more accurately an astrologer can position the planets in your chart by determining the correct rising sign.

How Your Rising Sign Can Influence Your Sun Sign

Your rising sign has an important relationship with your sun sign. Some will complement the sun sign; others hide it under a totally different mask, as if playing an entirely different role, making it difficult to guess the person's sun sign from outer appearances. This may be the reason why you might not look or act like your sun sign's archetype. For example, a Leo with a conservative Capricorn ascendant would come across as much more serious than a Leo with a fiery Aries or Sagittarius ascendant.

Though the rising sign usually creates the first impression you make, there are exceptions. When the sun sign is reinforced by other planets in the same sign, this might overpower the impression of the rising sign. For instance, a Leo sun plus a Leo Venus and Leo Jupiter would counteract the more conservative image that would otherwise be conveyed by the person's Capricorn ascendant.

Those born early in the morning when the sun was on the horizon will be most likely to project the image of their sun sign. These people are often called a "double Aries" or a "double Virgo" because the same sun sign and ascendant reinforce each other.

Find Your Rising Sign

Look up your rising sign from the chart at the end of this chapter. Since rising signs change every two hours, it is important to know your birth time as close to the minute as possible. Even a few minutes' difference could change the rising sign and therefore the setup of your chart. If you are unsure about the exact time, but know within a few hours, check the following descriptions to see which is most like the personality you project.

Aries Rising: Alpha Energy

You are the most aggressive version of your sun sign, with boundless energy that can be used productively if it's channeled in the right direction. Watch a tendency to overreact emotionally and blow your top. You come across as openly competitive, a positive asset in business or sports. Be on guard against impatience, which could lead to head injuries. Your walk and bearing could have the telltale head-forward Aries posture. You may wear more bright colors, especially red, than others of your sign. You may also have a tendency to drive your car faster.

Can you see the alpha Aries tendency in Barbra Streisand (a sun-sign Taurus) and Bette Midler (a sun-sign Sagittarius)?

Taurus Rising: Down to Earth

You're slow-moving, with a beautiful (or distinctive) speaking or singing voice that can be especially soothing or melodious. You probably surround yourself with comfort, good food, luxurious environments, and other sensual pleasures. You prefer welcoming others into your home to gadding about. You may have a talent for business, especially in trading, appraising, and real estate. A Taurus ascendant gives a well-padded physique that gains weight easily, like Liza Minnelli. This ascendant can also endow females with a curvaceous beauty.

Gemini Rising: A Way with Words

You're naturally sociable, with lighter, more ethereal mannerisms than others of your sign, especially if you're female.

You love to communicate with people, and express your ideas and feelings easily, like British prime minister Tony Blair. You may have a talent for writing or public speaking. You thrive on variety, a constantly changing scene, and a lively social life. However, you may relate to others at a deeper level than might be suspected. And you will be far more sympathetic and caring than you project. You will probably travel widely, changing partners and jobs several times (or juggle two at once). Physically, your nerves are quite sensitive. Occasionally, you would benefit from a calm, tranquil atmosphere away from your usual social scene.

Cancer Rising: Nurturing Instincts

You are naturally acquisitive, possessive, private, a moneymaker, like Bill Gates or Michael Bloomberg. You easily pick up on others' needs and feelings—a great gift in business, the arts, and personal relationships. But you must guard against overreacting or taking things too personally, especially during full moon periods. Find creative outlets for your natural nurturing gifts, such as helping the less fortunate, particularly children. Your insights would be helpful in psychology. Your desire to feed and care for others would be useful in the restaurant, hotel, or child-care industries. You may be especially fond of wearing romantic old clothes, collecting antiques, and, of course, dining on exquisite food. Since your body may retain fluids, pay attention to your diet. To relax, escape to places near water.

Leo Rising: Diva Dazzle

You may come across as more poised than you really feel. However, you play it to the hilt, projecting a proud royal presence. A Leo ascendant gives you a natural flair for drama, like Marilyn Monroe, and you might be accused of stealing the spotlight. You'll also project a much more outgoing, optimistic, sunny personality than others of your sign. You take care to please your public by always projecting your best star quality, probably tossing a luxuriant mane of hair, sporting a striking hairstyle, or dressing to impress. Females often dazzle with spectacular jewelry. Since you may have a strong parental nature, you could well be the regal family matriarch or patriarch, like George W. Bush.

Virgo Rising: High Standards

Virgo rising masks your inner nature with a practical, analytical outer image. You seem neat, orderly, more particular than others of your sign. Others in your life may feel they must live up to your high standards. Though at times you may be openly critical, this masks a well-meaning desire to have only the best for loved ones. Your sharp eye for details could be used in the financial world, or your literary skills could draw you to teaching or publishing. The healing arts, health care, and service-oriented professions attract many with a Virgo ascendant. You're likely to take good care of yourself, with great attention to health, diet, and exercise, like Madonna. You might even show some hypochondriac tendencies, like Woody Allen. Physically, you may have a very sensitive digestive system.

Libra Rising: The Charmer

Libra rising gives you a charming, social public persona, like Bill Clinton. You tend to avoid confrontations in relationships, preferring to smooth the way or negotiate diplomatically rather than give in to an emotional reaction. Because you are interested in all aspects of a situation, you may be slow to reach decisions. Physically, you'll have good proportions and symmetry. You will move with natural grace and balance. You're likely to have pleasing, if not beautiful, facial features, with a winning smile, like Cary Grant. You'll show natural good taste and harmony in your clothes and home decor. Legal, diplomatic, or public relations professions could draw your interest.

Scorpio Rising: An Air of Mystery

You project an intriguing air of mystery with this ascendant, as the Scorpio secretiveness and sense of underlying power combines with your sun sign. As with Jackie O, there's more to you than meets the eye. You seem like someone who is always in control and who can move comfortably in the world of power. Your physical look comes across as intense. Many of you have remarkable eyes, with a direct, penetrating gaze. But you'll never reveal your private agenda, and you tend to keep your true feelings under wraps (watch a tendency toward paranoia). You may have an interesting romantic history with secret love affairs, like Grace Kelly. Many of you heighten your air of mystery by wearing black. You're happiest near water and should provide yourself with a seaside retreat.

Sagittarius Rising: The Explorer

You travel with this ascendant. You may also be a more outdoor, sportive type, with an athletic, casual, outgoing air. Your moods are camouflaged with cheerful optimism or a philosophical attitude. Though you don't hesitate to speak your mind, like Ted Turner, who was called the Mouth of the South, you can also laugh at your troubles or crack a joke more easily than others of your sign. A Sagittarius ascendant can also draw you to the field of higher education or to spiritual life. You'll seem to have less attachment to things and people, and may explore the globe. Your strong, fast legs are a physical bonus.

Capricorn Rising: Serious Business

This rising sign makes you come across as serious, goal-oriented, disciplined, and careful with cash. You are not one of the zodiac's big spenders, though you might splurge occasionally on items with good investment value. You're the traditional, conservative type in dress and environment, and you might come across as quite normal and business-like, like Rupert Murdoch. You'll function well in a structured or corporate environment where you can climb to the top. (You are always aware of who's the boss.) In your personal life, you could be a loner or a single parent who is "father and mother" to your children.

Aquarius Rising: One of a Kind

You come across as less concerned about what others think and could even be a bit eccentric. You're more at ease with groups of people than others in your sign, and you may be attracted to public life, like Jay Leno. Your appearance may be unique, either unconventional or unimportant to you. Those of you whose sun is in a water sign (Cancer, Scorpio, Pisces) may exercise your nurturing qualities with a large group, an extended family, or a day-care or community center.

Pisces Rising: Romantic Roles

Your creative, nurturing talents are heightened and so is your ability to project emotional drama. And, like Antonio Banderas, your dreamy eyes and poetic air bring out the protective instinct in others. You could be attracted to the arts, especially theater, dance, film, and photography, or to psychology, spiritual practice, and charity work. You are happiest when you are using your creative ability to help others. Since you are vulnerable to mood swings, it is especially important for you to find interesting, creative work where you can express your talents and heighten your self-esteem. Accentuate the positive. Be wary of escapist tendencies, particularly involving alcohol or drugs to which you are supersensitive, like Whitney Houston.

RISING SIGNS—A.M. BIRTHS

	1 AM	2 AM	3 AM	4 AM	5 AM	6 AM	7 AM	8 AM	9 AM	10 AM	11 AM	12 NOON
Jan 1	Lib	Sc	Sc	Sc	Sag	Sag	Cap	Cap	Aq	Aq	Pis	Ar
Jan 9	Lib	Sc	Sc	Sag	Sag	Sag	Cap	Cap	Aq	Pis	Ar	Tau
Jan 17	Sc	Sc	Sc	Sag	Sag	Cap	Cap	Aq	Aq	Pis	Ar	Tau
Jan 25	Sc	Sc	Sag	Sag	Sag	Cap	Cap	Aq	Pis	Ar	Tau	Tau
Feb 2	Sc	Sc	Sag	Sag	Cap	Cap	Aq	Pis	Pis	Ar	Tau	Gem
Feb 10	Sc	Sag	Sag	Sag	Cap	Cap	Aq	Pis	Ar	Tau	Tau	Gem
Feb 18	Sc	Sag	Sag	Cap	Cap	Aq	Pis	Pis	Ar	Tau	Gem	Gem
Feb 26	Sag	Sag	Sag	Cap	Aq	Aq	Pis	Ar	Tau	Tau	Gem	Gem
Mar 6	Sag	Sag	Cap	Cap	Aq	Pis	Pis	Ar	Tau	Gem	Gem	Can
Mar 14	Sag	Cap	Cap	Aq	Aq	Pis	Ar	Tau	Tau	Gem	Gem	Can
Mar 22	Sag	Cap	Cap	Aq	Pis	Ar	Ar	Tau	Gem	Gem	Can	Can
Mar 30	Cap	Cap	Aq	Pis	Pis	Ar	Tau	Tau	Gem	Can	Can	Can
Apr 7	Cap	Cap	Aq	Pis	Ar	Ar	Tau	Gem	Gem	Can	Can	Leo
Apr 14	Cap	Aq	Aq	Pis	Ar	Tau	Tau	Gem	Gem	Can	Can	Leo
Apr 22	Cap	Aq	Pis	Ar	Ar	Tau	Gem	Gem	Gem	Can	Leo	Leo
Apr 30	Aq	Aq	Pis	Ar	Tau	Tau	Gem	Can	Can	Can	Leo	Leo
May 8	Aq	Pis	Ar	Ar	Tau	Gem	Gem	Can	Can	Leo	Leo	Leo
May 16	Aq	Pis	Ar	Tau	Gem	Gem	Can	Can	Can	Leo	Leo	Vir
May 24	Pis	Ar	Ar	Tau	Gem	Gem	Can	Can	Leo	Leo	Leo	Vir
June 1	Pis	Ar	Tau	Gem	Gem	Can	Can	Leo	Leo	Leo	Vir	Vir
June 9	Ar	Ar	Tau	Gem	Gem	Can	Can	Leo	Leo	Leo	Vir	Vir
June 17	Ar	Tau	Gem	Gem	Can	Can	Can	Leo	Leo	Vir	Vir	Vir
June 25	Tau	Tau	Gem	Gem	Can	Can	Leo	Leo	Leo	Vir	Vir	Lib
July 3	Tau	Gem	Gem	Can	Can	Can	Leo	Leo	Leo	Vir	Vir	Lib
July 11	Tau	Gem	Gem	Can	Can	Leo	Leo	Leo	Vir	Vir	Lib	Lib
July 18	Gem	Gem	Can	Can	Can	Leo	Leo	Vir	Vir	Vir	Lib	Lib
July 26	Gem	Gem	Can	Can	Leo	Leo	Vir	Vir	Vir	Lib	Lib	Lib
Aug 3	Gem	Can	Can	Can	Leo	Leo	Vir	Vir	Vir	Lib	Lib	Sc
Aug 11	Gem	Can	Can	Leo	Leo	Leo	Vir	Vir	Lib	Lib	Lib	Sc
Aug 18	Can	Can	Can	Leo	Leo	Vir	Vir	Vir	Lib	Lib	Sc	Sc
Aug 27	Can	Can	Leo	Leo	Leo	Vir	Vir	Lib	Lib	Lib	Sc	Sc
Sept 4	Can	Can	Leo	Leo	Leo	Vir	Vir	Vir	Lib	Lib	Sc	Sc
Sept 12	Can	Leo	Leo	Leo	Vir	Vir	Lib	Lib	Lib	Sc	Sc	Sag
Sept 20	Leo	Leo	Leo	Vir	Vir	Vir	Lib	Lib	Sc	Sc	Sc	Sag
Sept 28	Leo	Leo	Leo	Vir	Vir	Lib	Lib	Lib	Sc	Sc	Sag	Sag
Oct 6	Leo	Leo	Vir	Vir	Vir	Lib	Lib	Sc	Sc	Sc	Sag	Sag
Oct 14	Leo	Vir	Vir	Vir	Lib	Lib	Lib	Sc	Sc	Sag	Sag	Cap
Oct 22	Leo	Vir	Vir	Lib	Lib	Lib	Sc	Sc	Sc	Sag	Sag	Cap
Oct 30	Vir	Vir	Vir	Lib	Lib	Sc	Sc	Sc	Sag	Sag	Cap	Cap
Nov 7	Vir	Vir	Lib	Lib	Lib	Sc	Sc	Sc	Sag	Sag	Cap	Cap
Nov 15	Vir	Vir	Lib	Lib	Sc	Sc	Sc	Sag	Sag	Cap	Cap	Aq
Nov 23	Vir	Lib	Lib	Lib	Sc	Sc	Sag	Sag	Sag	Cap	Cap	Aq
Dec 1	Vir	Lib	Lib	Sc	Sc	Sc	Sag	Sag	Cap	Cap	Aq	Aq
Dec 9	Lib	Lib	Lib	Sc	Sc	Sag	Sag	Sag	Cap	Cap	Aq	Pis
Dec 18	Lib	Lib	Sc	Sc	Sc	Sag	Sag	Cap	Cap	Aq	Aq	Pis
Dec 28	Lib	Lib	Sc	Sc	Sag	Sag	Sag	Cap	Aq	Aq	Pis	Ar

RISING SIGNS—P.M. BIRTHS

	1 PM	2 PM	3 PM	4 PM	5 PM	6 PM	7 PM	8 PM	9 PM	10 PM	11 PM	12 MIDNIGHT
Jan 1	Tau	Gem	Gem	Can	Can	Can	Leo	Leo	Vir	Vir	Vir	Lib
Jan 9	Tau	Gem	Gem	Can	Can	Leo	Leo	Leo	Vir	Vir	Vir	Lib
Jan 17	Gem	Gem	Can	Can	Can	Leo	Leo	Vir	Vir	Vir	Lib	Lib
Jan 25	Gem	Gem	Can	Can	Leo	Leo	Leo	Vir	Vir	Lib	Lib	Lib
Feb 2	Gem	Can	Can	Can	Leo	Leo	Vir	Vir	Vir	Lib	Lib	Sc
Feb 10	Gem	Can	Can	Leo	Leo	Leo	Vir	Vir	Lib	Lib	Lib	Sc
Feb 18	Can	Can	Can	Leo	Leo	Vir	Vir	Vir	Lib	Lib	Sc	Sc
Feb 26	Can	Can	Leo	Leo	Leo	Vir	Vir	Lib	Lib	Lib	Sc	Sc
Mar 6	Can	Leo	Leo	Leo	Vir	Vir	Vir	Lib	Lib	Sc	Sc	Sc
Mar 14	Can	Leo	Leo	Vir	Vir	Vir	Lib	Lib	Lib	Sc	Sc	Sag
Mar 22	Leo	Leo	Leo	Vir	Vir	Lib	Lib	Lib	Sc	Sc	Sc	Sag
Mar 30	Leo	Leo	Vir	Vir	Vir	Lib	Lib	Sc	Sc	Sc	Sag	Sag
Apr 7	Leo	Leo	Vir	Vir	Lib	Lib	Lib	Sc	Sc	Sc	Sag	Sag
Apr 14	Leo	Vir	Vir	Vir	Lib	Lib	Sc	Sc	Sc	Sag	Sag	Cap
Apr 22	Leo	Vir	Vir	Lib	Lib	Lib	Sc	Sc	Sc	Sag	Sag	Cap
Apr 30	Vir	Vir	Vir	Lib	Lib	Sc	Sc	Sc	Sag	Sag	Cap	Cap
May 8	Vir	Vir	Lib	Lib	Lib	Sc	Sc	Sag	Sag	Sag	Cap	Cap
May 16	Vir	Vir	Lib	Lib	Sc	Sc	Sc	Sag	Sag	Cap	Cap	Aq
May 24	Vir	Lib	Lib	Lib	Sc	Sc	Sag	Sag	Sag	Cap	Cap	Aq
June 1	Vir	Lib	Lib	Sc	Sc	Sc	Sag	Sag	Cap	Cap	Aq	Aq
June 9	Lib	Lib	Lib	Sc	Sc	Sag	Sag	Sag	Cap	Cap	Aq	Pis
June 17	Lib	Lib	Sc	Sc	Sc	Sag	Sag	Cap	Cap	Aq	Aq	Pis
June 25	Lib	Lib	Sc	Sc	Sag	Sag	Sag	Cap	Cap	Aq	Pis	Ar
July 3	Lib	Sc	Sc	Sc	Sag	Sag	Cap	Cap	Aq	Aq	Pis	Ar
July 11	Lib	Sc	Sc	Sag	Sag	Sag	Cap	Cap	Aq	Pis	Ar	Tau
July 18	Sc	Sc	Sc	Sag	Sag	Cap	Cap	Aq	Aq	Pis	Ar	Tau
July 26	Sc	Sc	Sag	Sag	Sag	Cap	Cap	Aq	Pis	Ar	Tau	Tau
Aug 3	Sc	Sc	Sag	Sag	Sag	Cap	Cap	Aq	Pis	Ar	Tau	Gem
Aug 11	Sc	Sag	Sag	Sag	Cap	Cap	Aq	Pis	Ar	Tau	Tau	Gem
Aug 18	Sc	Sag	Sag	Cap	Cap	Aq	Pis	Pis	Ar	Tau	Gem	Gem
Aug 27	Sag	Sag	Sag	Cap	Cap	Aq	Pis	Ar	Tau	Tau	Gem	Gem
Sept 4	Sag	Sag	Cap	Cap	Aq	Pis	Pis	Ar	Tau	Gem	Gem	Can
Sept 12	Sag	Sag	Cap	Aq	Aq	Pis	Ar	Tau	Tau	Gem	Gem	Can
Sept 20	Sag	Cap	Cap	Aq	Pis	Pis	Ar	Tau	Gem	Gem	Can	Can
Sept 28	Cap	Cap	Aq	Aq	Pis	Ar	Tau	Tau	Gem	Gem	Can	Can
Oct 6	Cap	Cap	Aq	Pis	Ar	Ar	Tau	Gem	Gem	Can	Can	Leo
Oct 14	Cap	Aq	Aq	Pis	Ar	Tau	Tau	Gem	Gem	Can	Can	Leo
Oct 22	Cap	Aq	Pis	Ar	Ar	Tau	Gem	Gem	Can	Can	Leo	Leo
Oct 30	Aq	Aq	Pis	Ar	Tau	Tau	Gem	Can	Can	Can	Leo	Leo
Nov 7	Aq	Aq	Pis	Ar	Tau	Tau	Gem	Can	Can	Can	Leo	Leo
Nov 15	Aq	Pis	Ar	Tau	Gem	Gem	Can	Can	Can	Leo	Leo	Vir
Nov 23	Pis	Ar	Ar	Tau	Gem	Gem	Can	Can	Can	Leo	Leo	Vir
Dec 1	Pis	Ar	Tau	Gem	Gem	Can	Can	Can	Leo	Leo	Vir	Vir
Dec 9	Ar	Tau	Tau	Gem	Gem	Can	Can	Leo	Leo	Leo	Vir	Vir
Dec 18	Ar	Tau	Gem	Gem	Can	Can	Can	Leo	Leo	Vir	Vir	Vir
Dec 28	Tau	Tau	Gem	Gem	Can	Can	Leo	Leo	Vir	Vir	Vir	Lib

CHAPTER 8

Astrology's Magic Symbols: The Glyphs

One of the first things an astrology student learns is how to read the symbols on a horoscope chart. These symbols or *glyphs* represent a kind of code, a pictorial language understood by astrologers around the globe and used by all astrology software programs. You'll miss out if you don't learn the glyphs. Once you learn them, you can begin to find your way around the chart, beginning your journey to deeper understanding. You can also make use of free charts available on any number of Internet sites and perhaps purchase one of the many astrology software programs.

The glyphs are fascinating little pictures in themselves, with built-in clues to help you not only decipher which sign or planet each represents, but what the symbol means in a deeper, more esoteric sense. Actually the physical act of writing the symbol is a mystical experience in itself, a way to invoke the deeper meaning of the sign or planet through age-old visual elements that have been with us since time began.

Since there are only twelve signs and ten planets (not counting a few asteroids and other space objects some astrologers use), it's a lot easier than learning to read a foreign language. Here's a code cracker for the glyphs, beginning with the glyphs for the planets. To those who already know their glyphs, don't just skim over the chapter. These familiar graphics have hidden meanings you will discover!

The Glyphs for the Planets

The glyphs for the planets are easy to learn. They're simple combinations of the most basic visual elements: the circle, the semicircle or arc, and the cross. However, each component of a glyph has a special meaning in relation to the other parts of the symbol.

The circle, which has no beginning or end, is one of the oldest symbols of spirit or spiritual forces. Early diagrams of the heavens—spiritual territory—are shown in circular form. The never-ending line of the circle is the perfect symbol for eternity. The semicircle or arc is an incomplete circle, symbolizing the receptive, finite soul, which contains spiritual potential in the curving line.

The vertical line of the cross symbolizes movement from heaven to earth. The horizontal line describes temporal movement, here and now, in time and space. Combined in a cross, the vertical and horizontal planes symbolize manifestation in the material world.

The Sun Glyph ☉

The sun is always shown by this powerful solar symbol, a circle with a point in the center. The center point is you, your spiritual center, and the symbol represents your infinite personality incarnating (the point) into the finite cycles of birth and death.

The sun has been represented by a circle or disk since ancient Egyptian times when the solar disk represented the sun god, Ra. Some archaeologists believe the great stone circles found in England were centers of sun worship. This particular version of the symbol was brought into common use in the sixteenth century after German occultist and scholar Cornelius Agrippa (1486–1535) wrote a book called *Die Occulta Philosophia,* which became accepted as the authority in the field. Agrippa collected many medieval astrological and magical symbols in this book, which have been used by astrologers since then.

The Moon Glyph ☽

The moon glyph is the most recognizable symbol on a chart, a left-facing arc stylized into the crescent moon. As part of a circle, the arc symbolizes the potential fulfillment of the entire circle, the life force that is still incomplete. Therefore, it is the ideal representation of the reactive, receptive, emotional nature of the moon.

The Mercury Glyph ☿

Mercury contains all three elemental symbols: the crescent, the circle, and the cross in vertical order. This is the "Venus with a hat" glyph (compare with the symbol of Venus). With another stretch of the imagination, can't you see the winged cap of Mercury the messenger? Think of the upturned crescent as antennae that tune in and transmit messages from the sun, reminding you that Mercury is the way you communicate, the way your mind works. The upturned arc is receiving energy into the spirit or solar circle, which will later be translated into action on the material plane, symbolized by the cross. All the elements are equally sized because Mercury is neutral; it doesn't play favorites! This planet symbolizes objective, detached, unemotional thinking.

The Venus Glyph ♀

Here the relationship is between two components: the circle of spirit and the cross of matter. Spirit is elevated over matter, pulling it upward. Venus asks, "What is beautiful? What do you like best? What do you love to have done to you?" Consequently, Venus determines both your ideal of beauty and what feels good sensually. It governs your own allure and power to attract, as well as what attracts and pleases you.

The Mars Glyph ♂

In this glyph, the cross of matter is stylized into an arrowhead pointed up and outward, propelled by the circle of spirit. With a little imagination, you can visualize it as the shield and spear of Mars, the ancient god of war. You can deduce that Mars embodies your spiritual energy projected into the outer world. It's your assertiveness, your initiative, your aggressive drive, what you like to do to others, your temper. If you know someone's Mars, you know whether they'll blow up when angry or do a slow burn. Your task is to use your outgoing Mars energy wisely and well.

The Jupiter Glyph ♃

Jupiter is the basic cross of matter, with a large stylized crescent perched on the left side of the horizontal, temporal plane. You might think of the crescent as an open hand, because one meaning of Jupiter is "luck," what's handed to you. You don't have to work for what you get from Jupiter; it comes to you, if you're open to it.

The Jupiter glyph might also remind you of a jumbo jet plane, with a huge tail fin, about to take off. This is the planet of travel, mental and spiritual, of expanding your horizons via new ideas, new spiritual dimensions, and new places. Jupiter embodies the optimism and enthusiasm of the traveler about to embark on an exciting adventure.

The Saturn Glyph ♄

Flip Jupiter over, and you've got Saturn. This might not be immediately apparent because Saturn is usually stylized into an "h" form like the one shown here. The principle it expresses is the opposite of Jupiter's expansive tendencies. Saturn pulls you back to earth: the receptive arc is pushed down underneath the cross of matter. Before there are any rewards or expansion, the duties and obligations of the material world must be considered. Saturn says, "Stop, wait, finish your chores before you take off!"

Saturn's glyph also resembles the sickle of old "Father Time." Saturn was first known as Chronos, the Greek god of time, for time brings all matter to an end. When it was the most distant planet (before the discovery of Uranus), Saturn was believed to be the place where time stopped.

After the soul departed from earth, it journeyed back to the outer reaches of the universe and finally stopped at Saturn, or at "the end of time."

The Uranus Glyph ♅

The glyph for Uranus is often stylized to form a capital *H* after Sir William Herschel, who discovered the planet. But the more esoteric version curves the two pillars of the H into crescent antennae, or "ears," like satellite disks receiving signals from space. These are perched on the horizontal material line of the cross of matter and pushed from below by the circle of the spirit. To many sci-fi fans, Uranus looks like an orbiting satellite.

Uranus channels the highest energy of all, the white electrical light of the universal spiritual force that holds the cosmos together. This pure electrical energy is gathered from all over the universe. Because Uranus energy doesn't follow any ordinary celestial drumbeat, it can't be controlled or predicted (which is also true of those who are strongly influenced by this eccentric planet). In the symbol, this energy is manifested through the balance of polarities (the two opposite arms of the glyph) like the two polarized wires of a lightbulb.

The Neptune Glyph ♆

Neptune's glyph is usually stylized to look like a trident, the weapon of the Roman god Neptune. However, on a more esoteric level, it shows the large upturned crescent of the soul pierced through by the cross of matter. Neptune nails down, or materializes, soul energy, bringing impulses from the soul level into manifestation. That is why Neptune is associated with imagination or "imagining in," making an image of the soul. Neptune works through feelings, sensitivity, and the mystical capacity to bring the divine into the earthly realm.

The Pluto Glyph ♀

Pluto is written two ways. One is a composite of the letters *PL,* the first two letters of the word Pluto and coincidentally the initials of Percival Lowell, one of the planet's discoverers. The other, more esoteric symbol is a small circle above a large open crescent that surmounts the cross of matter. This depicts Pluto's power to regenerate. Imagine a new little spirit emerging from the sheltering cup of the soul. Pluto rules the forces of life and death. After this planet has passed a sensitive point in your chart, you are transformed, reborn in some way.

Sci-fi fans might visualize this glyph as a small satellite (the circle) being launched. It was shortly after Pluto's discovery that we learned how to harness the nuclear forces that made space exploration possible. Pluto rules the transformative power of atomic energy, which totally changed our lives and from which there is no turning back.

The Glyphs for the Signs

On an astrology chart, the glyph for the sign will appear after that of the planet. For example, when you see the moon glyph followed first by a number and then by another glyph representing the sign, this means that the moon was passing over a certain degree of that astrological sign at the time of the chart. On the dividing lines between the houses on your chart, you'll find the symbol for the sign that rules the house.

Because sun sign symbols do not contain the same basic geometric components of the planetary glyphs, we must look elsewhere for clues to their meanings. Many have been passed down from ancient Egyptian and Chaldean civilizations with few modifications. Others have been adapted over the centuries.

In deciphering many of the glyphs, you'll often find that the symbols reveal a dual nature of the sign, which is not always apparent in the usual sun sign descriptions. For instance, the Gemini glyph is similar to the Roman numeral for two, and reveals this sign's longing to discover a twin soul. The Cancer glyph may be interpreted as resembling either the nurturing breasts or the self-protective claws of a crab, both symbols associated with the contrasting qualities of this sign. Libra's glyph embodies the duality of the spirit balanced with material reality. The Sagittarius glyph shows that the aspirant must also carry along the earthly animal nature in his quest. The Capricorn sea goat is another symbol with dual emphasis. The goat climbs high, yet is always pulled back by the deep waters of the unconscious. Aquarius embodies the double waves of mental detachment, balanced by the desire for connection with others, in a friendly way. Finally, the two fishes of Pisces, which are forever tied together, show the duality of the soul and the spirit that must be reconciled.

The Aries Glyph ♈

Since the symbol for Aries is the Ram, this glyph is obviously associated with a ram's horns, which characterize one aspect of the Aries personality—an aggressive, me-first, leaping-headfirst attitude. But the symbol can be interpreted in other ways as well. Some astrologers liken it to a fountain of energy, which Aries people also embody. The first sign of the zodiac bursts on the scene eagerly, ready to go. Another analogy is to the eyebrows and nose of the human head, which Aries rules, and the thinking power that is initiated by the brain.

One theory of this symbol links it to the Egyptian god Amun, represented by a ram in ancient times. As Amun-Ra, this god was believed to embody the creator of the universe, the leader of all the other gods. This relates easily to the position of Aries as the leader (or first sign) of the zodiac, which begins at the spring equinox, a time of the year when nature is renewed.

The Taurus Glyph ♉

This is another easy glyph to draw and identify. It takes little imagination to decipher the bull's head with long curving horns. Like its symbol the Bull, the archetypal Taurus is slow to anger but ferocious when provoked, as well as stubborn, steady, and sensual. Another association is the larynx (and thyroid) of the throat area (ruled by Taurus) and the eustachian tubes running up to the ears, which coincides with the relationship of Taurus to the voice, song, and music. Many famous singers, musicians, and composers have prominent Taurus influences.

Many ancient religions involved a bull as the central figure in fertility rites or initiations, usually symbolizing the victory of man over his animal nature. Another possible origin is in the sacred bull of Egypt, who embodied the incarnate form of Osiris, god of death and resurrection. In early Christian imagery, the Taurus Bull represented St. Luke.

The Gemini Glyph ♊

The standard glyph immediately calls to mind the Roman numeral for two (II) and the Twins symbol, as it is called, for Gemini. In almost all drawings and images used for this sign, the relationship between two persons is emphasized. Usually one twin will be touching the other, which signifies communication, human contact, the desire to share.

The top line of the Gemini glyph indicates mental communication, while the bottom line indicates shared physical space.

The most famous Gemini legend is that of the twin sons, Castor and Pollux, one of whom had a mortal father while the other was the son of Zeus, king of the gods. When it came time for the mortal twin to die, his grief-stricken brother pleaded with Zeus, who agreed to let them spend half the year on earth in mortal form and half in immortal life, with the gods on Mount Olympus. This reflects a basic duality of humankind, which possesses an immortal soul yet is also subject to the limits of mortality.

The Cancer Glyph ♋

Two convenient images relate to the Cancer glyph. It is easiest to decode the curving claws of the Cancer symbol, the Crab. Like the crab's, Cancer's element is water. This sensitive sign also has a hard protective shell to protect its tender interior. The crab must be wily to escape predators, scampering sideways and hiding under rocks. The crab also responds to the cycles of the moon, as do all shellfish. The other image is that of two female breasts, which Cancer rules, showing that this is a sign that nurtures and protects others as well as itself.

In ancient Egypt, Cancer was also represented by the scarab beetle, a symbol of regeneration and eternal life.

The Leo Glyph ♌

Notice that the Leo glyph seems to be an extension of Cancer's glyph, with a significant difference. In the Cancer glyph, the lines curve inward protectively. The Leo glyph expresses energy outwardly. And there is no duality in the symbol, the Lion, or in Leo, the sign.

Lions have belonged to the sign of Leo since earliest times. It is not difficult to imagine the king of beasts with his sweeping mane and curling tail from this glyph. The upward sweep of the glyph easily describes the positive energy of Leo: the flourishing tail, the flamboyant qualities. Anther analogy, perhaps a stretch of the imagination, is that of a heart leaping up with joy and enthusiasm, also very typical of Leo, which also rules the heart. In early Christian imagery, the Leo Lion represented St. Mark.

The Virgo Glyph ♍

You can read much into this mysterious glyph. For instance, it could represent the initials of "Mary Virgin," or a young woman holding a staff of wheat, or stylized female genitalia, all common interpretations. The M shape might also remind you that Virgo is ruled by Mercury. The cross beneath the symbol reveals the grounded, practical nature of this earth sign.

The earliest zodiacs link Virgo with the Egyptian goddess Isis, who gave birth to the god Horus after her husband

Osiris had been killed, in the archetype of a miraculous conception. There are many ancient statues of Isis nursing her baby son, which are reminiscent of medieval Virgin and Child motifs. This sign has also been associated with the image of the Holy Grail, when the Virgo symbol was substituted with a chalice.

The Libra Glyph ♎

It is not difficult to read the standard image for Libra, the Scales, into this glyph. There is another meaning, however, that is equally relevant: the setting sun as it descends over the horizon. Libra's natural position on the zodiac wheel is the descendant, or sunset position (as the Aries natural position is the ascendant, or rising sign). Both images relate to Libra's personality. Libra is always weighing pros and cons for a balanced decision. In the sunset image, the sun (male) hovers over the horizontal earth (female) before setting. Libra is the space between these lines, harmonizing yin and yang, spiritual and material, male and female, ideal and real worlds. The glyph has also been linked to the kidneys, which are associated with Libra.

The Scorpio Glyph ♏

With its barbed tail, this glyph is easy to identify as the Scorpion for the sign of Scorpio. It also represents the male sexual parts, over which the sign rules. From the arrowhead, you can draw the conclusion that Mars was once its ruler. Some earlier Egyptian glyphs for Scorpio represent it as an erect serpent, so the Serpent is an alternate symbol.

Another symbol for Scorpio, which is not identifiable in this glyph, is the Eagle. Scorpios can go to extremes, either in soaring like the eagle or self-destructing like the scorpion. In early Christian imagery, which often used zodiacal symbols, the Scorpio Eagle was chosen to symbolize the intense apostle St. John the Evangelist.

The Sagittarius Glyph ♐

This is one of the easiest to spot and draw: an upward pointing arrow lifting up a cross. The arrow is pointing skyward, while the cross represents the four elements of the material world, which the arrow must convey. Elevating materiality into spirituality is an important Sagittarius quality, which explains why this sign is associated with higher learning, religion, philosophy, travel—the aspiring professions. Sagittarius can also send barbed arrows of frankness in the pursuit of truth, so the Archer symbol for Sagittarius is apt. (Sagittarius is also the sign of the supersalesman.)

Sagittarius is symbolically represented by the centaur, a mythological creature who is half man, half horse, aiming his arrow toward the skies. Though Sagittarius is motivated by spiritual aspiration, it also must balance the powerful appetites of the animal nature. The centaur Chiron, a figure in Greek mythology, became a wise teacher who, after many adventures and world travels, was killed by a poisoned arrow.

The Capricorn Glyph ♑

One of the most difficult symbols to draw, this glyph may take some practice. It is a representation of the sea goat: a mythical animal that is a goat with a curving fish's tail. The goat part of Capricorn wants to leave the waters of the emotions and climb to the elevated areas of life. But the fish tail is the unconscious, the deep chaotic psychic level that draws the goat back. Capricorn is often trying to escape the deep, feeling part of life by submerging himself in work, steadily ascending to the top. To some people, the glyph represents a seated figure with a bent knee, a reminder that Capricorn governs the knee area of the body.

An interesting aspect of this glyph is the contrast of the sharp pointed horns—which represent the penetrating, shrewd, conscious side of Capricorn—with the swishing tail—which represents its serpentine, unconscious, emotional force. One Capricorn legend, which dates from Roman times, tells of the earthy fertility god, Pan, who tried to save himself from uncontrollable sexual desires by jumping into the Nile. His upper body then turned into a goat, while the lower part became a fish. Later, Jupiter gave him a safe haven as a constellation in the skies.

The Aquarius Glyph ≈

This ancient water symbol can be traced back to an Egyptian hieroglyph representing streams of life force. Symbolized by the Water Bearer, Aquarius is distributor of the waters of life—the magic liquid of regeneration. The two waves can also be linked to the positive and negative charges of the electrical energy that Aquarius rules, a sort of universal wavelength. Aquarius is tuned in intuitively to higher forces via this electrical force. The duality of the glyph could also refer to the dual nature of Aquarius, a sign that runs hot and cold and that is friendly but also detached in the mental world of air signs.

In Greek legends, Aquarius is represented by Ganymede, who was carried to heaven by an eagle in order to become the cupbearer of Zeus and to supervise the annual flooding of the Nile. The sign later became associated with aviation and notions of flight.

The Pisces Glyph)(

Here is an abstraction of the familiar image of Pisces, two Fishes swimming in opposite directions yet bound together by a cord. The Fishes represent the spirit—which yearns for the freedom of heaven—and the soul—which remains attached to the desires of the temporal world. During life on earth, the spirit and the soul are bound together. When they complement each other, instead of pulling in opposite directions, they facilitate the Pisces creativity. The ancient version of this glyph, taken from the Egyptians, had no connecting line, which was added in the fourteenth century.

In another interpretation, it is said that the left fish indicates the direction of involution or the beginning of a cycle, while the right fish signifies the direction of evolution, the way to completion of a cycle. It's an appropriate grand finale for Pisces, the last sign of the zodiac.

CHAPTER 9

High-Tech Astrology: The Best Software for Your Budget and Ability

After you've acquired some basic knowledge—the signs, houses, planets, and glyphs—you have the tools to take astrology to the next level by reading charts and relating the planets to the lives of friends, relatives, and daily events.

If you have a computer, the easiest way to do this is to use astrology software that can put a chart on the screen in seconds and even help you interpret it.

When it comes to astrology software, there are endless options. How do you make the right choice? First, define your goals. Do you want to do charts of friends and family, study celebrity charts, or check the aspects every day on your Palm Pilot? Do you want to invest in a more comprehensive program that adapts to your changing needs as you learn astrology?

The good news is that there's a program for every level of interest in all price points—starting with free. For the dabbler, there are the affordable Winstar Express and Time Passages. For the serious student, there are Astrolog (free), Solar Fire, Kepler, Winstar Plus—software that does every technique on planets and gives you beautiful chart printouts. You can do a chart of someone you've just met on your PDA with Astracadabra. If you're a Mac user, you'll be satisfied with the wonderful IO and Time Passages software.

However, since all the programs use the astrology symbols, or glyphs, for planets and signs, rather than written words, you should learn the glyphs before you purchase your software. Our chapter on the glyphs in this book will help you do just that. Here are some software options for you to explore.

Easy for Beginners

Time Passages

Designed for either a Macintosh or Windows computer, Time Passages is straightforward and easy to use. It allows you to generate charts and interpretation reports for yourself or friends and loved ones at the touch of a button. If you haven't yet learned the astrology symbols, this might be the program for you; just roll your mouse over any symbol of the planets, signs, or house cusps, and you'll be shown a description in plain English below the chart. Then click on the planet, sign, or house cusp and up pops a detailed interpretation. It couldn't be easier. A new basic edition, under fifty dollars at this writing, is bargain priced and ideal for beginners.

Time Passages
(866) 772-7876 (866-77-ASTRO)
Web site: www.astrograph.com

Growth Opportunities

Astrolabe

Astrolabe is one of the top astrology software resources. Check out the latest version of their powerful Solar Fire software for Windows. A breeze to use, it will grow with your increasing knowledge of astrology to the most sophisticated levels. This company also markets a variety of programs for all levels of expertise and a wide selection of computer-generated astrology readings. This is a good resource for innovative software as well as applications for older computers.

The Astrolabe Web site is a great place to start your astrology tour of the Internet. Visitors to the site are greeted with a chart of the time you log on. And you can get your chart calculated, also free, with an interpretation e-mailed to you.

Astrolabe
Box 1750-R
Brewster, MA 02631
Phone: (800) 843-6682
Web site: www.alabe.com

Matrix Software

You'll find a wide variety of software at student and advanced levels in all price ranges, demo disks, and lots of interesting readings. Check out Winstar Express, a powerful but reasonably priced program suitable for all skill levels. The Matrix Web site offers lots of fun activities for Web surfers, such as free readings from the *I Ching,* the runes, and the tarot. There are many free desktop backgrounds with astrology themes. Go here to connect with news groups and online discussions. Their online almanac helps you schedule the best day to sign on the dotted line, ask for a raise, or plant your tomatoes.

Matrix Software
126 South Michigan Avenue
Big Rapids, MI 49307
Phone: (800) 416-3924
Web site: www.astrologysoftware.com

Astro Communications Services (ACS)

Books, software for Mac and IBM compatibles, individual charts, and telephone readings are offered by this California company. Their freebies include astrology greeting cards and new moon reports. Find technical astrology materials here, such as *The American Ephemeris* and PC atlases. ACS will calculate and send charts to you, a valuable service if you do not have a computer.

ACS Publications
P.O. Box 1646
El Cajon, CA 92022-1646
Phone: (800) 514-5070
Fax: (619) 631-0180
Web site: www.astrocom.com

Air Software

Here you'll find powerful, creative astrology software, and current stock market analysis. Financial astrology programs for stock market traders are a specialty. There are some interesting freebies at this site; check out the maps of eclipse paths for any year and a free astrology clock program.

Air Software
115 Caya Avenue
West Hartford, CT 06110
Phone: (800) 659-1247
Web site: www.alphee.com

Kepler: State of the Art

Here's a program that has everything. Gorgeous graphic images, audio-visual effects, and myriad sophisticated chart options are built into this fascinating software. It's even got an astrological encyclopedia, plus diagrams and images to help you understand advanced concepts. This program is expensive, but if you're serious about learning astrology, it's an investment that will grow with you! Check out its features at www.astrologysoftwareshop.com.

Time Cycles Research: For Mac Users

Here's where Mac users can find astrology software that's as sophisticated as it gets. If you have a Mac, you'll love their beautiful graphic IO Series programs.

Time Cycles Research
P.O. Box 797
Waterford, CT 06385
Web site: www.timecycles.com
(800) 827-2240

Shareware and Freeware: The Price Is Right!

Halloran Software: A Super Shareware Program

Check out Halloran Software's Web site (www.halloran. com), which offers several levels of Windows astrology software. Beginners should consider their Astrology for Windows shareware program, which is available in unregistered demo form as a free download and in registered form for a very reasonable price.

Halloran Software
P.O. Box 75713
Los Angeles, CA 90075
(800) 732-4628

Astrolog

If you're computer-savvy, you can't go wrong with Walter Pullen's amazingly complete Astrolog program, which is offered absolutely free at the site. The Web address is www.astrolog.org/astrolog.htm.

Astrolog is an ultrasophisticated program with all the features of much more expensive programs. It comes in versions for all formats—DOS, Windows, Mac, UNIX—and has some cool features, such as a revolving globe and a constellation map. If you are looking for astrology software with bells and whistles that doesn't cost big bucks, this program has it all!

Programs for the Pocket PDA and Palm Pilot

Would you like to have astrology at your fingertips everywhere you go? No need to drag along your laptop. You can check the chart of the moment or of someone you've just met on your pocket PDA or Palm Pilot. As with most other programs, you'll need to know the astrological symbols in order to read the charts.

For the pocket PC that has the Microsoft Pocket PC 2002 or the Microsoft Windows Mobile 2003 operating system, there is the versatile Astracadabra, which can interchange charts with the popular Solar Fire software. It can be ordered at www.leelehman.com or www.astrologysoftwareshop.com.

For the Palm OS5 and compatible handheld devices, there is Astropocket from www.yves.robert.org/features.html. This is a shareware program, which allows you to use all the features free. However, you cannot store more than one chart at a time until you pay a mere twenty-eight-dollar registration fee for the complete version.

CHAPTER 10

Travel the World of Astrology

There's a world of astrology waiting to welcome you, and thanks to the Internet, it's now possible to connect instantly with astrology fans and events around the globe. There are so many ways out there to expand your knowledge and share with others. Consider studying with a famous astrologer or attending a local astrology club or regional workshop. You could even combine your vacation with an astrological workshop in an exotic locale such as Bali or Mexico.

You need only type the word *astrology* into any Internet search engine and watch hundreds of listings of astrology-related sites pop up. There are local meetings and international conferences where you can connect with other astrologers, and books and tapes to help you study at home.

To help you sort out the variety of options available, here are our top picks of the Internet and the astrological community at large.

Nationwide Astrology Organizations and Conferences

Meet the World's Best Astrologers at UAC!

From May 14 to 21, 2008, the best astrologers from around the world will gather in Denver, Colorado, site of the United

Astrology Conference. UAC is jointly sponsored by three nonprofit educational organizations: AFAN (Association for Astrological Networking), ISAR (International Society for Astrological Research), and NCGR (National Council for Geocosmic Research). This conference attracts astrology fans from North and South America, Europe, Russia, India, Japan, South Africa, Australia, and New Zealand.

Here's your chance to meet and socialize with the world's top astrologers, who'll be participating in a global forum on modern astrology. There will be an all-star lineup of lectures on a variety of financial, metaphysical, psychological, and scientific topics for astrology professionals, students, and beginners. Whatever your level of expertise, there's a track for you at UAC.

Preview the conference at the convention site Web site, www.uacastrology.com.

National Council for Geocosmic Research (NCGR)

Whether you'd like to know more about such specialties as financial astrology or techniques for timing events, or if you'd prefer the psychological or mythological approach, you'll meet the top astrologers at conferences sponsored by the National Council for Geocosmic Research. NCGR is dedicated to providing quality education, bringing astrologers and astrology fans together at conferences, and promoting fellowship. Their course structure provides a systematized study of the many facets of astrology. The organization sponsors educational workshops, taped lectures, conferences, and a directory of professional astrologers. For an annual membership fee, you get their excellent publications and newsletters, plus the opportunity to network with other astrology buffs at local chapter events. (At this writing there are chapters in twenty-six states and four countries.)

To join NCGR for the latest information on upcoming events and chapters in your city, consult their Web site: www.geocosmic.org.

American Federation of Astrologers (AFA)

Established in 1938, this is one of the oldest astrological organizations in the United States. AFA offers conferences, conventions, and a thorough correspondence course. If you are looking for a reading, their interesting Web site will refer you to an accredited AFA astrologer.

AFA
6535 S. Rural Road
Tempe, AZ 85283
Phone: (888) 301-7630 or (480) 838-1751
Fax: (480) 838-8293
Web site: www.astrologers.com

Association for Astrological Networking (AFAN)

Did you know that astrologers are still being harassed for practicing astrology? AFAN provides support and legal information and works toward improving the public image of astrology. AFAN's network of local astrologers links with the international astrological community. Here are the people who will go to bat for astrology when it is attacked in the media. Everyone who cares about astrology should join!

AFAN
8306 Wilshire Boulevard
PMB 537
Beverly Hills, CA 90211
Phone: (800) 578-2326
E-mail: info@afan.org
Web site: www.afan.org

International Society for Astrology Research (ISAR)

An international organization of professional astrologers dedicated to encouraging the highest standards of quality in the field of astrology with an emphasis on research. Among ISAR's benefits are a quarterly journal, a weekly e-mail newsletter, frequent conferences, and a free membership directory.

ISAR
P.O. Box 38613
Los Angeles, CA 90038
Fax: (805) 933-0301
Web site: www.isarastrology.com

Astrology Magazines

In addition to articles by top astrologers, most of these have listings of astrology conferences, events, and local happenings.

Horoscope Guide
Kappa Publishing Group
6198 Butler Pike
Suite 200
Blue Bell, PA 19422-2600
Web site: www.kappapublishing.com/astrology

Dell Horoscope
Their Web site (www.dellhoroscope.com) features a listing of local astrological meetings.

Customer Service
6 Prowitt Street
Norwalk, CT 06855
(800) 220-7443

The Mountain Astrologer

A favorite magazine of astrology fans! *The Mountain Astrologer* also has an interesting Web site featuring the latest news from an astrological point of view, plus feature articles from the magazine.

The Mountain Astrologer
P.O. Box 970
Cedar Ridge, CA 95924
Phone: (800) 247-4828
Web site: www.mountainastrologer.com

Astrology College

Kepler College of Astrological Arts and Sciences

A degree-granting college, which is also a center of astrology, has long been the dream of the astrological community and is a giant step forward in providing credibility to the profession. Therefore, the opening of Kepler College in 2000 was a historical event for astrology. It is the only college in the western hemisphere authorized to issue B.A. and M.A. degrees in Astrological Studies. Here is where to study with the best scholars, teachers, and communicators in the field. A long-distance study program is available for those interested.

For more information, contact:

Kepler College of Astrological Arts and Sciences
4630 200th Street SW
Suite A-1
Lynnwood, WA 98036
Phone: (425) 673-4292
Fax: (425) 673-4983
Web site: www.kepler.edu

Our Favorite Web Sites

Of the thousands of astrological Web sites that come and go on the Internet, these have stood the test of time and are likely to still be operating when this book is published.

Astrodienst (www.astro.com)

Don't miss this fabulous international site that has long been one of the best astrology resources on the Internet. It's also a great place to view and download your own astrology chart. The world atlas on this site will give you the accurate longitude and latitude of your birthplace for setting up your horoscope. Then you can print out your free chart in a range of easy-to-read formats. Other attractions: a list of famous people born on your birth date, a feature that helps you choose the best vacation spot, plus articles by world-famous astrologers.

AstroDatabank (www.astrodatabank.com)

When the news is breaking, you can bet this site will be the first to get accurate birthdays of the headliners. The late astrologer Lois Rodden was a stickler for factual information and her meticulous research is being continued, much to the benefit of the astrological community. The Web site specializes in charts of current newsmakers, political figures, and international celebrities. You can also participate in discussions and analysis of the charts and see what some of the world's best astrologers have to say about them. Their AstroDatabank program, which you can purchase at the site, provides thousands of verified birthdays sorted into categories. It's an excellent research tool.

StarIQ (www.stariq.com)

Find out how top astrologers view the latest headlines at the must-see StarIQ site. Many of the best minds in astrology comment on the latest news, stock market ups and downs, political contenders. You can sign up to receive e-mail forecasts at the most important times keyed to your individual chart. (This is one of the best of the many online forecasts.)

Astro-Noetics (www.astro-noetics.com)

For those who are ready to explore astrology's interface with politics, popular culture, and current events, here is a sophisticated site with in-depth articles and personality profiles. Lots of depth and content here for the astrology-savvy surfer.

Astrology Books (www.astroamerica.com)

The Astrology Center of America sells a wide selection of books on all aspects of astrology, from the basics to the most advanced, at this online bookstore. Also available are many hard-to-find and recycled books.

Astrology Scholars' Sites

See what one of astrology's great teachers, Robert Hand, has to offer on his site: www.robhand.com. A leading expert on the history of astrology, he's on the cutting edge of the latest research.

The Project Hindsight group of astrologers is devoted to restoring the astrology of the Hellenistic period, the primary source for all later Western astrology. There are fascinating articles for astrology fans on this site, www.project-hindsight.com.

Financial Astrology Sites

Financial astrology is a hot specialty, with many tipsters, players, and theorists. There are online columns, newsletters, specialized financial astrology software, and mutual funds run by astrology seers. One of the more respected financial astrologers is Ray Merriman, whose stock market comments on www.mmacycles.com are a must read for those following the bulls and bears. Other top financial astrologers offer tips and forecasts at the www.afund.com and www.alphee.com sites.

CHAPTER 11

Is It Time for a Personal Reading?

Looking for answers to a burning personal question? A reading with a professional astrologer might help. A reading can be an empowering experience if you want to reach your full potential. You could use it for sizing up a lover or business situation to find out what the future has in store. If you're in a quandary about a problem, some astrological perspective could be an eye-opener. It might help you make over your life by choosing a more satisfying career or moving to a more favorable location. You could use it to find the optimum time for an important event such as a wedding or get the competitive edge in a meeting.

Another good reason for a reading is to refine your knowledge of astrology by consulting with someone who has years of experience analyzing charts. You might choose someone with a special technique that intrigues you. Armed with the knowledge of your chart that you have acquired so far, you can then learn to interpret subtle nuances or gain insight on your talents and abilities.

How do you choose when there are so many different kinds of readings available, especially since the Internet has brought astrology into the mainstream? Besides individual one-on-one readings with a professional astrologer, there are personal readings by mail, telephone, Internet, and tape. Well-advertised computer-generated reports and celebrity-sponsored readings are sure to attract your attention on commercial Web sites and in magazines. Then there are astrologers who specialize in certain areas such as finance or medical astrology. And unfortunately, there are many questionable practitioners who range from streetwise gypsy fortune-tellers to unscrupulous scam artists.

The following basic guidelines can help you sort out your options to find the reading that's right for you.

One-on-One Consultations with a Professional Astrologer

Nothing compares to a one-on-one consultation with a professional astrologer who has analyzed thousands of charts and can pinpoint the potential in yours. During your reading, you can get your specific questions answered. For instance, how to get along better with your mate or coworker. There are many astrologers who now combine their skills with training in psychology and are well-suited to help you examine your alternatives.

To give you an accurate reading, an astrologer needs certain information from you: the date, time, and place where you were born. (A horoscope can be cast about anyone or anything that has a specific time and place.) Most astrologers will then enter this information into a computer, which will calculate a chart in seconds. From the resulting chart, the astrologer will do an interpretation.

If you don't know your exact birth time, you can usually locate it at the Bureau of Vital Statistics at the city hall or county seat of the state where you were born. If you still have no success in getting your time of birth, some astrologers can estimate an approximate birth time by using past events in your life to determine the chart. This technique is called *rectification*.

How to Find an Astrologer

Choose your astrologer with the same care as you would any trusted adviser such as a doctor, lawyer, or banker. Unfortunately, anyone can claim to be an astrologer—to date, there is no licensing of astrologers or universally established professional criteria. However, there are nation-wide organizations of serious, committed astrologers that can help you in your search.

Good places to start your investigation are organizations such as the American Federation of Astrologers (AFA) or the National Council for Geocosmic Research (NCGR), which offer a program of study and certification. If you live near a major city, there is sure to be an active NCGR chapter or astrology club in your area; many are listed in astrology magazines available at your local newsstand. In response to many requests for referrals, both the AFA and the NCGR have directories of professional astrologers listed on their Web sites; these directories include a glossary of terms and an explanation of specialties within the astrological field. Contact the NCGR and AFA headquarters for information (see chapter 10 in this book).

Warning Signals

As a potentially lucrative freelance business, astrology has always attracted self-styled experts who may not have the knowledge or the counseling experience to give a helpful reading. These astrologers can range from the well-meaning amateur to the charlatan or street-corner gypsy who has for many years given astrology a bad name. Be very wary of astrologers who claim to have occult powers or who make pretentious claims of celebrated clients or miraculous achievements. You can often tell from the initial phone conversation if the astrologer is legitimate. He or she should ask for your birthday time and place, then conduct the conversation in a professional manner. Any astrologer who gives a reading based only on your sun sign is highly suspect.

When you arrive at the reading, the astrologer should be prepared. The consultation should be conducted in a private, quiet place. The astrologer should be interested in your problems of the moment. A good reading involves feedback on your part. So if the reading is not relating to your concerns, you should let the astrologer know. You should feel free to ask questions and get clarifications of technical terms. The more you actively participate, rather than expecting the astrologer to carry the reading or come forth with oracular predictions, the more meaningful your experience will be. An astrologer should help you validate your current experience and be frank about possible negative happenings, but also suggest a positive course of action.

In their approach to a reading, some astrologers may be more literal, others more intuitive. Those who have had counseling training may take a more psychological approach. Though some astrologers may seem to have an almost psychic ability, extrasensory perception or any other parapsychological talent is not essential. A very accurate picture can be drawn from the data in your horoscope chart.

An astrologer may do several charts for each client, including one for the time of birth and a *progressed chart*, showing the evolution from birth to the present time. According to your individual needs, there are many other possibilities, such as a chart for a different location if you are contemplating a change of place. Relationships between any two people, things, or events can be interpreted with a chart that compares one partner's horoscope with the other's. A composite chart, which uses the midpoint between planets in two individual charts to describe the relationship, is another commonly used device.

An astrologer will be particularly interested in transits, those times when cycling planets activate the planets or sensitive points in your birth chart. These indicate important events in your life.

Many astrologers offer tape-recorded readings, another option to consider, especially if the astrologer you choose lives at a distance. In this case, you'll be mailed a taped reading based on your birth chart. This type of reading is more personal than a computer printout and can give you valuable insights, though it is not equivalent to a live dialogue with the astrologer when you can discuss your specific interests and issues of the moment.

The Telephone Reading

Telephone readings come in two varieties: a dial-in taped reading, usually recorded in advance by an astrologer, or a live consultation with an "astrologer" on the other end of the line. The taped readings are general daily or weekly forecasts, applied to all members of your sign and charged by the minute. The quality depends on the astrologer. One caution: Be aware that these readings can run up quite a telephone bill, especially if you get into the habit of calling every day. Be sure that you are aware of the per-minute cost of each call beforehand.

Live telephone readings also vary with the expertise of the astrologer. Ideally, the astrologer at the other end of the line enters your birth date into a computer, which then quickly calculates your chart. This chart will be referred to during the consultation. The advantage of a live telephone reading is that your individual chart is used and you can ask about a specific problem. However, before you invest in any reading, be sure that your astrologer is qualified and that you fully understand in advance how much you will be charged. There should be no unpleasant financial surprises later.

Computer-Generated Reports

Companies that offer computer programs (such as ACS, Matrix, Astrolabe) also offer a variety of computer-generated horoscope readings. These can be quite comprehensive, offering a beautiful printout of the chart plus many pages of detailed information about each planet and aspect of the chart. You can then study it at your convenience. Of course, the interpretations will be general, since there is no personal input from you, and may not cover your immediate concerns. Since computer-generated horoscopes are much lower in cost than live consultations, you might consider one as either a supplement or a preparation for an eventual live reading. You'll then be more familiar with your chart and able to plan specific questions in advance. They also make terrific gifts for astrology fans. There are several companies, listed in chapter 9, that offer computerized readings prepared by reputable astrologers.

Whichever option you decide to pursue, may your reading be an empowering one!

CHAPTER 12

Your Baby-scope: Children Born in 2008

Parents of several children may see a marked difference between children born in 2008 and their older siblings, as the cosmic atmosphere is changing, which should imprint the personalities of this year's children.

Astrologers look to the slow-moving outer planets—Uranus, Neptune, and Pluto—to describe a generation. This year, Uranus and Neptune are still passing through Pisces and Aquarius, both visionary and spiritual signs. However, there is also much more earth-sign emphasis than in previous years due to the earthly pull of Pluto in Capricorn, plus the closer planets, Jupiter and Saturn, also in earth signs, which will counterbalance this spirituality with extreme practicality and pragmatism. This generation will be focused on getting the job done, on fixing up the planet, and on making things work.

Astrology can be an especially helpful tool that can be used to design an environment that will enhance and encourage each child's positive qualities. Some parents start before conception, planning the birth of their child as far as possible to harmonize with the signs of other family members. However, each baby has its own schedule, so if yours arrives a week early or late, or elects a different sign than you'd planned, recognize that the new sign may be more in line with the mission your child is here to accomplish. In other words, if you were hoping for a Libra child and he arrives during Virgo, that Virgo energy may be just what is needed to stimulate or complement your family. Remember that there are many astrological elements besides the sun sign that indicate strong family ties. Usually each child will share a particular planetary placement, an emphasis on a particular sign or house, or a certain chart configuration with his parents and other family members. Often there is a significant planetary angle that will define the parent-child relationship, such as family sun signs that form a T-square or a triangle.

One important thing you can do is to be sure the exact moment of birth is recorded. This will be essential in calculating an accurate astrological chart. The following descriptions can be applied to the sun or moon sign (if known) of a child—the sun sign will describe basic personality and the moon sign indicates the child's emotional needs.

The Aries Child

Baby Aries is quite a handful! This energetic child will walk—and run—as soon as possible and perform daring feats of exploration. Caregivers should be vigilant. Little Aries seems to know no fear (and is especially vulnerable to head injuries). Many Aries children, in their rush to get on with life, seem hyperactive and are easily frustrated when they can't get their own way. Violent temper tantrums and dramatic physical displays are par for the course with these children, necessitating a time-out chair.

The very young Aries should be monitored carefully, since he is prone to take risks and may injure himself. An Aries loves to take things apart and may break toys easily, but with encouragement, the child will develop formidable coordination. Aries's bossy tendencies should be molded into leadership qualities, rather than bullying. Otherwise, the me-first Aries will have many clashes with other strong-willed youngsters. Encourage these children to take out aggressions and frustrations in active, competitive sports, where they usually excel. When a young Aries learns to focus his energies long enough to master a subject and learns consideration for others, the indomitable Aries spirit will rise to the head of the class.

Aries born in 2008 will be a more subdued version of

this sign, but still loaded with energy. The Capricorn effect should make little Aries easier to discipline and more focused on achievement. A natural leader!

The Taurus Child

This is a cuddly, affectionate child who eagerly explores the world of the senses, especially the senses of taste and touch. The Taurus child can be a big eater and will put on weight easily if not encouraged to exercise. Since this child likes comfort and gravitates to beauty, try coaxing little Taurus to exercise to music or take him outdoors for hikes or long walks. Though Taurus may be a slow learner, this sign has an excellent retentive memory and generally masters a subject thoroughly. Taurus is interested in results and will see each project patiently through to completion, continuing long after others have given up. This year's earth-sign planet will give him a wonderful sense of support and accomplishment.

Choose Taurus toys carefully to help develop innate talents. Construction toys, such as blocks or erector sets, appeal to their love of building. Paints or crayons develop their sense of color. Many Taurus have musical talents and love to sing, which is apparent at a young age.

This year's Taurus will want a pet or two and a few plants of his own. Give little Taurus a minigarden and watch the natural green thumb develop. This child has a strong sense of acquisition and an early grasp of material value. After filling a piggy bank, Taurus graduates to a savings account, before other children have started to learn the value of money.

This year's Taurus gets a bonanza of good luck and support from Jupiter, Pluto, and Saturn—all in compatible earth signs. These should give little Taurus an especially easygoing disposition and provide many opportunities to live up to his sign's potential.

The Gemini Child

Little Gemini will talk as soon as possible, filing the air with questions and chatter. This is a friendly child who enjoys social contact, seems to require company, and adapts quickly to different surroundings. Geminis have quick minds that easily grasp the use of words, books, and telephones and will probably learn to talk and read at an earlier age than most. Though they are fast learners, Gemini may have a short attention span, darting from subject to subject. Projects and games that help focus the mind could be used to help them concentrate. Musical instruments, typewriters, and computers help older Gemini children combine mental with manual dexterity. Geminis should be encouraged to finish what they start before they go on to another project. Otherwise, they can become jack-of-all-trade types who have trouble completing anything they do. Their dispositions are usually cheerful and witty, making these children popular with their peers and delightful company at home.

This year's Gemini baby should go to the head of the class. Uranus in Pisces could inspire Gemini to make an unusual career choice, perhaps in a financial field. When he grows up, this year's Gemini may change jobs several times before he finds a position that satisfies his need for stimulation and variety.

The Cancer Child

This emotional, sensitive child is especially influenced by patterns set early in life. Young Cancers cling to their first memories as well as their childhood possessions. They thrive in calm emotional waters, with a loving, protective mother, and usually remain close to her (even if their relationship with her was difficult) throughout their lives. Divorce, death—anything that disturbs the safe family unit—

are devastating to Cancers, who may need extra support and reassurance during a family crisis.

They sometimes need a firm hand to push the positive, creative side of their personality and discourage them from getting swept away by emotional moods or resorting to emotional manipulation to get their way. Praised and encouraged to find creative expression, Cancer will be able to express his positive side consistently on a firm, secure foundation.

This year's Cancer baby should be a social, cooperative child, oriented toward others, thanks to Jupiter and Pluto blessing relationships.

The Leo Child

Leo children love the limelight and will plot to get the lion's share of attention. These children assert themselves with flair and drama and can behave like tiny tyrants to get their way. But in general, they have sunny, positive dispositions and are rarely subject to blue moods. At school, they're the ones who are voted most popular, head cheerleader, or homecoming queen. Leo is sure to be noticed for personality, if not for stunning looks or academic work; the homely Leo will be a class clown and the unhappy Leo may be the class bully.

Above all, a Leo child cannot tolerate being ignored for long. Drama or performing-arts classes, sports, and school politics are healthy ways for Leo to be a star. But Leos must learn to take lesser roles occasionally, or they will have some painful put-downs in store. Usually, the popularity of Leos is well earned; they are hard workers who try to measure up to their own high standards—and usually succeed.

This year's Leo should be a less flamboyant, more down-to-earth version of his sign, as the earthy planets exert their influence. This should add more financial and practical talents to the expressive Leo personality.

The Virgo Child

The young Virgo can be a quiet, rather serious child, with a quick, intelligent mind. Early on, little Virgo shows far more attention to detail and concern with small things than other children do. Little Virgo has a built-in sense of order and a fascination with how things work. It is important for these children to have a place of their own, which they can order as they wish and where they can read or busy themselves with crafts and hobbies.

This child's personality can be very sensitive. Little Virgo may get hyper and overreact to seemingly small irritations, which can take the form of stomach upsets or delicate digestive systems. But this child will flourish where there is mental stimulation and a sense of order. Virgos thrive in school, especially in writing or language skills, and seem truly happy when buried in books. Chances are, young Virgo will learn to read ahead of classmates. Hobbies that involve detail work or that develop fine craftsmanship are especially suited to young Virgos.

Baby Virgo of 2008 is likely to be an especially high achiever with Saturn also in Virgo, adding focus and discipline, while Jupiter transiting the house of self-expression endows extra creativity.

The Libra Child

The Libra child learns early about the power of charm and appearance. This is often a very physically appealing child with an enchanting dimpled smile, who is naturally sociable and enjoys the company of both children and adults. It is a rare Libra child who is a discipline problem, but when their behavior is unacceptable, they respond better to calm discussion than displays of emotion, especially if the discussion revolves around fairness. Because young Libras without a strong direction tend to drift with the mood of the group, these children should be encouraged to develop their unique talents and powers of discrimination so they can later stand on their own.

In school, this child is usually popular and will often have to choose between social invitations and studies. In the teen years, social pressures mount as the young Libra begins to look for a partner. This is the sign of best friends, so Libra's choice of companions can have a strong effect on his future direction. Beautiful Libra girls may be tempted to go steady or have an unwise early marriage. Chances are, both sexes will fall in and out of love several times in their search for the ideal partner.

Little Libra of 2008 is an especially social, talkative child who gets along well with siblings because Jupiter in Capricorn enhances family life. This child is endowed with much imagination and creativity, as well as communication skills.

The Scorpio Child

The Scorpio child may seem quiet and shy, but will surprise others with intense feelings and formidable willpower. Scorpio children are single-minded when they want something and intensely passionate about whatever they do. One of a caregiver's tasks is to teach this child to balance activities and emotions, yet at the same time to make the most of his or her great concentration and intense commitment.

Since young Scorpios do not show their depth of feelings easily, parents will have to learn to read almost imperceptible signs that troubles are brewing beneath the surface. Both Scorpio boys and girls enjoy games of power and control on or off the playground. Scorpio girls may take an early interest in the opposite sex, masquerading as tomboys, while Scorpio boys may be intensely competitive and loners. When their powerful energies are directed into work, sports, or challenging studies, Scorpio is a superachiever, focused on a goal. With trusted friends, young Scorpio is devoted and caring—the proverbial friend through thick and thin, loyal for life.

Scorpio 2008 has a strong financial emphasis, which could make these children big money earners in adulthood. Uranus in Pisces in their house of creativity should put them on the cutting edge of whichever field they choose.

The Sagittarius Child

This restless, athletic child will be out of the playpen and off on adventures as soon as possible. Little Sagittarius is remarkably well-coordinated, attempting daredevil feats on any wheeled vehicle from scooters to skateboards. These natural athletes need little encouragement to channel their energies into sports. Their cheerful, friendly dispositions earn them popularity in school, and once they have found a subject where their talent and imagination can soar, they will do well academically. They love animals, especially horses, and will be sure to have a pet or two, if not a home zoo. When they are old enough to take care of themselves, they'll clamor to be off on adventures of their own, away from home, if possible.

This child loves to travel, will not get homesick at summer camp, and may sign up to be a foreign-exchange student or spend summers abroad. Outdoor adventure appeals to little Sagittarius, especially if it involves an active sport, such as skiing, cycling, or mountain climbing. Give them enough space and encouragement, and their fiery spirit will propel them to achieve high goals.

Baby Sagittarius of 2008 has a natural generosity of spirit and an optimistic, expansive nature. He will also demand a great deal of freedom. He may need reality checks from time to time, since he may be a risk taker, especially in the financial area. He should learn early in life how to handle money.

The Capricorn Child

These purposeful, goal-oriented children will work to capacity if they feel this will bring results. They're not ones who enjoy work for its own sake—there must be an end in sight. Authority figures can do much to motivate these children, but once set on an upward path, young Capricorns will mobilize energy and talent and work harder, and with more perseverance, than any other sign. Capricorn has built-in self-discipline that can achieve remarkable results, even if lacking the flashy personality, quick brain power, or penetrating insight of others. Once involved, young Capricorn will stick to a task until it is mastered. These children also know how to use others to their advantage and may well become team captains or class presidents.

A wise parent will set realistic goals for the Capricorn child, paving the way for the early thrill of achievement. Youngsters should be encouraged to express their caring, feeling side to others, as well as their natural aptitude for leadership. Capricorn children may be especially fond of grandparents and older relatives and will enjoy spending time with them and learning from them. It is not uncommon for young Capricorns to have an older mentor or teacher who guides them. With their great respect for authority, Capricorn children will take this influence very much to heart.

The Capricorn born in 2008 will have an upbeat, cheerful personality, thanks to the presence of lucky Jupiter in Capricorn. This child should have a generous, expansive nature and be more outgoing than the usual member of this sign.

The Aquarius Child

The Aquarius child has an innovative, well-focused mind that often streaks so far ahead of those of peers that this child seems like an oddball. Routine studies never hold the restless youngster for long; he will look for another, more experimental place to try out his ideas and develop his inventions. Life is a laboratory to the inquiring Aquarius mind. School politics, sports, science, and the arts offer scope for such talents. But if there is no room for expression within approved social limits, Aquarius is sure to rebel. Questioning institutions and religions comes naturally, so these children may find an outlet elsewhere, becoming rebels with a cause. It is better not to force this child to conform, but rather to channel forward-thinking young minds into constructive group activities.

This year's Aquarius will have far-out glamour as well as charisma, thanks to his ruler, Uranus, in a friendly bond with Neptune. This could be a rock star, a statesman, or a scientist.

The Pisces Child

Give young Pisces praise, applause, and a gentle, but firm, push in the right direction. Lovable Pisces children may be abundantly talented, but may be hesitant to express themselves, because they are quite sensitive and easily hurt. It is a parent's challenge to help them gain self-esteem and self-confidence. However, this same sensitivity makes them trusted friends who'll have many confidants as they develop socially. It also endows many Pisces with spectacular creative talent.

Pisces adores drama and theatrics of all sorts; therefore, encourage them to channel their creativity into art forms rather than indulging in emotional dramas. Understand that they may need more solitude than other children, as they develop their creative ideas. But though daydreaming can be creative, it is important that these natural dreamers not dwell too long in the world of fantasy. Teach them practical coping skills for the real world. Since Pisces are physically sensitive, parents should help them build strong bodies with proper diet and regular exercise. Young Pisces may gravitate to more individual sports, such as swimming, sailing, and skiing, rather than to team sports. Or they may prefer more artistic physical activities like dance or ice skating.

Born givers, these children are often drawn to the underdog (they fall quickly for sob stories) and attract those who might take advantage of their empathic nature. Teach them to choose friends wisely and to set boundaries in relationships, to protect their emotional vulnerability—invaluable lessons in later life.

With the planet Uranus now in Pisces, the 2008 baby

belongs to a generation of Pisces movers and shakers. This child may have a rebellious streak that rattles the status quo. But this generation also has a visionary nature, which will be much concerned with the welfare of the world at large.

CHAPTER 13

Your Leap Year Guide to Love

The year 2008 is a leap year, when ladies traditionally make the first romantic moves. However, it's no longer unusual for women to pursue the object of their desire aggressively, no matter what the year. So if you want to charm a Capricorn, hook a Pisces, or corral a Taurus, here are sun-sign seduction tips guaranteed to keep your lover begging for more.

How to Love Every Sign

Aries: Daredevil Lover

This highly physical sign is walking dynamite with a brief attention span. Don't be too easy to get, ladies. A little challenge, a lively debate, and a merry chase only heat up your admirers. They want to see what you're made of. Once you've lured them into your lair, be a challenge, a bit of a daredevil, and pull out your X-rated tricks. Don't give your all—let them know there's more where that came from. Make it exciting, show you're up for adventure. Wear bright red somewhere interesting. Since Aries rules the head and face, be sure to focus on these areas in your lovemaking. Use your lips, tongue, breath, and even your eyelashes to the max. Practice scalp massages and deep-kissing techniques. Aries won't wait, so when you make your move, be sure you're ready to follow through. No head games or teasing!

To keep you happy, you've got to voice your own needs, because this lover will be focused on his. Teach him how to please, or this could be a one-sided adventure.

Taurus: Sweet Treats

Taurus wins as the most sensual sign, with the most sexual stamina. This man is earthy and lusty in bed; he can go on all night. This is not a sign to tease. Like the Bull, he'll see red, not bed. So make him comfortable, then bombard all his senses. Good food gets Taurus in the mood. So do the right music and fragrance, revealing clothes, and luxurious bed linens. Give him a massage with delicious-smelling and -tasting oils; focus on the neck area.

Don't forget to turn off the phone! Taurus hates interruptions. Since they can be very vocal lovers, choose a setting where you won't be disturbed. And don't ever rush; enjoy a long, slow, delicious encounter.

Gemini: Playtime

Playful Gemini loves games, so make your seduction fun. Be their lost twin soul, their confidant. Good communication is essential, so share deep secrets, live out fantasies. This sign adores variety. Nothing bores Gemini more than making love the same way all the time, or bringing on the heavy emotions. So trot out all the roles you've been longing to play. Here's the perfect partner. But remember to keep it light and fun. Gemini's turn-on zone is the hands, and this sign gives the best massages. Gadgets that can be activated with a touch amuse Gemini. This sign is great at doing two things at once, like making love while watching an erotic film. Turn the cell phone off unless you want company. On the other hand, Gemini is your sign for superhot phone sex.

Gemini loves a change of scene. So experiment on the floor, in the shower, or on the kitchen table. Borrow a friend's apartment or rent a room in a hotel for variety.

Cancer: In the Mood

The key to Cancer is to get this moon child in the mood. Consult the moon—a full moon is best. Wining, dining, old-fashioned courtship, and breakfast in bed are turn-ons. Whatever makes your Cancer feel secure will promote shedding inhibitions in the sack. (Don't try any of your Aries daredevil techniques here!) Cancer prefers familiar, comfortable, homey surroundings. Cancer's turn-on zone is the breasts. Cancer women often have naturally inflated chests. Cancer men may fantasize about a well-endowed playmate. If your breasts are enhanced, show them off. Cancer will want to know all your deepest secrets, so invent a few good ones. But lots of luck delving into their innermost thoughts!

A sure thing: Take your Cancer near water. The sight and sound of the sea can be their aphrodisiac. A moonlit beach, a deserted swimming pool, a Jacuzzi, and a bubble bath are good seduction spots. Listen to the rain patter on the roof in a mountain cabin.

Leo: The Royal Treatment

Leo must be the best and hear it from you often. In return, they'll perform for you, telling you just what you want to hear (true or not). They like a lover with style and endurance, to be swept off their feet and into bed. Leos like to go first-class all the way, so build them up with lots of attention, wining and dining, special gifts.

Never mention other lovers or make them feel like second best. A sure signal for Leo to look elsewhere is a competitive spouse. Leos take great pride in their body, so you should pour on the admiration. A few well-placed mirrors could inspire them. So would a striptease of beautiful lingerie, expensive fragrance on the sheets, and, if female, an occasional luxury hotel room, with champagne and caviar delivered by room service. Leo's erogenous zone is the lower back, so a massage with expensive oils would make your lion purr with pleasure.

Virgo: Pedestal Perfect

Virgo's standards are so sky-high that you may feel intimidated at first. The key to pleasing fussy Virgo lovers is to look for the hot fantasy beneath their cool surface. Secret tip: They're really looking for someone to make over. So let Virgo play teacher and you play willing student; the doctor-patient routine works as well.

Let Virgo help you improve your life, quit smoking, learn French, or diet. Read an erotic book together, then practice the techniques. Or study the esoteric, erotic exercises from Asia.

The Virgo erogenous zone is the tummy area, which should be your base of operations. Virgo likes things pristine and clean. Fall into crisp, immaculate white sheets. Wear a sheer white nightie. Smell shower-fresh with no heavy perfume. Be sure your surroundings pass the hospital test. A shower together afterward (with great-smelling soap) could get the ball rolling again.

Libra: The Beauty Lover

Libra must be turned on aesthetically. Make sure you look as beautiful as possible and wear something stylishly seductive but never vulgar. Have a mental affair first, as you flirt and flatter this sign. Then proceed to the physical. Approach Libra like a dance partner, ready to waltz or tango.

Libra must be in the mood for love; otherwise, forget it. Any kind of ugliness is a turnoff. Provide the right atmosphere, elegant and harmonious. No loud noise, clashing colors, or uncomfortable beds. Libra is not an especially spontaneous lover, so it is best to spend time warming them up. Libra's back is his erogenous zone, your cue to provide back rubs with scented potions. Once in bed, you can be a bit aggressive sexually. Libra loves strong, decisive moves. Set the scene, know what you want, and let Libra be happy to provide it.

Scorpio: The Legendary Lover

Scorpio is legendary in bed, often called the sex sign of the zodiac. But seducing them is often a power game. Scorpio likes to be in control, even the quiet, unassuming ones. Scorpio loves a mystery, so don't tell all. Keep them guessing about you, offering tantalizing hints along the way. The hint of danger often turns Scorpio on, so you'll find members of this sign experimenting with the exotic and highly erotic forms of sex. Sadomasochism and bondage, anything that tests the limits of power could be a turn-on for Scorpio.

Invest in some sexy black leather and some powerful music (depending on your tastes). Clothes that lace, buckle, or zip tempt Scorpio to untie you. Present yourself as a mysterious package just waiting to be unwrapped.

Once in bed, there are no holds barred with Scorpio. They'll find your most pleasurable pressure points and touch you as you've never been touched before. They are quickly aroused (the genital area belongs to this sign) and willing to try anything. But they can be possessive. Don't expect your Scorpio to share you with anyone. It's all or nothing for them.

Sagittarius: The Sexual Athletes

Sagittarius men are the Don Juans of the zodiac, love-'em-and-leave-'em types who are difficult to pin down. Your seduction strategy is to join them in their many pursuits, then hook them with love on the road. Sagittarius enjoys sex in venues that suggest movement: planes, SUVs, or boats. But a favorite turn-on place is outdoors, in nature. A deserted hiking path, a field of tall grass, a remote woodland glade all give the Centaur sexy ideas. Athletic Sagittarius might go for some personal training in an empty gym. Join your Sagittarius for amorous aerobics, meditate together, or explore the tantric forms of sex. Lovemaking after hiking and skiing would be healthy fun.

Sagittarius enjoys lovers from exotic ethnic backgrounds or lovers met in spiritual pursuits or on college campuses. Sagittarius are great cheerleaders and motivators, and will enjoy feeling that they have inspired you to be all that you can be.

There may be a canine or feline companion sharing your Sagittarius lover's bed with you, so check your allergies. And bring Fido or Felix a toy to keep him occupied.

Capricorn: Animal Instincts

The great news about Capricorn lovers is that they improve with age. They are probably the sexiest seniors. So stick around, if you have a young one. They're lusty in bed (it's not the sign of the Goat for nothing), and can be quite raunchy and turned on by X-rated words and deeds. If this is not your thing, let them know. The Capricorn erogenous zone is the knees. Some discreet fondling in public places could be your opener. Capricorn tends to think of sex as part of a game plan for the future. They are well-organized, and might regard lovemaking as relaxation after a long day's work. This sign often combines business with pleasure. So look for a Capricorn where there's a convention, trade show, or work-related conference.

Getting Capricorn's mind off his agenda and onto yours could take some doing. Separate him from his buddies by whispering sexy secrets in his ear. Then convince him you're an asset to his image and a boon to his health. Though he may seem uptight at first, you'll soon discover he's a love animal who makes a wonderful and permanent pet.

Aquarius: Far-Out Lover

This sign really does not want an all-consuming passion or an all-or-nothing relationship. Aquarius need space. But once they feel free to experiment with a spontaneous and exciting partner, Aquarius can give you a far-out sexual adventure.

Passion begins in the mind, so a good mental buildup is key. Aquarius is an inventive sign who believes love is a playground without rules. Plan surprise, unpredictable encounters in unusual places. Find ways to make love transcendental, an extraordinary and unique experience. Be ready to try anything Aquarius suggests, if only once. Calves and ankles are the special Aquarius erogenous zones, so perfect your legwork.

Be careful not to be too possessive. Your Aquarius needs lots of space, tolerance for friends (including old lovers), and their many outside interests.

Pisces: Fantasy Time

Pisces is the sign of fantasy and imagination. This sign has great theatrical talent. Pisces looks for lovers who will take care of them. Pisces will return the favor! Here is someone who can psych out your deepest desires without mentioning them. Pisces falls for sob stories and is always ready to empathize. It wouldn't hurt to have a small problem for Pisces to help you overcome. It might help if you cry on his shoulder, for this sign needs to be needed. Use your imagination when setting the scene for love. A dramatic setting brings out Pisces theatrical talents. Or creatively use the element of water. Rain on the roof, waterfalls, showers, beach houses, waterbeds, and Jacuzzis could turn up the heat. Experiment with pulsating jets of water. Skinny-dip at midnight in deserted pools.

The Pisces erogenous zone is the feet. This is your cue to give a sensuous foot massage using scented lotions. Let him paint your toes. Beautiful toenails in sexy sandals are a special turn-on.

Your Hot Planets: Mars and Venus Tango Together

Here's a tip for finding your hottest love match. If your lover's Mars sign makes favorable aspects to your Venus, is in the same element (earth, air, fire, water), or is in the same sign, your lover will do what you want done! Mars influences how we act when we make love, while Venus shows what we like done to us. Sometimes fighting and making up is the sexiest fun of all. If you're the type who needs a spark to keep lust alive (you know who you are!), then look for Mars and Venus in different signs of the same quality (fixed or cardinal or mutable). For instance, a fixed sign (Taurus, Leo, Scorpio, Aquarius) paired with another fixed sign can have a sexy standoff, a hot tug of war before you finally surrender. Two cardinal signs (Aries, Cancer, Libra, Capricorn) set off passionate fireworks when they clash. Mutable signs (Gemini, Virgo, Sagittarius, Pisces) play a fascinating game of cat and mouse, never quite catching each other.

The Best Time for Love

The best time for love is when Venus is in your sign, making you the most desirable sign in the zodiac. This only lasts about three weeks (unless Venus is retrograde), so don't waste time! And find out the time this year when Venus is in your sign by consulting the Venus chart at the end of chapter 6.

Who's the Sexiest Sign of the Zodiac?

It depends on what sign you are. Astrology has traditionally given this honor to Scorpio, the sign associated with the sex organs. However, we are all a combination of different signs (and turn-ons). Gemini's communicating ability and manual dexterity could deliver the magic touch. Cancer's tenderness and understanding could bring out your passion more than regal Leo.

Who'll Be Faithful?

The earth signs of Capricorn, Taurus, and Virgo are usually the most faithful. They tend to be more home-oriented and family-oriented, and they are usually choosy about their mates. It's impractical, inconvenient, and probably expensive to play around, so they think.

Who's Most Likely to Cheat?

The mutable signs of Gemini, Pisces, and Sagittarius win the playboy or playgirl sweepstakes. These signs tend to be changeable, fickle, and easily bored. But they're so much fun!

CHAPTER 14

Signs of Success: Wealth-Building Advice from the Stars

Are you a serial spender or a savvy saver? Here's where to find out your sign's bottom line when it comes to managing money. Though no sign wins the financial sweepstakes—all have their share of billionaires and paupers—the signs of success are those who make the most of their particular financial talents. This year's financial winners are the earth signs (Taurus, Virgo, and especially Capricorn), who should profit from the lucky rays of Jupiter in Capricorn. Yet all of us could benefit from some of Capricorn's self-discipline when it comes to spending wisely and budgeting carefully.

Aries

You've got a taste for fast money, quick turnover, and edgy investments, with no patience for gradual long-term gains. You're an impulse buyer with the nerve for risky tactics that could backfire. On the other hand, you're a pioneer who can see into the future, who dares to take a gamble on a new idea or product that could change the world . . . like Sam Walton of the Wal-mart stores who changed the way we shop. You need a backup plan in case one of your big ideas burns out. To protect your money, get a backup plan you can follow without thinking about it. Have an automatic percentage of your income put into a savings or retirement plan. Then give yourself some extra funds to play with. Your weak point is your impatience; you're not one to wait out a slow market or watch savings slowly accumulate.

Taurus

You're a saver who loves to see your cash accumulate, as well as your possessions. You have no qualms about steadily increasing your fortune. You're a savvy trader and a shrewd investor, in there for long-term gains. You have low toleration for risk, hate to lose anything. But you do enjoy luxuries, may need to reward yourself frequently. You might pass up an opportunity because it seems too risky. Take a chance once in a while. You're especially lucky in real estate.

Gemini

With Gemini, the cash can flow in and then out just as quickly. You naturally multitask and are sure to have several projects going at once, as well as several credit cards, which can easily get out of hand. Saving is not one of your strong points . . . too boring. You fall in and out of love with different ideas, have probably tried a round of savings techniques. Diversification is your best strategy. Have several different kinds of investments—at least one should be a long-term plan. Set savings goals and then regularly deposit small amounts into your accounts.

Cancer

You can be a natural moneymaker with your peerless intuition. You can spot a winner that everyone else misses. Consider Cancer success stories like those of cosmetics queen Estée Lauder and Roxanne Quimby, of Burt's Bees, who turned her friend's stash of beeswax into a thriving cosmetics business. Who knew? So trust your intuition. You are a saver who always has a backup plan just in case. Remember to treat and nurture yourself as well as others. Investments in the food industry, restaurants, hotels, shipping, and water-related industries are Cancer territory.

Leo

You love the first-class lifestyle, but may not always have the resources to support it. Finding a way to fund your extravagant tastes is the Leo challenge. Some courses in money management or an expert financial coach could set you on the right track. However, you're also a terrific salesperson, fabulous in high-profile jobs that pay a lot. You're the community tastemaker. Satisfy your appetite for "the best" by working for a quality company that sells luxury goods, splendid real estate, dream vacations, first-class travel—that way you'll have access to the lifestyle without having to pay for it.

Virgo

Your sign is a stickler for details and that includes your money management. You like to follow your spending and saving closely and enjoy planning and budgeting and price comparison. Your sign usually has no problem sticking to a savings or investment plan. You have a critical eye for quality and like to bargain—shop to get the best value. In fact, Virgo billionaire Warren Buffet is known for value investing. You buy cheap and sell at a profit. Investing in health care and organic products and food could be profitable for you.

Libra

Oh, do you ever love to shop! And you often have an irresistible urge to acquire an exquisite object, like a designer dress you can't really afford, or splurge on the perfect antique armoire once you've found it. You don't like to settle for second-rate or bargain buys. Learning to prioritize your spending is especially difficult for your sign, so try to find a good money manager to do it for you. Following a strictly balanced budget is your key to financial success. With Libra's keen eye for quality and good taste, you are a savvy picker at auctions and antiques fairs, so you might be able to turn around your purchase for a profit.

Scorpio

Scorpios prefer to stay in control of their finances at all times. You're sure to have a financial-tracking program on your computer. You're not an impulse buyer, unless you see something that immediately turns you on. Rely on your instincts! Scorpio is the sign of credit cards, taxes, and loans, so you are able to use these tools cleverly. Investing for Scorpio is rarely casual. You'll do extensive research and track your investments—reading the financial pages, annual reports, and profit-and-loss statements.

Sagittarius

Sagittarius is a natural gambler, with a high tolerance for risk. It's important for you to learn when to hold 'em, and when to fold 'em, as the song goes, by setting limits on your risk taking and covering your assets. You enjoy the thrill of playing the stock market, where you could win big and lose big. Money itself is rarely the object for Sagittarius—it's the game that counts. Since your sign rarely saves for a rainy day, your best strategy might be an automatic-savings plan that deducts a certain amount without your knowing it. Regular bill-paying plans are another strategy to keep you on track. You could benefit from an inspirational money manager who gets you fired up about an investment plan.

Capricorn

You're one of the strongest money managers in the zodiac, which should serve you well this year when Jupiter, the planet of luck and expansion, is blessing Capricorn. You're a born bargain hunter and clever negotiator, a saver rather than a spender. You are the sign of self-discipline, which works well when it comes to sticking with a budget and living frugally while waiting for resources to accumulate. You are likely to plan carefully for your elder years, profiting from long-term investments. You have a keen sense of value and will pick up a bargain, then turn it around at a nice profit.

Aquarius

The Aquarius trait of unpredictability extends to your financial life, where you surprise us all with your ability to turn something totally unique into a money spinner. Consider your wealthy sign mates Oprah Winfrey and Paris Hilton, who are able to intuit what the public will buy at a given moment. Some of your ideas might sound far-out, but turn out to be right on the money. Investing in high-tech companies that are on the cutting edge of their field is good for Aquarius. You'll probably intuit which ones will stay the course. You'll feel good about investing in companies that improve the environment, such as new types of fuel, or ones that are related to your favorite cause.

Pisces

The typical Pisces is probably the sign least interested in money management. However, there are many billionaires born under your sign, such as Michael Dell, David Geffen, and Steve Jobs. Generally they have made money from innovative ideas and left the details to others. That might work for you. Find a Scorpio, Capricorn, or Virgo to help you set a profitable course and systematically save (which is not in your nature). Sign up for automatic bill paying, so you won't have to think about it. If you keep in mind how much less stressful life will be and how much more you can do when you're not worried about paying bills, you might be motivated enough to stick to a sensible budget. Investmentwise, consider anything to do with water—offshore drilling, water conservation and purifying, shipping, and seafood. Petroleum is also ruled by your sign, as are institutions related to hospitals.

CHAPTER 15

Keep Father Time in His Place: Antiaging Tips

In 2008, both Jupiter and Pluto enter the sign of Capricorn, the Saturn-ruled sign associated with Father Time and the elder years. This is especially meaningful for the baby boomer generation, the millions of Americans born between 1946 and 1964. For the post–World War II generation, who are looking forward to a long and vital life span, age sixty is the beginning of middle age, not old age. This active generation will be reinventing our concept of how to spend the senior years, as they play a much more vocal and demanding role in society.

It will not be unusual to live to be over one hundred, say the experts, but baby boomers will be concerned with how well they live, not just how long. Innovative medical technologies in areas such as joint replacement and management of cardiovascular disease assure this generation of more pep and productivity, while drugs like Viagra boost their sex lives. Americans will be well able to skip retirement and continue in the workforce or choose to start a second, more rewarding career.

Astrology has many ideas for keeping baby boomers healthy and happy. Each sign is associated with a part of the body that could become vulnerable in later years. Within the personality of a sign are other clues for having a productive old age.

Aries

The Aries baby boomer is one who plans on staying forever young. You'll stay up-to-date and may identify with the younger generation rather than your peers. If something is wrong physically, you'll fix it quickly with the latest medical technology. It's important, Aries, that you learn to pace yourself and be realistic about what you can do. (You are the sign that goes snowboarding at age sixty.) Be sure to take physical precautions to safeguard yourself when doing sports. Guard your head area with the right gear and rein in your impulsiveness when in crowded or traffic situations. More patience could be the greatest gift of your elder years.

Taurus

As the zodiac's gourmet, Taurus needs to watch your diet and craving for sweets as you grow older, since you're more likely to overindulge and gain weight. Exercise is not your favorite activity, so trick yourself by combining a workout with a walk in a beautiful nature preserve or bike path. Since you are a great shopper, you could combine bargain hunting with a power walk in your local mall. Gardening and playing with a lively pet are pleasant ways to get moving or get a fun workout playing with young grandchildren. Combining movement with your everyday activities is the key for sedentary Taurus.

Gemini

Yours is one of the active signs that rarely has a serious weight problem. Your lungs may be vulnerable, however, so do everything you can to stop smoking, get regular flu shots, and improve the air quality in your home. Gemini thrives on social contact and mental stimulation and should remain active in the community. Expand your social network as much as possible to include young people with innovative ideas. Take courses at your local college and challenge yourself by learning new skills. It is important for Gemini to protect your nerve pathways, so be sure your chairs are ergonomic and watch for carpal tunnel syndrome if you use a computer.

Cancer

Cancer is family-oriented in the elder years and thrives on close contact with loving relatives. It is even better if your home is near water, where you can exercise with long walks on the beach and swimming. If not, join a local water-aerobics class at your local pool. Cancer can be moody, so combat any tendency to get depressed by doing creative projects and spending time with loved ones. A positive attitude is one of your best antiaging techniques.

Leo

Leo's vulnerable area is the heart, which you should check frequently as you grow older, even if you appear to be the picture of health, like Leos Arnold Schwarzenegger and Bill Clinton, who have had cardiac surgery. Adopting a heart-healthy diet will help stave off problems. Sun-ruled Leos should take preventive measures to avoid skin cancer by using a high SPF sunscreen, especially if you live in a Southern climate. Leos thrive on the attention they get from performing, so why not share skills by lecturing or teaching a local class. Share that hard-won wisdom!

Virgo

As one of the most health-conscious signs, Virgo usually sticks to a sensible diet and gets regular checkups. Staying mentally active can ward off age-related depression, so investigate your local community college, take education-oriented trips, and expand your social circle with new friends. Virgo thrives when being of service to the community and should seek opportunities to do volunteer work. Teaching or coaching young people can be especially rewarding to your sign.

Libra

Libra's key to youth is to keep the social, family, mental, and physical areas of your life in balance. Strengthen your body with balancing exercises like tai chi and yoga or artistic and social exercises like dancing. Exercises done in a sociable group are more to Libra's liking. Your back and kidneys are vulnerable areas to keep in good condition. In later years, Libra has the time to become more involved in intellectual pursuits and arts and crafts. Libra enjoys entertaining and throwing parties for friends and family. Cultivating relationships with like-minded friends by joining a club or group with a common cause is a good idea.

Scorpio

You're the sexy senior! The sign of Scorpio is associated with the sex organs and known for having an active sex life in the senior years. Your partner may well need Viagra! Scorpio is often likened to a phoenix rising from the ashes for your ability to survive illness and regain health. However, you should pay special attention to the elimination and sexual functions of the body with regular examinations and colonoscopies. Water sports and vacations near the sea are excellent therapy for stressed-out Scorpios. Getting involved in something you care passionately about keeps Scorpio young at heart.

Sagittarius

You're no stay-at-home senior! You'll enjoy the independence you have, which gives you the chance to pursue your many interests, including travel to places you've always wanted to explore and having fun times with pals. Active Sagittarius is one of the most athletic signs and may continue to play your favorite sports in senior years, right alongside your grandchildren. Now's your time to motivate the younger generation, so find ways to pass on your hard-won wisdom via teaching or writing, perhaps continuing your career on a part-time basis. Many Sagittarius will get involved in promoting an idealistic or political cause.

Capricorn

The Capricorn senior likes to stay actively involved in community life. Yours is a disciplined, organized sign that may not retire from business or may continue your career on a part-time basis. Some may pursue an entirely different career, with great success. You could well represent the seniors in your community on boards and committees. It is important for Capricorn to continue doing productive work, even if it is on a volunteer basis. Physically Capricorn is one of the longer-lived signs. It is associated with bones and knees, so protect these areas and watch a tendency toward arthritis and osteoporosis.

Aquarius

Aquarius is on the cutting edge and usually on top of the latest trends, even later in life. You won't let advanced years hold you back! You're likely to play computer games with grandchildren and even have your own Web site. You remain young if you stay involved in a cause and pursue your multiple interests. You'll share your wisdom by teaching a class, lecturing, or writing. Physically, protect yourself against airborne allergies, and exercise to prevent circulation problems. Group activities appeal to Aquarius, especially if you are promoting a cause.

Pisces

Elder Pisces is happiest when pursuing creative activities, such as filmmaking, painting, writing, or a hobby or craft in which you can express your imagination. Places near water are particularly healthful for Pisces. Water sports, especially swimming, can maintain your health. Avoid addictive substances and stick to a balanced diet of organic foods, including plenty of fish. Lymphatic drainage massage is good therapy for Pisces, which is associated with the lymphatic system. Pay special attention to the condition of your feet, and wear the appropriate shoes for each activity.

CHAPTER 16

The Mystic Properties of Your Birthstone

Who hasn't at one time or another received a special piece of jewelry with a birthstone? We enjoy the idea that wearing a special gem resonates with our personality and might even bring us luck. However, there is quite a bit of confusion over which stone is best for each sign, because we are often given birthstones according to the month of our birthday rather than our zodiac sign. You may be wondering if the amethyst is more suitable for a February-born Pisces than the aquamarine, or you might prefer the gems associated with your moon sign, which resonate with your emotional nature, or your Venus sign, which appeal to your sense of fashion and good taste.

There are many ways to approach the subject of birthstones. Lovers of precious gems could choose one that reflects the element of your sun sign. Earth signs (Taurus, Virgo, Capricorn) resonate to the bright green emerald. Fire signs (Aries, Leo, Sagittarius) belong to the flaming ruby. Water signs (Cancer, Scorpio, Pisces) might prefer the deep blue sapphire. And air signs (Gemini, Libra, Aquarius) may gravitate to the clear, brilliant diamond.

If you don't care for your birthstone, you could choose a talisman by color. Choose a stone that is associated with your sun, moon, or Venus sign. An Aries with moon in Cancer might prefer a pale lunar jewel like the pearl or moonstone. A Pisces with Venus in Aries might love to wear bright red stones like ruby or spinel.

In ancient India, Egypt, and Babylonia, rare and beautiful gemstones were thought to have magical properties. People are said to have consulted astrologers for advice on wearing the appropriate gem for each occasion. Ancient Egyptians carried scarabs and tiny figures of their gods for protection and luck. These were carved in semi-precious stones like lapis lazuli, carnelian, and turquoise. In India, one of the most powerful talismans was an amulet designed with precious stones representing the known planets at the time. Another astrological connection was the wearing of gems associated with a planet on that planet's special day. Mars-ruled rubies would be worn on the Mars day, Tuesday, for instance. It is still possible to find special astrological talismans created by astrologer-jewelers, who will make up a special pendant or necklace displaying your horoscope's special stones in a beautiful design.

In the Judeo-Christian tradition, the astrological association with gemstones dates from the sacred twelve-gem breastplate of Aaron, recorded in Exodus. Each gem symbolized one of the twelve tribes of Israel. Later these gems became connected with the twelve signs of the zodiac. However, it was not until the eighteenth century that people began to wear their special birthstones. For more information on the history and mystery of gemstones, including their astrological use, read *The Curious Lore of Precious Stones* by George Frederick Kunz.

Here are some suggestions for choosing stones associated with a given zodiac sign. Bear in mind that there are no hard-and-fast rules; you might find yourself attracted to a certain gem without fully understanding why. That might well be the gem you are supposed to wear, regardless of your sign.

Aries

Though most sources give the birthstone for April as the diamond, Aries may feel more affinity for Mars-ruled stones with red hues, such as ruby, spinels, fire opals, garnets, coral, and carnelian.

Taurus

Emeralds are most associated with Taurus. However, Taurus might gravitate toward some of the earthy agates and green stones such as tourmaline, jade, serpentine (which is believed to draw good fortune), and green quartz.

Gemini

Pearls and agates are associated with Gemini, but you might prefer fascinating gems like alexandrite or tanzanite, which change color according to the angle of light. Or watermelon tourmaline, which has dual colorations. Interesting rutilated quartzes with fine hairlike inclusions are associated with communication and might be perfect for your sign.

Cancer

July has often been linked with the ruby; however, that fiery stone might be better suited to Leos born in late July. Cancer seems to resonate more with the elegant blue sapphire, moonstone, chalcedony, and the deep blue flashes of laboradorite and rainbow moonstone.

Leo

The yellow-green peridot and all golden stones belong to sun-ruled Leos. You may also love the ruby, yellow diamonds, amber, and citrine. Go for the golden tones!

Virgo

Sapphires, which come in many colors, carnelian, onyx, and pink jasper are associated with Virgo. You may also respond to the earthy agates and the green tones of emerald and jade.

Libra

Opal, which was once considered exclusive to Libra, comes in many variations. In fact, the opal was deemed unlucky for any other sign. This beautiful stone comes in many color variations, from the deeper Australian opals to the pale Russian opals. You might try the blue-and-pink Peruvian opal or the mysterious, earthy boulder opal. Libra is also associated with the color pink, as in rose quartz, pink sapphires, pink diamonds, and kunzite. Apple green chrysoprase is another beautiful choice.

Scorpio

This mysterious sign was given the topaz, which comes in blue or golden variations. You might also respond to the deep tones of smoky quartz, tiger's eye, black onyx, rainbow obsidian, black diamonds, or black South Sea pearls.

Sagittarius

Visionary Sagittarius responds to turquoise, the mystical stone of Native Americans and Tibetans. No medicine man's outfit was complete without a turquoise. It was treasured by the Persians, who believed that turquoise could protect from evil and bring good fortune. Also consider lapis lazuli, blue topaz, and ruby.

Capricorn

The burgundy red garnet is the usual stone for Capricorn, but garnets are now available in many other colors, such as the green tsavorite garnet. Also consider the beautifully marked green malachite. Onyx in all its color variations is compatible with Capricorn.

Aquarius

Aquarius is associated with the purple amethyst, a type of quartz that was once thought to prevent drunkenness. This sign might respond to some of the newer stones on the market, such as laboradorite, a gray stone that flashes electric blue, or to some of the other purple stones, such as sugilite, tanzanite, or purple jade. The colorful quartzes, which are able to conduct electricity, could be your gem. Diamonds of all kinds also resonate with Aquarius, according to the glamorous Aquarius Gabor sisters and Carol Channing, who sang "Diamonds Are a Girl's Best Friend."

Pisces

The blue-green aquamarine and the earthy bloodstone are usually associated with Pisces. During the sixteenth century, bloodstone was believed to cure hemorrhages caused by the plague. Jasper is also a Pisces stone, now available in many beautiful colors such as "picture jasper" and "poppy jasper," which look like miniature paintings. Pisces also responds to jewels from the sea: pearls and coral and ocean blue sapphires. Elizabeth Taylor, a great Pisces jewel collector, owns the famous Peregrina pearl as well as many deep blue sapphires.

CHAPTER 17

Give the Perfect Gift to Every Sign

So often we're in a quandary about what to give a loved one, someone who has everything, that hard-to-please friend, or a fascinating new person in your life, or about the right present for a wedding, birthday, or hostess gift. Why not let astrology help you make the perfect choice by appealing to each sun sign's personality. When you're giving a gift, you're also making a memory, so it should be a special occasion. The gift that's most appreciated is one that touches the heart, reminds you both of a shared experience, or shows that the giver has really cared enough to consider the recipient's personality.

In general, the water signs (Cancer, Pisces, Scorpio) enjoy romantic, sentimental, and imaginative gifts given in a very personal way. Write your loved one a poem or a song to express your feelings. Assemble an album of photos or mementos of all the good times you've shared. Appeal to their sense of fantasy. Scorpio Richard Burton had the right idea when he gave Pisces Elizabeth Taylor a diamond bracelet hidden in lavender roses (her favorite color).

Fire signs (Aries, Leo, Sagittarius) appreciate a gift presented with lots of flair. Pull out the drama, like the actor who dazzled his Aries sweetheart by presenting her with trash cans overflowing with daisies.

Air signs (Gemini, Libra, Aquarius) love to be surprised with unusual gifts. The Duke of Windsor gave his elegant Gemini duchess, Wallis Windsor, fabulous jewels engraved with love notes and secret messages in their own special code.

Earth signs (Taurus, Virgo, Capricorn) value solid, tangible gifts or ones that appeal to all the senses. Delicious gourmet treats, scented body lotions, the newest CDs, the gift of a massage, or stocks and bonds are sure winners! Capricorn Elvis Presley once received a gold-plated piano from his wife.

Here are some specific ideas for each sign:

Aries

These are the trendsetters of the zodiac, who appreciate the latest thing! For Aries, it's the excitement that counts, so present your gift in a way that will knock their socks off. Aries is associated with the head, so a jaunty hat, hair ornaments, chandelier earrings, sunglasses, and hair-taming devices are good possibilities. Aries love games of any kind that offer a real challenge, like war video games, military themes, or rousing music with a beat. Anything red is a good bet: red flowers, red gems, and red accessories. How about giving Aries a way to let off steam with a gym membership or aerobic-dancing classes? Monogram a robe with a nickname in red.

Taurus

These are touchy-feely people who love things that appeal to all their senses. Find something that sounds, tastes, smells, feels, or looks good. And don't stint on quality or comfort. Taurus know the value of everything and will be aware of the price tag. Taurus foodies will appreciate chef-worthy kitchen gadgets, the latest cookbook, and gourmet treats. Taurus is a great collector. Find out what their passion is and present them with a rare item or a beautiful storage container such as an antique jewelry box. Green-thumb Taurus would love some special plants or flowers, garden tools, beautiful plant containers. Appeal to their sense of touch with fine fabrics—high-thread-count sheets, cashmere, satin, and mohair. One of the animal-loving signs, Taurus might appreciate a retractable leash or soft bed for the dog or cat. Get them a fine wallet or checkbook cover. They'll use it often.

Gemini

Mercury-ruled Gemini appreciates gifts that appeal to their mind. The latest book or novel, a talked-about film, a CD from a hot new singer, or a high-tech gadget might appeal. A beautiful diary or a tape recorder would record their adventures. Since Geminis often do two things at once, a telephone gadget that leaves their hands free would be appreciated. In fact, a new telephone device or superphone would appeal to these great communicators. Gloves, rings, and bracelets accent their expressive hands. Clothes from an interesting new designer appeal to their sense of style. You might try giving Gemini a variety of little gifts in a beautiful box or a Christmas stocking. A tranquil massage at a local spa would calm Gemini's sensitive nerves. Find an interesting way to wrap your gift. Nothing boring, please!

Cancer

Cancer is associated with home and family, so anything to do with food, entertaining at home, and family life is a good bet. Beautiful dishes or serving platters, silver items, fine crystal and linen, gourmet cookware, cooking classes or the latest DVD from a cooking teacher might be appreciated. Cancer designers Vera Wang and Giorgio Armani have perfected the Cancer style and have many home products available, as well as their elegant designer clothing. Naturally, anything to do with the sea is a possibility: pearls, coral, or shell jewelry. Boat and water-sports equipment might work. Consider cruise wear for traveling Cancers. Sentimental Cancer loves antiques and silver frames for family photos. Cancer people are often good photographers, so consider frames, albums, and projectors to showcase their work. Present your gift in a personal way with a special note.

Leo

Think big with Leo and appeal to this sign's sense of drama. Go for the gold (Leo's color) with gold jewelry, designer clothing, or big attention-getting accessories. Follow their signature style, which could be superelegant, like Jacqueline Onassis, or superstar, like Madonna or Jennifer Lopez. This sign is always ready for the red carpet and stays beautifully groomed, so stay within these guidelines when choosing your gift. Feline motifs and animal prints are usually a hit. The latest grooming aids, high-ticket cosmetics, and mirrors reflect their best image. Beautiful hairbrushes tame their manes. Think champagne, high-thread-count linens, and luxurious loungewear or lingerie. Make Leo feel special with a custom portrait or photo shoot with your local star photographer. Be sure to go for spectacular wrapping, with beautiful paper and ribbons. Present your gift with a flourish!

Virgo

Virgo usually has a special subject of interest and would appreciate relevant books, films, lectures, or classes. Choose health-oriented things: gifts to do with fitness and self-improvement. Virgo enjoys brainteasers, crossword puzzles, computer programs, organizers, and digital planners. Fluffy robes, bath products, and special soaps appeal to Virgo's sense of cleanliness. Virgo loves examples of good, practical design: efficient telephones, beautiful briefcases, computer cases, desk accessories. Choose natural fibers and quiet colors when choosing clothes for Virgo. Virgo has high standards, so go for quality when choosing a gift.

Libra

Whatever you give this romantic sign, go for beauty and romance. Libra loves accessories, decorative objects, whatever makes him or his surroundings more aesthetically pleasing. Beautiful flowers in pastel colors are always welcome. Libras are great hosts and hostesses, who might appreciate a gift related to fine dining: serving pieces, linens, glassware, flower vases. Evening or party clothes please since Libra has a gadabout social life. Interesting books, objets d'art, memberships to museums, and tickets to cultural events are good ideas. Fashion or home-decorating magazine subscriptions usually please Libra women. Steer away from anything loud, garish, or extreme. Think pink, one of their special colors, when giving Libra jewelry, clothing, or accessories. It's a very romantic sign, so be sure to remember birthdays, holidays, and anniversaries with a token of affection.

Scorpio

Scorpios love mystery, so bear that in mind when you buy these folks a present. You could take this literally and buy them a good thriller DVD, novel, or video game. Scorpios are power players, so a book about one of their sign might please. Bill Gates, Jack Welch, Condoleezza Rice, and Hillary Clinton are hot Scorpio subjects. Scorpios love black leather, suede, fur, anything to do with the sea, power tools, tiny spy tape recorders, and items with secret compartments or intricate locks. When buying a handbag for Scorpio, go for simple shapes with lots of interior pockets. Sensuous Scorpios appreciate hot lingerie, sexy linens, body lotions, and perfumed candles. Black is the favored color for Scorpio clothing—go for sexy textures like cashmere and satin in simple shapes by designers like Calvin Klein. This sign is fascinated with the occult, so give them an astrology or tarot-card reading, beautiful crystals, or an astrology program for the computer.

Sagittarius

For these outdoor people, consider adventure trips, designer sportswear, gear for their favorite sports. A funny gift or something for their pets pleases Sagittarius. For clothing and accessories, the fashionista of this sign tends to like bright colors and dramatic innovative styles. Otherwise, casual sportswear is a good idea. These travelers usually have a favorite getaway place; give them a travel guide, DVD, novel, or history book that would make their trip more interesting. Luggage is also a good bet. Sleek carry-ons, travel wallets, ticket holders, business-card cases, and wheeled computer bags might please these wanderers. Anything that makes travel more comfortable and pleasant is good for Sagittarius, including a good book to read en route. This sign is the great gambler of the zodiac, so gifts related to their favorite gambling venue would be appreciated.

Capricorn

For this quality-conscious sign, go for a status label from the best store in town. Get Capricorns something good for their image and career. They could be fond of things Spanish, like flamenco or tango music, or of country-and-western music and motifs. In the bookstore, go for biographies of the rich and famous, or advice books to help Capricorn get to the top. Capricorns take their gifts seriously, so steer away from anything too frivolous. Garnet, onyx, or malachite jewelry, Carolina Herrera fragrance and clothing, and beautiful briefcases and wallets are good ideas. Glamorous status tote bags carry business gear in style. Capricorns like golf, tennis, and sports that involve climbing, cycling, or hiking, so presents could be geared to their outdoor interests. Elegant evening accessories would be fine for this sign, which often entertains for business.

Aquarius

Give Aquarius a surprise gift. This sign is never impressed with things that are too predictable. So use your imagination to present the gift in an unusual way or at an unexpected time. With Aquarius, originality counts. When in doubt, give them something to think about, a new electronic gadget, perhaps a small robot, or an advanced computer game. Or something New Age, like an amethyst-crystal cluster. Aquarius like innovative materials with a space-age look. They are the ones with the wraparound glasses, the titanium computer cases. This air sign loves to fly—an airplane ticket always pleases. Books should be on innovative subjects, politics, or adventures of the mind. Aquarius goes for unusual color combinations—especially electric blue or hot pink—and abstract patterns. They like the newest, coolest looks on the cutting edge of fashion and are not afraid to experiment. Think of Paris Hilton's constantly changing looks. Look for an Aquarius gift in an out-of-the-way boutique or local hipster hangout. They'd be touched if you find out Aquarius's special worthy cause and make a donation. Spirit them off to hear their favorite guru.

Pisces

Pisces respond to gifts that have a touch of fantasy, magic, and romance. Look for mystical gifts with a touch of the occult. Romantic music (a customized CD of favorite love songs) and love stories appeal to Pisces sentimentalists. Pisces is associated with perfume and fragrant oils, so help this sign indulge with their favorite scent in many forms. Anything to do with the ocean, fish, and water sports appeals to Pisces. How about a whirlpool, a water-therapy spa treatment, or a sea salt rub. Appeal to this sign with treats for the feet: foot massages, pedicures, ballet tickets, and dance lessons. Cashmere socks and metallic evening sandals are other Pisces pleasers. A romantic dinner overlooking the water is Pisces paradise. A case of fine wine or another favorite liquid is always appreciated. Write a love poem and enclose it with your gift.

CHAPTER 18

The Meaning of Numbers

What exactly is a number 9 day, and how did it get to be that number? If you've been reading the dailies, you've no doubt seen such numerological references. Usually you'll find these numbers on the days when the moon is transiting from one sign to another.

If you're familiar with numerology, you probably know your life-path number, which is derived from your birth date. That number represents who you were at birth and the traits that you'll carry throughout your life. There are numerous books and Web sites that will provide you with details on what the numbers mean regarding your life path.

The numbers used in the dailies are found by adding the numbers related to the astrological sign (1 for Aries, 2 for Taurus, etc.), the year, the months, and the day. For example, June 14, 2008 for a Libra would be 7 for Libra, plus 1 (adding together the numbers in 2008), plus 6 for June, plus 7 (1+6) for the day. That would be 7+1+6+5 (sign+year+month+day)=19=1 (1+9=10 [1+0=1]).

So on that number 1 day, you might be advised that you're getting a fresh start, a new beginning. You can take the lead on something new. Stress originality and creativity. Explore and discover. You're inventive and make connections that others overlook.

Briefly, here are the meanings of the numbers, which are included in more detail in the dailies themselves.

1: taking the lead, getting a fresh start, a new beginning
2: cooperation, partnership, a new relationship, sensitivity
3: harmony, beauty, pleasures of life, warm, receptive

4: getting organized, hard work, being methodical, re-building, fulfilling your obligations
5: freedom of thought and action, change, variety, thinking outside the box
6: a service day, being diplomatic, generous, tolerant, sympathetic
7: mystery, secrets, investigations, research, detecting deception, exploration of the unknown, of the spiritual realms
8: your power day, financial success, unexpected money, a windfall
9: finishing a project, looking beyond the immediate, setting your goals, reflection, expansion

—Rob MacGregor

Rob MacGregor is the author of seventeen novels and ten nonfiction books, including *Psychic Power*, *Star Power for Teens*, and *Romancing the Raven*. For more information, go to www.robmacgregor.net.

CHAPTER 19

All About Gemini: Your Personality, Family, Career, Relationships, and Lifestyle

Have you tapped in to your Gemini power? Knowing and using your positive Gemini sun-sign traits (and downplaying the negative ones) could be your key to achieving more happiness and success in all areas of your life. That's because every part of your life has a strong Gemini influence. That includes what and whom you like, your family relationships, your strengths on the job, even the decor of your home. The more you understand the Gemini in you, the better you can use your personal solar power to help you make good decisions. You can use it every day from something as basic as choosing what to wear to more important issues such as getting along with your boss or spicing up your love life.

So get ready for your close-up! In the following chapters, you'll be empowered with tools to control your destiny and make your dreams come true by moving in harmony with your natural inclinations.

Before we begin, here's how we determine what a Gemini personality is. Astrologers describe a Gemini using a type of recipe. The basic characteristics of a Gemini are determined by blending several ingredients. First there's your Gemini element: air. Air signs are distinguished by their mental orientation. Next, consider that Gemini functions as a mutable sign, constantly changing. Then there's your sign's polarity, which adds a positive, masculine, yang dimension. Let's not forget your planetary ruler: Mercury, the planet of communication and mental functioning. Add your sign's zodiac location in the third house of communication. Finally, stir in your symbol, the Twins, which reveals that Gemini has a dual nature.

This combination of ingredients influences everything we say about Gemini. For example, you could easily deduce that an air sign with a Mercury ruling planet should have a quick mind and a facility with words. Is a Gemini likely to sit around the house? Only if there's a dual-line phone or a party going on. Changeable Gemini is the ruler of multitasking, easily able to do two things at once. If you're a typical, social Gemini, a deserted island is unlikely to be your favorite vacation spot. But your total astrological personality contains a blend of many other planets, colored by the signs they occupy, plus factors such as the sign coming over the horizon at the exact moment of your birth. However, the more Gemini planets in your horoscope, the more likely you'll follow your sun sign's prototype. On the other hand, if many planets are grouped together in a different sign, they will color your horoscope accordingly, sometimes making a communicative sign like yours appear more withdrawn. So if the Gemini traits mentioned here don't describe you, there could be other factors flavoring your cosmic stew. (Look up your other planets in the tables in this book to find out what they might be!)

The Gemini Man: Multiple Choices

The Gemini man is on a perpetual journey in search of the new. You seem to be forever in motion. Even when you're sitting still, your mind is racing. You are a lover of games on every level who can make a game of the most complicated situations. On the negative side, it is difficult for you to take anything or anyone too seriously. Weighty matters tend to drag you down, unless your mind is challenged by a crisis situation. You'd rather dabble in lots of different projects, then fly off when things get sticky.

In childhood, Gemini is the bright, funny little boy who gets bored in school and could devise some jolly pranks to amuse himself. You'll have many interests, which keep changing constantly. In your early years you should learn self-discipline as well as the satisfaction of setting goals and reaching them. Otherwise, you'll have a tendency to skim the surface of life, with much activity but few real accomplishments.

Young adulthood is an experimental time, and you're not about to deny yourself any adventures. Like the characters portrayed by Gemini idol Johnny Depp, you're the elusive and scintillating lover who dazzles, then disappears. A born flirt and charming chameleon who can't resist an exciting affair of the heart, you usually opt for several romantic experiences at once. This could result in your becoming a perennial playboy, even to leading a double life, both hazards of the ever-curious and charming Gemini man.

In a Relationship

The woman who succeeds in tying Gemini down would be well advised to give him lots of rope and keep an open mind. This is likely to be a nontraditional marriage—exciting but not particularly stable. Though Gemini is not naturally inclined to be monogamous, he will stick with a woman who is bright, entertaining, sociable, interesting, and companionable. It would help if she is involved in his professional life, too, as well as having strong interests of her own. His hot-cold temperament and roving eye could cause his mate a great deal of insecurity, unless she is an independent person as well. This mercurial man makes the perfect husband for an intelligent woman who longs for a witty conversationalist, a flirtatious and inventive lover, and an ever-youthful companion throughout life. With Gemini, she'll never be bored.

The Gemini Woman: The Great Communicator

It's no surprise that the comedienne whose signature line is "Can we talk?" is a Gemini—Joan Rivers. Your verbal skills are legendary, giving you the ability to talk yourself into or out of any situation. The written and spoken word is your means of seduction, sales, and self-defense. You'll talk with your expressive hands (the Gemini part of the body), and use body language to add extra emphasis.

You're highly charged with nervous energy, seeming to be everywhere at once. And you have enough sides to your personality to dazzle even those close to you. One moment you are a capable executive, the next a little girl filled with wonder, the next an earthy sensualist, the next an expert in verbal karate, the next a comedienne. It's no wonder there are so many actresses under this sign. And, best of all, you do everything with a light, quicksilver touch, so the effort never shows.

While your brain is busily skipping about, juggling many people and projects at once, you manage to skip away from heavy emotional involvements. You're not one to be tied down in any way. However, though variety may be the spice of your life, it can also be hard to digest. You need a substantial anchor and truly caring relationships to get you through the tough times. If you learn to live with a few normal human flaws and foibles (you can't laugh everything off!) instead of constantly changing your mind, you'll find your twin sides working together more smoothly. Then you will have a much better idea of what you're really looking for.

The little Gemini girl is the bright, precocious one who learns to read and write ahead of everyone. She is very well-coordinated, moves quickly, and talks even more rapidly. She bores easily with her toys, and may even invent new games to play with them.

Gemini's problem is making up her mind. There is always something more interesting to do, a more exciting place to go, people who might be more fun. You must learn early to stick to one thing until you have mastered it—or you'll end up being the proverbial "jill-of-all-trades."

Propelled by a great reservoir of nervous energy, the young Gemini is likely to have more than one job, more than one boyfriend, and a full schedule of social activities. Juggling is second nature to you. The more balls in the air, the less likely you are to get bored. One challenge is to find situations that give you a chance to grow. Otherwise, you'll skip from job to job, love affair to love affair, at a great strain on your nerves.

When you find a man who stimulates you mentally as well as emotionally and physically, you may be tempted to take a chance on love. It is important that you separate dream from reality here—and not confuse surface attraction with true communication. Otherwise, you may marry on impulse, quickly tire of the situation, and search for excitement elsewhere. Since you often retain your looks and youthful outlook, it is not unusual for you to finally settle with a much younger man.

In a Relationship

Keeping your foothold in the working world after marriage provides you with the outside stimulation you need and also the financial means to delegate the more boring routine tasks of housekeeping to someone else. If you apply your creativity to making the marriage special, you can keep the union lively, with no need to look for greener pastures. You're sure to promote a social life, entertain frequently, and decorate with flair and originality. Your relationship may also benefit if you take an active part in your husband's business. But too much togetherness can seem confining for your restless sign. If your husband is too possessive and demanding, you may be tempted to take flight. However, if you can negotiate enough room for personal freedom, you'll provide a life of sparkle and variety.

Gemini in the Family

The Gemini Parent

Geminis take a great interest in their child's different stages, watching the young personality unfold. You may find the early babyhood years most difficult, when the child is dependent and needs steady, routine care. After the child learns to communicate, you'll take on the role of teacher, introducing the child to the world of ideas and mental pursuits, helping with homework, and making difficult subjects easier to understand. One of your greatest assets as a parent is your own insatiable curiosity about the world, which you can communicate to the children by introducing them early to the world of ideas and books. You are also an excellent coach, teaching your child social abilities and the art of handling others at an early age. As your child matures, your youthful, ever fresh outlook makes you a wonderful friend and companion through the years.

The Gemini Stepparent

Your verbal skills and sense of humor will often come to the rescue in the initial stages of starting up a new family. You're a communicator who can quickly get shy youngsters to open up and difficult personalities to communicate. Your natural sociability and flair for entertainment encourages everyone to have fun, making family get-togethers seem like parties. Since you have many outside activities and interests, the children will be able to have as much time as they need alone with their parent. Soon your new family will find that you are a fun-loving addition to their lives, a wise adviser, and an excellent noncompetitive companion.

The Gemini Grandparent

You're an upbeat grandparent who still finds life an interesting adventure. You're always the life of the party, up on all the latest family gossip, as well as what's happening with the rest of the world. Visits with you are full of laughter and good stories! You'll take a special interest in your grandchildren's education and support them in whatever career path they choose. Like Barbara Bush, you may have a large extended family that reaches out to the children of your community. You'll give your own children plenty of space to rear the grandchildren as they please, never interfering with Mother's rules or taking over the grandchildren's upbringing.

"Never complain" was the motto of the Duchess of

Windsor (a Gemini), and it could be yours, too. You accentuate the positive and keep a cheerful attitude. Your mentor should be the famous Gemini pastor Norman Vincent Peale, author of *The Power of Positive Thinking,* one of the most influential self-help books of all time. Dr. Peale lived a productive life well into his nineties, still writing and preaching. You, too, realize how the right mental attitude can influence any situation for the better, and you'll be sure to pass on your wisdom to your grandchildren.

CHAPTER 20

The Gemini Lifestyle: How to Make Your Gemini Sign Shine

Astrology's personal insights follow through to the way you dress and live. Here's how to polish your Gemini image with tips tailored specifically for your sign, and improve your atmosphere by using your best colors and surrounding yourself with Gemini-loving sounds. Find out how to create a living environment that reflects your personality, where you'll feel totally at home. And how to make the most of your sign's special fashion flair. Even your vacations might be more fun and relaxing if you tailor them to your sun sign's natural inclinations.

The Gemini Fashion Image

Gemini always likes to do something interesting with your clothes and have fun with fashion, and never take your fashion image too seriously. Nicole Kidman dresses with great Gemini flair in clothes that get people talking. Annette Bening opts for simple, elegant clothes that set off her delicate beauty. Other Gemini beauties, like Liz Hurley, who once attended the Academy Awards in a gown held together with safety pins, and Angelina Jolie enjoy looking downright outrageous, keeping their fans guessing! Some Geminis, like the late Marilyn Monroe, love to flaunt their sex appeal, making a game of it. And then there is Joan Rivers, mistress of the red carpet, whose fashion flair and crusade for more elegance has literally transformed the way celebrities dress!

Since you have such a changeable personality, you'll probably experiment before you find the style that suits you. Double-duty clothes that change personality with a scene-stealing accessory or two are ideal for your gadabout life, when you're just too busy to fuss. A hairstyle that can be combed several different ways would satisfy your need for constant change. Add a witty, scene-stealing jewel or two, a dramatic scarf, or trendy shoes and handbag to quickly change your outfit's personality and you're ready to go!

Gemini often talks with the hands, so make your gestures count. Stay well-manicured and accent your expressive hands with hot-colored nail polish and fabulous rings.

Gemini's Fashion Colors

The Gemini palette—soft silvery-gray, pale yellow, and airy Wallis Windsor blue—consists of great background colors, elegant ones you can live with over a period of time. They adapt to different seasons and climates, won't compete with your personality or distract from your total image. You can change the look of these colors at will, accenting them with bright touches or blending with other pastels. And they can tolerate a frequent change of accessories according to your mood of the moment.

Your Gemini Fashion Role Models

Some legendary fashion icons, like the late Duchess of Windsor, were born under your sign and you couldn't find better inspiration than this scandalous siren who made fashion history as well. We remember Wallis Simpson for her witty way with accessories, like those fabulous jewels she wore with casual aplomb (some engraved with secret messages from the Duke). Yet she never varied her signature swept-back hairdo or her elegantly simple style of dressing.

The fashion duo Dolce & Gabbana, the with-it looks of

Anna Sui, or the newest androgynous menswear styles would be fun for you to try on for size. Gemini models who express your flair, like Naomi Campbell and Heidi Klum, have the ability to change their image with their hair style, be a vamp one moment, an innocent girl next door the next.

Gemini at Home

Your home should be multipurpose to accommodate your many interests and ongoing projects, yet it should also be a place where you can conduct your active social life, and finally, a relaxing haven. Keep your atmosphere and colors light and airy. Give heavy drapes, intense colors, and dark furniture a pass.

Let the colors of your room be a background for all the interesting things that will happen there. Pale neutrals and pastels on the walls are versatile and easy to live with over a period of time. (You might get quickly bored with more vibrant shades.) Then shift into color with bright slipcovers and accessories to give your room a quick change of personality.

Since you may have several activities going on at once, your decor strategy should help you avoid confusion and stay on top of your schedule. Choose furniture that can be rearranged in different combinations and settings. Clever cabinets and storage containers allow you to sweep your projects out of sight when friends drop in. Line a room with bookcases if you're one of the Gemini readers who collect the latest magazines, books, and newspapers.

Set up your communications center carefully. (You're the sign with a telephone on both sides of the bed and along-side the bathtub.) Have a separate room or corner with a desk where you can organize lists, equipment, and books so you won't waste time looking for them. Many Geminis have houses in more than one place (you're often bicoastal), so you can switch environments. At each place, there should be a space to stash whatever you need to stay connected to your network. With a laptop computer, you can work wherever you go.

Geminis love to entertain casually and frequently, so your kitchen should be set up for impromptu parties, with plenty of glassware and buffet plates handy. Have multipurpose tables that can be set up anywhere and folding chairs for instant group seating. Then get ready to party!

Gemini Background Music

Gemini has sophisticated, eclectic musical tastes, and perhaps has accumulated a varied collection of sounds. You may enjoy instrumentals that require manual dexterity, such as piano concertos. In popular music, you pay attention to the words as well as the melody, so the witty lyrics of Cole Porter and the poetry of Bob Dylan appeal, as do the hottest rap artist and the latest experiment of Sir Paul McCartney. You like abstract classical music, but nothing too heavy or loud that might distract from conversation or bring on the blues. You're a natural disk jockey, so customize your own mix of musical moods on an iPod or CD recorder. Paula Abdul, Miles Davis, Alanis Morrisette, rap music, Kylie Minogue, Cole Porter, Prince, Judy Garland, and continental tunes from Charles Aznavour would give you the full range of Gemini sounds.

Gemini Travel Guide

Sometimes you just have to get away from it all! But Gemini never likes to get too far away from civilization. Stay away from desert islands, unless you need some peace and quiet to write your novel. Stick to places where there's a lively social scene, some interesting scenery, local characters who provide good conversation, and an Internet café to keep up with your e-mail.

Improve your language skills by visiting a foreign country; you'll have no trouble communicating in sign language, if necessary. Consider a language school in the south of France or in Switzerland, where you'll mix with fellow students of many nationalities while you perfect your accent. In the USA, visit some of the Gemini states: Wisconsin, Tennessee, Kentucky, Rhode Island, South Carolina, and Arkansas.

Lightness is the key to Gemini travel. Don't weigh yourself down with luggage. Dare to travel with an empty suitcase, then acquire clothes and supplies at your destination. Imagine how fast you'll speed through the airport! Invest in a fabulous carry-on that you can throw your life in and go.

Keep a separate tiny address book for each city, so the right numbers are always handy. Invest in beautifully designed travel cases and briefcases, since you're on the go so much. Spend some time looking for the perfect luggage, portable notebook computer (with a modem and Wi-Fi), and a worldwide mobile phone to keep you in touch at all times.

CHAPTER 21

Gemini Health and Well-Being

Astrology can clue you in to the tendencies that contribute to good or ill health (especially when it comes to controlling your appetite). So follow these tips on how best to lose those extra pounds, and make this your healthiest year ever.

Make a Game of It

Gemini is an on-the-go sign that does not usually have a weight problem, as long as you keep moving. If life circumstances force you to be sedentary, however, you may eat out of boredom and watch the pounds pile on. Your active social life can also sabotage your weight with sumptuous party buffets and restaurant meals where you enjoy sampling everything. Your challenge is to find a healthy eating system with enough variety so you won't get bored. Develop a strategy for eating out—at parties or restaurants—and fill up the buffet plates with salad or veggies before you taste all the desserts. Sociable Geminis on a diet can benefit from group support in a system like Weight Watchers. Or find a diet twin who'll support you and have fun losing weight together.

Calm Your Nerves

Gemini is associated with the nervous system, our body's lines of communication. If your nerves are on edge, you may be trying to do too many things at once, leaving no time for fun and laughter. When you've overloaded your circuits, it's time to get together with friends, go out to parties, do things in groups to release tension and bring perspective into your life. Investigate natural tension relievers such as yoga or meditation. Doing things with your hands—playing the piano, typing, craftwork—is also helpful.

Guard Your Lungs

Gemini is also associated with the lungs, which are especially sensitive. If you smoke, please consider quitting. Yoga, which incorporates deep breathing into physical exercise, brings oxygen into your lungs. Among its many benefits are the deep relaxation and tranquillity so needed by your sign. If you work in a closed environment, with inadequate ventilation, consider getting an air purifier to combat airborn flu viruses. If you are a frequent flyer, bolster your immune system with vitamins and antioxidants before you travel and plan your schedule ahead of time to make travel as stress-free as possible.

Exercise with Friends

Combine healthful activities with social get-togethers for fun and plenty of fringe benefits for everyone. Include friends in your exercise routines; join an exercise class or jogging club. Gemini excels at sports that require good timing and manual dexterity as well as communication with others, like tennis or golf. These are sports that usually take place in a clubby social atmosphere, which should motivate you to exercise frequently as you continue to improve your skills. Racquet sports are also good for travelers, who can easily find courts or clubs in other cities, enabling you to make new friends wherever you go.

Those who jog may want to add hand weights or upper-body exercises, which will strengthen the arms and hands. If you spend long hours at the computer, try an ergonomic keyboard for comfort and protection against carpal tunnel syndrome.

CHAPTER 22

Your Gemini Career Guide: What It Takes to Succeed in 2008

Find the Right Career for You

Gemini has a special combination of talents and abilities that can make you a natural winner. Develop and nurture these sun-sign strengths, and you'll be likely to find a career you truly enjoy, one where you'll be most successful. The great philosopher and teacher Joseph Campbell gave you the best advice: Follow your bliss!

Your Ideal Work Environment

Follow your natural Gemini tendencies. Gemini has many winning cards to play in the career game. Your quick mind works best in a career where there is enough mental stimulation to keep you from getting bored. High-pressure situations that would be stressful to others are stimulating to you. Many things happening simultaneously—phones ringing off the hook, daily client meetings, constant changes—create a situation in which you thrive, getting to use all your communications skills. Consider the way the Gemini mayor of New York City, Rudolph Giuliani, masterfully handled the World Trade Center crisis, for the prime example of Gemini grace under pressure.

Your ability to communicate with a variety of people

works well in sales, journalism, public relations, politics, agent or broker work, personnel, or consulting—literally any job that requires verbal or writing skills. You who learn languages easily could be a language teacher or interpreter. Manual dexterity is another Gemini gift that can find craft, musical, or medical expression (especially surgery or chiropractic work).

What to avoid: a job that is too isolated, routine, detail-oriented, or confining. Stay away from companies that are hidebound, with rigid rules. Instead, look for a place that gives you strong backup as well as free rein. Gemini often succeeds in a freelance position, provided you have a solid support system to help with the details and routine chores.

The Gemini Leader

Gemini's natural analytical mind and way with words can be used to wheel and deal your way to the top. Master deal maker and real estate tycoon Donald Trump has written several books on his techniques that should make fascinating reading for ambitious Geminis. Be inspired and entertained by this colorful tycoon, who changed the skyline of New York and became a TV star, as well.

As a leader, Gemini is fun to work for—sociable, witty, and clever. Your office will be a beehive of activity, with telephone lines buzzing and clients coming and going. What is lacking in job security, you make up in opportunities for others to experiment, to develop flexibility and a sense of gamesmanship.

You operate best as a deal maker or an entrepreneur rather than a designer or producer. You often change your mind, so you should hire assistants who are adaptable enough to keep up with you, yet who can provide organization, follow-up, and structure. You rule by multitasking, and sometimes have so many projects going on at once that others are dizzy, yet you are known for innovative ideas and cool analysis of problems. You are especially gifted in making a deal, coordinating the diverse aspects of a project.

The Gemini Team Player

You work beautifully on a team, where your light sense of humor, friendliness, and ability to express yourself clearly are appreciated. Your position should deal with the public in sales or communications. You are also skilled at office politics. It's all part of the game to you; you rarely get emotionally involved. Let someone else do the record keeping, financial management, or accounting. As a Gemini you can handle a position where you report to several different people or juggle several different assignments, though you may do less well if the job requires intense concentration, patience, and perseverance.

The Gemini Way to Get Ahead

As a Gemini, you bring some important assets to the table, such as your ability to think on your feet, to act quickly, and to get results. It's up to you to decide how to best utilize your talents and abilities to bring you the very highest return on the investment of your time and energy. Look for a job with plenty of variety and mental stimulation. Play up these attributes:

- Verbal and written communication skills
- Ability to handle several tasks at once
- Charm and sociability
- Manual dexterity
- Ability to learn quickly
- Analytical ability

CHAPTER 23

Gemini on the Red Carpet

Are you a fan of tabloids and gossip columns? Your fascination with the rich and famous could have a fringe benefit. It's also a terrific way to learn more about astrology. A celebrity's attraction for the public tells much about the planetary influences of a given time and the special star quality of his or her sun sign. You may even have a celebrity astro twin who shares both your birthday and the same year.

You're sure to have many of the same traits as your famous sun-sign siblings. Like Joan Rivers and Rudolph Giuliani, you may have Gemini's virtuoso verbal skills. Or the mercurial sexiness of Angelina Jolie and Marilyn Monroe. Gemini males combine intelligence with charm, like Johnny Depp, John F. Kennedy, and Bill Moyers. Consider how Judy Garland, the Olsen twins, and Nicole Kidman have handled fame and fortune.

The lives of the famous can be fascinating textbooks with full-color illustrations of the different planetary combinations. If someone intrigues you, explore his personality further by looking up his other planets using the tables in this book. Then apply the effects of Venus, Mars, Saturn, and Jupiter to his sun-sign traits. It's a fun way to get up close and personal with your famous friend, maybe learn some secrets not revealed to the public.

Then why not move on from the red carpet to world leaders and current newsmakers? You can find accurate data online at Internet sites such as www.Stariq.com or www.astrodatabank.com, which have the charts of world events and headline makers. Then compare notes with other fans, including many professional astrologers who frequent the forums on these sites.

Gemini Celebrities

Raymond Burr (5/21/17)
Laurence Olivier (5/22/1907)
Naomi Campbell (5/22/70)
Douglas Fairbanks (5/23/1883)
Drew Carey (5/23/58)
Bob Dylan (5/24/41)
Priscilla Presley (5/24/45)
Roseanne Cash (5/24/50)
Kristin Scott-Thomas (5/24/60)
Dixie Carter (5/25/39)
Sir Ian McKellen (5/25/39)
Connie Selleca (5/25/55)
Mike Myers (5/25/63)
Anne Heche (5/25/69)
John Wayne (5/26/1907)
Peggy Lee (5/26/20)
Miles Davis (5/26/26)
Stevie Nicks (5/26/48)
Lenny Kravitz (5/26/64)
Helena Bonham-Carter (5/26/66)
Vincent Price (5/27/11)
Henry Kissinger (5/27/23)
Tony Hillerman (5/27/25)
Louis Gossett, Jr. (5/27/36)
Siouxie Sioux (5/27/57)
Joseph Fiennes (5/27/70)
Paul Bethany (5/27/71)
Gladys Knight (5/28/44)
Rudolph Giuliani (5/28/44)
Kylie Minogue (5/28/68)
Bob Hope (5/29/1903)
John F. Kennedy (5/29/17)
Kevin Conway (5/29/42)

Anthony Geary (5/29/47)
Annette Bening (5/29/58)
Rupert Everett (5/29/59)
Benny Goodman (5/30/1909)
Prince Ranier (5/31/23)
Clint Eastwood (5/31/30)
Peter Yarrow (5/31/38)
Sharon Gless (5/31/43)
Tom Berenger (5/31/50)
Joe Namath (5/31/50)
Lea Thompson (5/31/61)
Brooke Shields (5/31/65)
Andy Griffith (6/1/26)
Marilyn Monroe (6/1/26)
Edward Woodward (6/1/30)
Pat Boone (6/1/34)
Morgan Freeman (6/1/37)
Rene Auberjonois (6/1/40)
Jonathan Pryce (6/1/47)
Ron Wood (6/1/47)
Heidi Klum (6/1/73)
Alanis Morrisette (6/1/74)
Hedda Hopper (6/2/1890)
Sally Kellerman (6/2/37)
Stacey Keach (6/2/41)
Marvin Hamlisch (6/2/44)
Tony Curtis (6/3/25)
Curtis Mayfield (6/3/42)
Deniece Williams (6/3/51)
Anderson Cooper (6/3/67)
Dr. Ruth Westheimer (6/4/28)
Bruce Dern (6/4/36)
Michelle Phillips (6/4/44)
Parker Stevenson (6/4/52)
Angelina Jolie (6/4/75)
Bill Moyers (6/5/34)
Mark Wahlberg (6/5/71)
Sandra Bernhard (6/6/55)
Jessica Tandy (6/7/1909)
James Ivory (6/7/28)
Tom Jones (6/7/40)

Liam Neeson (6/7/52)
Prince (6/7/58)
Anna Kournikova (6/7/81)
Barbara Bush (6/8/25)
Joan Rivers (6/8/33)
Kathy Baker (6/8/50)
Juliana Margulies (6/8/66)
Cole Porter (6/9/1892)
Helena Rubenstein (6/9/1892)
Charles Saatchi (6/9/43)
Michael J. Fox (6/9/61)
Johnny Depp (6/9/63)
Natalie Portman (6/9/81)
Prince Philip (6/10/21)
Lionel Jeffries (6/10/26)
Grace Mirabella (6/10/30)
Elizabeth Hurley (6/10/65)
Tara Lipinski (6/10/82)
Gene Wilder (6/11/35)
Chad Everett (6/11/37)
Adrienne Barbeau (6/11/45)
George Bush (6/12/24)
Timothy Busfield (6/12/57)
Basil Rathbone (6/13/1892)
Christo (6/13/35)
Tim Allen (6/13/53)
Ashley and Mary Kate Olsen (6/13/86)
Donald Trump (6/14/46)
Boy George (6/14/61)
Steffi Graf (6/14/69)
Mario Cuomo (6/15/32)
Waylon Jennings (6/15/37)
Helen Hunt (6/15/63)
Courteney Cox Arquette (6/15/64)
Corin Redgrave (6/16/39)
Sonia Braga (6/16/50)
Yasmine Bleeth (6/16/68)
Dean Martin (6/17/17)
Joe Piscopo (6/17/51)
Jason Patric (6/17/66)
E. G. Marshall (6/18/10)

Roger Ebert (6/18/42)
Paul McCartney (6/18/42)
Isabella Rossellini (6/18/52)
Gena Rowlands (6/19/34)
Phylicia Rashad (6/19/48)
Kathleen Turner (6/19/54)
Paula Abdul (6/19/63)
Danny Aiello (6/20/33)
Lionel Richie (6/20/40)
John Goodman (6/20/52)
Cyndi Lauper (6/20/53)
Nicole Kidman (6/20/67)

CHAPTER 24

Star Wars or Passionate Supernovas? How Gemini Partners with Every Other Sign

After learning all about your own sun sign, it's time to consider how you interact with others. Knowing how your sun sign works with other signs can give you valuable insight into the future of all your relationships. Once you understand how another sun sign is likely to view yours, you'll be in a much better position to judge whether this combination will burn and crash or have lasting happiness potential.

The celebrity couples are used as examples to help you visualize each sun-sign combination. Note that some legendary couples have stood the test of time, others blazed brightly and then burned out, and a few existed only in the fantasy world of film or television (but still captured our imagination). Is there a magic formula for compatibility? Traditional astrological wisdom holds that signs of the same element, in your case other air signs (Libra and Aquarius), are naturally compatible. So are signs of complementary elements, such as air signs with fire signs. In these relationships, communication supposedly flows easily and you'll feel most comfortable with each other. However, there are no hard-and-fast rules with sun-sign combinations. Many lasting marriages happen between incompatible sun signs, while some ideally matched couples fizzle after a few years.

When sparks fly, and an irresistible magnetic pull draws you together, when disagreements and challenges fuel intrigue, mystery, passion, and sexy sparring matches, don't rule the relationship out. That person may provide the diversity, excitement, and challenge you need for an unforgettable romance, a stimulating friendship, or a successful business partnership!

Gemini/Aries

THE ATTRACTION:

There is fast-paced action here. Gemini gets a charge of excitement. Aries gets constant changes to keep up with. Both are spontaneous, optimistic, and energetic. Differences of opinion only keep the atmosphere stimulating.

THE ISSUES:

Juggling life with you could have Aries seeing double. Aries is direct and to the point, but Gemini can't or won't be pinned down. This hyperactive combination could get on both your nerves unless you give each other plenty of space. Gemini, tone down the flirting. Aries must be number one!

SIGN MATES:

Gemini Annette Bening and Aries Warren Beatty

Gemini/Taurus

THE ATTRACTION:

The sign next door can be your best friend as well as lover. In this case, you drag Taurus out of the house and into social life, adding laughter to love. Taurus has a soothing, stabilizing quality that supports your restlessness and allows you to be more creative than ever.

THE ISSUES:

Homebody Taurus usually wants one-on-one relations, while social Gemini loves to flirt with a crowd. You will have to curb roving eyes and bodies and plan to spend more time at home, which might cramp your style and leave you gasping for air. Infidelity can be serious business with Taurus, but taken lightly by Gemini. The line between freedom and license swings and sways here. You could feel Taurus is holding you back.

SIGN MATES:

Gemini Liam Neeson and Taurus Natasha Richardson
Gemini Steffi Graf and Taurus Andre Agassi
Gemini Anna Kournikova and Taurus Enrique Iglesias

Gemini/Gemini

THE ATTRACTION:

When Gemini twins find each other, you know you'll never be bored. There is enough multifaceted mental activity, games, and delightful social life to double your pleasure. Your partner will understand the complexities of your sign as only a fellow Gemini can.

THE ISSUES:

When the realities of life hit, you may go off in four directions at once. This combination lacks focus. It functions best in a light, creative atmosphere where there are no financial concerns. Serious practical problems could split your personalities and send you running elsewhere for protection and guidance.

SIGN MATES:

Twins Mary Kate and Ashley Olsen

Gemini/Cancer

THE ATTRACTION:

This is a very public pair with charisma to spare. Your sparkling wit sets off Cancer poise with the perfect light touch. Cancer adds warmth and caring to Gemini. This sign's shrewd insight can make your ideas happen. You can go places together!

THE ISSUES:

It's not easy for Gemini to deliver the kind of devotion Cancer needs. There are too many other exciting options. Nor do you react well to the Cancer need to mother you or to Cancer pleas for sympathy. Their up-and-down moods get on your nerves. Why can't they learn to laugh away their troubles or to find new interests? When Cancer clings, Gemini does a vanishing act. You need to have strong mutual interests or projects to hold this combo together. But it has been done!

SIGN MATES:

Gemini Michael J. Fox and Cancer Tracy Pollan
Gemini Nicole Kidman and Cancer Tom Cruise

Gemini/Leo

THE ATTRACTION:

Gemini good humor, ready wit, and social skills delight and complement Leo. Here is someone who can share the spotlight without trying to steal the show from the regal lion. This is one of the most entertaining combinations. Steady Leo provides the focus Gemini often lacks, and directs the twins toward achieving goals and status.

THE ISSUES:

Gemini loves to flirt and flit among many interests, romantic and otherwise. This is sure to irritate the lion, who does one thing at a time and does it well. Gemini might be a bit bored with Leo self-promotion, and might poke fun at this sign's notorious vanity. The resulting feline roar will be no laughing matter!

SIGN MATES:

Gemini President J.F.K. and Leo Jacqueline Kennedy

Gemini/Virgo

THE ATTRACTION:

You are both Mercury-ruled, and your deepest bond will be mental communication and appreciation of each other's intelligence. The Virgo Mercury is earthbound and analytical, while the Gemini Mercury is a jack-of-all trades. Gemini shows Virgo the big picture; Virgo takes care of the details. Your combined talents make a stimulating partnership. Virgo becomes the administrator here, Gemini the idea person.

THE ISSUES:

Your different priorities can be irritating to each other. Virgo needs a sense of order. Gemini needs to experiment and is forever the gadabout. An older Gemini who has slowed down somewhat makes the best partner here.

SIGN MATES:

Gemini Courteney Cox and Virgo David Arquette

Gemini/Libra

THE ATTRACTION:

Air signs Gemini and Libra have both mental and physical rapport. This is an outgoing combination, full of good talk. You'll never be bored. Libra's good looks and charm, as well as fine mind, could keep restless Gemini close to home.

THE ISSUES:

Both of you have a low tolerance for boredom and practical chores. The question of who will provide, do the dirty work, and clean up can be the subject of many a debate. There could be more talk than action here, leaving you turning elsewhere for substance.

SIGN MATES:

Tiger tamers Gemini Siegfried Fischbacher and Libra Roy Horn

Gemini/Scorpio

THE ATTRACTION:

You're a fascinating mystery to each other. Gemini is immune from Scorpio paranoia, laughs away dark moods, and matches wits in power games. Scorpio intensity, focus, and sexual magnetism draw Gemini like a moth to a flame. You're intrigued by Scorpio secrets. Here's a puzzle that would be fun to solve! And steamy Scorpio brings intensity and a new level of thrills to your sex life.

THE ISSUES:

Scorpio gets heavy, possessive, and jealous, which Gemini doesn't take seriously. To make this one last, Gemini needs to treat Scorpio like the one and only, while Scorpio must use a light touch, and learn not to take Gemini flirtations to heart.

SIGN MATES:

Gemini Prince Ranier and Scorpio Grace Kelly
Gemini Nicole Kidman and Scorpio Keith Urban

Gemini/Sagittarius

THE ATTRACTION:

These polar opposites shake each other up happily. Sagittarius helps Gemini see higher truths, to look beyond the life of the party and the art of the deal. Gemini adds mental challenge and flexibility to Sagittarius.

THE ISSUES:

Gemini pokes holes in Sagittarius theories. Sagittarius can brand Gemini as a superficial party animal. Work toward developing nonthreatening, nonjudgmental communication. However, you can't talk away practical financial realities. You need a carefully thought-out program to make things happen.

SIGN MATES:

Gemini Marilyn Monroe and Sagittarius Joe DiMaggio
Gemini Angelina Jolie and Sagittarius Brad Pitt

Gemini/Capricorn

THE ATTRACTION:

Capricorn benefits from the Gemini abstract point of view and lighthearted sense of fun. Gemini shows Capricorn how to enjoy the rewards of hard work. Support and structure are Capricorn gifts to Gemini. (Taking that literally, Capricorn Howard Hughes designed the famous bra that supported Gemini sexpot Jane Russell's physical assets!)

THE ISSUES:

Capricorn can be ultraconservative and tightfisted with money, which Gemini will not appreciate. The Gemini freespirited, fun-loving attitude could grate against the Capricorn driving ambition. Gemini will have to learn to take responsibility and to produce solid results.

SIGN MATES:

Gemini Kylie Minogue and Capricorn Olivier Martinez

Gemini/Aquarius

THE ATTRACTION:

In this open and spontaneous relationship, the pressure's off. You two air signs have room to breathe freely. At the same time, you can count on each other for friendship, understanding, and mental stimulation plus highly original romantic ideas. You'll keep each other entertained, and your love life will be fresh and stimulating.

THE ISSUES:

Be sure to leave time in your busy schedule for each other. If there is no commitment, you could both fly off. A sharing of causes, projects, or careers could hold you together.

SIGN MATES:

Gemini Lisa Hartman and Aquarius Clint Black

Gemini/Pisces

THE ATTRACTION:

You are both dual personalities in mutable, freedom-loving signs. You fascinate each other with ever-changing facets. You keep each other from straying by providing constant variety and new experiments to try together.

THE ISSUES:

At some point, you'll need a frame of reference for this relationship to hold together. Since neither likes structure, this could be a problem. Overstimulation is another monster that can rise to the surface. Pisces sensitive feelings and Gemini hyperactive nerves could send each other searching for more soothing, stabilizing alternatives.

SIGN MATES:

Gemini Donald Trump and Pisces Ivana Trump

CHAPTER 25

The Big Picture for Gemini in 2008

Welcome to 2008, Gemini! It's your year for laying foundations and building on them. Your communication skills are as strong as usual, and you get help from Saturn in Virgo, your fourth house. This planet helps to structure what you want to say and how you say it, and it aids you in finding the right venue. Your home life may be a bit more structured.

Saturn left Leo late last year. Even though it forms a challenging angle with your sun, you need the structure and the restrictions it brings. You may feel at times that you're burdened by your family, one of your parents, or your personal environments. You eventually get used to whatever Saturn brings, but to make this transit more positive, meet your obligations and responsibilities.

At the tail end of 2007, lucky and expansive Jupiter entered Capricorn; it will be there through the end of this year, in your eighth house. This transit indicates that it's a good year to get a mortgage or car loan and that your spouse or partner may get a substantial raise. You could find yourself signing up for workshops or seminars on esoteric topics. You may even be writing about these topics.

Pluto enters Capricorn on January 25, joining Jupiter in your eighth house. It then retrogrades for a while and goes back into Sagittarius from mid-June to late November. During the months it's in Capricorn, it works to transform your joint finances. This can be good or bad, depending on the present state of the finances you share with a partner. However, Jupiter always seeks to expand what it touches, and Pluto always transforms.

While Jupiter and Pluto are forming this angle with your sun, you are called upon to adjust your attitude about joint finances. In fact, the sooner you adjust, the happier you'll be.

Neptune continues it lengthy transit through Aquarius and your ninth house. If you're a writer or involved in the publishing industry, law, or higher education, this transit has been adding spiritual insights to your work. Your compassion has accelerated. But since Neptune represents our blind spots, the areas represented could cause you to feel disillusioned or victimized. The most positive way to handle this energy is to do things for others without expecting compensation and to deepen your spiritual practices.

Uranus continues its transit through Pisces and your tenth house. Uranus is the planet that symbolizes sudden, unexpected change, and your career and professional life have been going through a lot of abrupt changes in the last few years. But you get bored easily, anyway, so this isn't necessarily a bad thing. Use Uranus's energy to attract unusual and idiosyncratic people into your professional life.

Best Time for Romance

You'll enjoy the period between June 5 and July 18, when Venus is in your sign. Your love life picks up big time, your creativity gains momentum, and others see you much differently. Another great time for romance falls between August 30 and September 23, when Venus transits through Libra, your fifth house of love.

Best Time for Career Decision

With Uranus creating unpredictability in your career, timing is everything. With Jupiter forming a favorable angle to Uranus, mark the following dates for making career decisions: Between January 1 and May 9, and between September 7 and the end of the year. During these periods, Jupiter is moving direct, and its energy flows nicely with that of Uranus.

Mercury Retrograde

Every year, your ruler, Mercury, turns retrograde three times. During these periods, it's wisest not to negotiate or sign contracts, to travel, to submit manuscripts, or to make major decisions. Granted, we can't live our lives entirely by Mercury retrogrades! However, if you have to travel during the periods listed below, expect changes in your itinerary. If you have to sign a contract, expect to revisit it. Communications are bumpy. It's easy to be misunderstood. It's a good time to revise, review, and rewrite.

During these periods, back up computer files before Mercury turns retrograde. Quite often, computers and other communication devices act up. Be sure your virus software is up-to-date. Pay special attention to the house in which a Mercury retrograde falls. It will tell you the area of your life most likely to be impacted. The periods to watch for in 2008 are:

January 28–February 18: retrograde in Aquarius, your ninth house of long-distance travel.

May 26–June 19: retrograde in Gemini, your sun sign and first house of self.

September 24–October 15: retrograde in Libra, your fifth house of love and creativity.

Eclipses

Every year, there are four eclipses, two solar and two lunar. Solar eclipses trigger external events that allow us to see something that eluded us before. When an eclipse hits one of your natal planets, it's especially important. Take note of the sign and house placement. Lunar eclipses bring up emotional issues related to the sign and house into which they fall. If you have your birth chart, check to see if the eclipses hit any natal planets. If they do, pay special attention to events that occur for up to six months after the eclipse.

Here are the dates to watch for:

February 6: Solar eclipse at 17 degrees Aquarius, your ninth house of long-distance travel, higher education, and worldview. Those of you born between June 6 and 10 are likely to feel the most positive impact of this eclipse.

February 20: Lunar eclipse at 10 degrees Virgo, in your fourth house of home and family.

August 1: Solar eclipse, 9 degrees Leo, in your third house of siblings, community, and conscious thoughts. If you were born between May 28 and June 1, this eclipse will impact you strongly, in a positive way.

August 16: Lunar eclipse at 24 degrees Aquarius, your eleventh house of friends, wishes, and dreams.

Luckiest Days in 2008

Every year, Jupiter forms a beneficial angle with the sun, usually a conjunction, when both planets are in the same sign. In 2008, the angle is a lovely trine, and it occurs during two time periods: May 11–13 and September 3–5. If you're going to buy a Lotto ticket, do it during these periods!

Now let's take a look at what 2008 has in store for you day by day.

CHAPTER 26

Eighteen Months of Day-by-Day Predictions—July 2007 to December 2008

Moon sign times are calculated for Eastern Standard Time and Eastern Daylight Time. Please adjust for your local time zone.

JULY 2007

Sunday, July 1 (Moon in Capricorn) The summer is heating up. But with the moon in Capricorn, you're forced to be grounded and practical today. If you've been thinking of buying a home, don't apply for a mortgage until after Mercury turns direct on July 9.

Monday, July 2 (Moon in Capricorn to Aquarius 1:25 a.m.) Escape from your routine. Create an adventure. Get out of town. Pretend you're being pursued by government agents who want information that only you possess. Use your imagination, Gemini!

Tuesday, July 3 (Moon in Aquarius) Continuing with yesterday's journey, you're in a town you've never visited. You aren't sure which way to turn. But you find friends in unlikely places, and you are able to rest for the night.

Wednesday, July 4 (Moon in Aquarius to Pisces 6:53 a.m.) Happy Independence Day! Stop thinking about your career. It's not time for that, Gemini. Today is for family, friends, neighborhoods, celebrations. It's about understanding the Bill of Rights and what constitutes a democracy.

Thursday, July 5 (Moon in Pisces) If you have the day off, indulge yourself by doing something that appeals to your artistic or intuitive senses. It could be something as simple as visiting an art museum or as complex as taking a workshop on intuitive development.

Friday, July 6 (Moon in Pisces to Aries 10:57 a.m.) Good thing it's Friday! From midmorning forward, you'll be restless. Whether you hang with friends this evening or head to a class or a bookstore or seek out the company of a special romantic partner, the day will be enjoyable.

Saturday, July 7 (Moon in Aries) In two days, your ruler, Mercury, will turn direct. You may be feeling a slight difference in the air already, but don't pack your bags just yet. If the weather is good, go hiking or canoeing or rafting.

Sunday, July 8 (Moon in Aries to Taurus 1:54 p.m.) This afternoon, the moon joins Mars in Taurus in your solar twelfth house. This combination of planets may grate on you. Best to take the energy and head to the gym or pour it into some other form of physical activity.

Monday, July 9 (Moon in Taurus) Mercury turns direct. Checks you've expected start to arrive, and any financial hassles you've had straighten out. Put on your traveling shoes and get out of town!

Tuesday, July 10 (Moon in Taurus to Gemini 4:10 p.m.) By this afternoon, you're swinging from the trees! The moon is in your sign, and you certainly need the energy it brings. Gone is the angst of the past few weeks. You're rushing ahead on a half dozen projects; your main dilemma is deciding which is most important.

Wednesday, July 11 (Moon in Gemini) You and your partner steal away for an evening together. But your idea

225

of an evening together may not be a candlelight dinner; it's probably the newest art film or a bookstore with a great café. Be sure your partner has the same agenda.

Thursday, July 12 (Moon in Gemini to Cancer 6:40 p.m.)   As the moon joins Mercury in your solar second house, your intuitive certainty about an investment or financial opportunity may be at odds with what your left brain is telling you. Wait until the moon or Mercury moves out of Cancer before you decide.

Friday, July 13 (Moon in Cancer)   Putter around your house, fix what needs to be fixed, and generally tidy things up. You should enhance the prosperity area of your house through some feng shui techniques. If you work at home, determine which area of your office is your prosperity corner.

Saturday, July 14 (Moon in Cancer to Leo 10:44 p.m.)   Venus moves into Virgo and your solar fourth house. If you and your partner live together, this transit should spell smooth sailing. Your relationship with your family improves. You may feel compelled to beautify your home before this transit ends in November.

Sunday, July 15 (Moon in Leo)   Talk over that investment opportunity with a trusted friend or sibling, and make your decision. Still thinking about how much fun you had on the Fourth of July? Start planning for just as much pleasure over Labor Day weekend.

Monday, July 16 (Moon in Leo)   If you have an anniversary, be sure to do something special for and with your partner. Whether you've been together three months or thirty years, renew your commitment.

Tuesday, July 17 (Moon in Leo to Virgo 5:40 a.m.)   As the moon joins Venus in Virgo, you're in the mood for romance and nurturing. If you're not involved with anyone, this energy may manifest itself as good fortune in the arts or money. If you're going to buy a new appliance or some other expensive item, do it before Venus turns retrograde on July 27.

Wednesday, July 18 (Moon in Virgo) If you can, work out of your house. After all, if you performed feng shui magic on your home office, the energy is excellent. You may have to shut the door to your office so you can maintain your privacy.

Thursday, July 19 (Moon in Virgo to Libra 3:54 p.m.) It's a fine day for your creative projects. In fact, you won't be able to avoid being artistic. Your aesthetic senses are enhanced; you have the drive and will to follow your heart.

Friday, July 20 (Moon in Libra) You may find yourself in the midst of a dispute. If so, appoint yourself the mediator. You'll be able to argue both sides. Your intervention won't be immediately appreciated, but by tomorrow, hard feelings on both sides will be gone.

Saturday, July 21 (Moon in Libra) Balance is the toughest quality to find. You may need to ask for help, perhaps by assigning duties or tasks to the people around you, thus freeing your time for something else.

Sunday, July 22 (Moon in Libra to Scorpio 4:19 a.m.) Information is power. So you're empowered because you simply won't relinquish your search for something you or someone else needs. You dig, research, and investigate.

Monday, July 23 (Moon in Scorpio) Just think, Gemini. The intensity of your will and emotions can shatter obstacles. If there are things you don't like about your daily work environment, apply your powerful will to change them. Your point of power lies in the present.

Tuesday, July 24 (Moon in Scorpio to Sagittarius 4:31 p.m.) Sign contracts. You have the larger picture of the issues involved; the Sagittarius moon fills you with optimism. Even though this moon is opposed to your sun, it lights up your seventh house of partnerships.

Wednesday, July 25 (Moon in Sagittarius)   The deeper truth you're looking for is spiritual. As a Gemini, you're seeking ways to incorporate that spirituality into your ordinary life and to teach it without being dogmatic. Obviously, this can't be done in a day. Commit to a long-term quest.

Thursday, July 26 (Moon in Sagittarius)   Set your course. Be clear about where you want to go. Then connect the dots between the two points and make it happen. This requires commitment and pure intention on your part. Are you up to the challenge?

Friday, July 27 (Moon in Sagittarius to Capricorn 2:23 a.m.)   Venus turns retrograde in Virgo, your solar fourth house. This doesn't mean that your love life, home life, or family life is going to hit the skids. It doesn't mean your marriage will unravel. You may be revisiting your concepts and feelings about relationships, the arts, and even your attitude toward money. The retrograde period lasts until September 8.

Saturday, July 28 (Moon in Capricorn)   You could be spending time with an elderly person who needs help and emotional support. Don't resist the flow of events. Try to remain emotionally detached.

Sunday, July 29 (Moon in Capricorn to Aquarius 9:14 a.m.)   The Aquarius moon suits you much better than earth-sign moons. It's all about mind, groups, and the individual's place within the universe. How you apply Aquarius principles will determine how you live.

Monday, July 30 (Moon in Aquarius)   What can you do for people who are less fortunate or stray animals? Do something that helps someone else. Volunteer your time or make a charitable contribution.

Tuesday, July 31 (Moon in Aquarius to Pisces 1:41 p.m.) As the moon changes signs, your career comes into play. Or you may have to deal with some aspect of authority. Deal with the person directly. In the end, that will get you past the situation much faster.

AUGUST 2007

Wednesday, August 1 (Moon in Pisces) Whenever the moon joins Uranus in your solar tenth house, your emotional reactions are unusual. A colleague or boss annoys you with unfair criticism. Keep your opinion to yourself. It's not worth arguing about.

Thursday, August 2 (Moon in Pisces to Aries 4:43 p.m.) As the moon moves into your solar eleventh house, you have several invitations from friends. Any publicity or public speaking you do is well-received. Promote yourself or your product.

Friday, August 3 (Moon in Aries) With Venus still moving retrograde in your solar fourth house and the moon in your eleventh, you're restless for change. Don't make any renovations to your home. Wait until after Venus turns direct on September 8.

Saturday, August 4 (Moon in Aries to Taurus 7:16 p.m.) Mercury moves into Leo, stimulating all of your communications abilities. If you're a writer, this transit should light a fire under you. Things really pick up in about four days, when Mars moves into your sign.

Sunday, August 5 (Moon in Taurus) With the moon in your solar twelfth house, you need time for solitude and reflection. Security issues may surface. You could worry about money or insurance coverage. Try not to fret and obsess. It's just the Taurus moon reminding you to pay attention to what makes you feel emotionally secure.

Monday, August 6 (Moon in Taurus to Gemini 10:02 p.m.) Jupiter turns direct in Sagittarius and your solar ninth house. This movement should feel very good for you. Opportunities in publishing, education, and overseas travel surface until the end of the year.

Tuesday, August 7 (Moon in Gemini) Mars moves into your sign, a booster rocket that impacts every area of your life. Your energy and sexuality are at a high. You feel as if you can do anything; you won't shy away from anything that comes your way. Be careful not to overcommit. Otherwise you'll find yourself in a time crunch.

Wednesday, August 8 (Moon in Gemini) With the moon and Mars in your sign, you have a powerful combination at your fingertips. Mars may make you impatient. If you're in a hurry, you could be more accident-prone. Slow down!

Thursday, August 9 (Moon in Gemini to Cancer 1:37 a.m.) The moon moves into your solar second house. This lunar transit compels you to bring your ideas down to earth, to be more practical and efficient. Anything you take on will be done with those attributes in mind.

Friday, August 10 (Moon in Cancer) If there are minor issues surfacing at home, deal with them directly and immediately. You may have to slow down on your spending until checks arrive.

Saturday, August 11 (Moon in Cancer to Leo 6:42 a.m.) The Leo moon may accelerate things, just as Mars in your sign does. Slow down; pace yourself. There's plenty of time to get things done.

Sunday, August 12 (Moon in Leo) You have plenty of star power. Finish your novel or screenplay, complete any communications projects. Your partnerships are humming right along now that Jupiter is moving direct in your solar seventh house.

Monday, August 13 (Moon in Leo to Virgo 2:04 p.m.)   Finish up projects and get emotional issues straightened out before September 2, when Saturn moves into Virgo and your fourth house. For the next two and a half years, Saturn will impose structures through which you and your family must live.

Tuesday, August 14 (Moon in Virgo)   Since Mars will be in your sign until September 28, make a list of everything you would like to accomplish by that date. This can include anything from practicalities to the esoteric, from home improvement to self-improvement.

Wednesday, August 15 (Moon in Virgo)   When the moon moves into Libra early tomorrow, you'll feel the shift. Stay up a little later, and figure out how you can clear your schedule so that you can devote tomorrow and the next day to *your* creativity.

Thursday, August 16 (Moon in Virgo to Libra 12:05 a.m.)   If you did clear your schedule, where will you start with your creativity? The question won't puzzle you for very long. Like many Geminis, you probably have a number of writing projects you've started and stuck away somewhere. Dust them off and set to work.

Friday, August 17 (Moon in Libra)   Your kids take up part of your day, but you love every second of it. After all, time is marching inexorably forward, and they won't be at home forever. Enjoy them while you can.

Saturday, August 18 (Moon in Libra to Scorpio 12:14 p.m.)   Detach from emotional issues as much as possible. It's all too easy to be led into an argument about some hot topic, and then find yourself boxed in, with no way out. This is particularly true if the topic involves religion or politics.

Sunday, August 19 (Moon in Scorpio)   Mercury moves into Virgo and your fourth house. This transit should stimulate activity on the home front. Out-of-town visitors are possible before September 5; there are more e-mails than usual in your in-box.

Monday, August 20 (Moon in Scorpio)   Your spiritual beliefs or worldview comes into play. You may try to incorporate one or both of these areas into your ordinary life. An Aries or a Leo has advice you should listen to.

Tuesday, August 21 (Moon in Scorpio to Sagittarius 12:45 a.m.)   You really do enjoy this moon. It's especially fine because it shares space with direct-moving Jupiter. Your opportunities in education, publishing, and overseas travel are expanding. You may also be called for jury duty!

Wednesday, August 22 (Moon in Sagittarius)   How far can you run with an idea? Discover just how passionate you feel about an idea or project and how determined you are to make this idea or project a reality.

Thursday, August 23 (Moon in Sagittarius to Capricorn 11:20 a.m.)   As the moon moves into Capricorn, you suddenly feel fatigued. The Capricorn moon is dampening your spirits and great mood. But this moon also compels you to become more grounded and aware of your surroundings.

Friday, August 24 (Moon in Capricorn)   If you pay quarterly taxes, get your tax forms in order. You may sign up for a course in something as mundane as estate law or as mysterious as past lives.

Saturday, August 25 (Moon in Capricorn to Aquarius 6:35 p.m.)   When the moon joins Neptune in your ninth house, you can expect some vagueness and confusion about what you feel and experience. Higher inspiration and spirituality ride along with this combination.

Sunday, August 26 (Moon in Aquarius)   You feel exhilarated by the promise of newness in the air. Friends figure into the activities, specifically those whose goals are like yours. Your political involvement may increase this fall.

Monday, August 27 (Moon in Aquarius to Pisces 10:35 p.m.)   Try to chill out; don't run yourself ragged. A colleague may turn to you for advice or emotional support. Be as gentle with this person as possible. Listen.

Tuesday, August 28 (Moon in Pisces)   The insight you have from dreams and meditation concerns a professional issue or someone involved in your professional life. Take the insight into account, weigh the issues, and make your decision when the moon moves into Aries.

Wednesday, August 29 (Moon in Pisces)   Be prepared for the moon's transit into Aries. Make lists, contact people by e-mail, and check your schedule for the next few days. Any public speaking you do in the next two days is well-received.

Thursday, August 30 (Moon in Pisces to Aries 12:25 a.m.)   A visit to a psychic may be in order. This person will be able to provide you with information or insight you need concerning a friendship or perhaps one of your goals. List your questions before you go. If the psychic is really good, you won't even have to ask the questions.

Friday, August 31 (Moon in Aries)   It's the end of another month, and your energy might be low. Kick back and relax this weekend if you don't have plans. Fall is coming, so enjoy the good weather while you can.

SEPTEMBER 2007

Saturday, September 1 (Moon in Aries to Taurus 1:36 a.m.) Tomorrow, Saturn moves into Virgo and remains there for about two and a half years. You can prepare for this by listing the goals you have for your home and family.

Sunday, September 2 (Moon in Taurus)   Saturn moves into Virgo and your solar fourth house. This transit may delay any moves you had hoped to make, but brings the proper structure into your life. With Venus still moving retrograde in your fourth house, you may encounter physical discomforts that relate to the environment.

Monday, September 3 (Moon in Taurus to Gemini 3:31 a.m.)   Early this morning, the moon moves into your sign, signaling a high time of the month. Look to friends to help you achieve your goals. Don't hesitate to delegate.

Tuesday, September 4 (Moon in Gemini)   You do your share of catching up with friends you haven't seen for a while. A Libra or an Aquarius brings you information you've been searching for. If you can squeeze in time to read, get to that book you haven't yet started.

Wednesday, September 5 (Moon in Gemini to Cancer 7:09 a.m.)   Mercury moves into Libra; this transit feels very good! It stimulates activity in your love life and with your creativity. In fact, get busy with your book.

Thursday, September 6 (Moon in Cancer)   Feeling somewhat security conscious, Gemini? Blame the Cancer moon. This moon also enhances your intuition and your nurturing instincts.

Friday, September 7 (Moon in Cancer to Leo 1:00 p.m.)   Pluto turns direct in your seventh house. This movement benefits both personal and professional partnerships. Whether partnerships begin or end, the transformation is profound and, in the long run, works to your benefit.

Saturday, September 8 (Moon in Leo)   Venus turns direct, so whatever bumps you've been experiencing at home will iron out. Friends gather at your place this evening, perhaps for a cookout. You end up on center stage as a storyteller.

Sunday, September 9 (Moon in Leo to Virgo 9:11 p.m.)   In two days, there's a solar eclipse in Virgo and your solar fourth house. Take steps to maximize this eclipse's energy. You'll be glad you did.

Monday, September 10 (Moon in Virgo)   Make your lists, prioritize, and tackle one item at a time. Be a perfectionist. As long as you don't criticize others for not living up to your ideal of perfection, you can achieve a great deal.

Tuesday, September 11 (Moon in Virgo)   You might feel like getting off by yourself for some meditation. You'll be glad you did. Spend the rest of the day with loved ones.

Wednesday, September 12 (Moon in Virgo to Libra 7:32 a.m.)   You're looking for balance in your creative work and your personal life. How you achieve the balance depends on how you allot your time. Get to work!

Thursday, September 13 (Moon in Libra)   You're on a creative roll! With both the moon and Mercury in your solar fifth house, you express yourself well regardless of what creative venue you're pursuing.

Friday, September 14 (Moon in Libra to Scorpio 7:37 p.m.)   An emotional issue related to employees surfaces. Postpone any decision until Monday, when the moon is in Sagittarius. Then you'll be able to see the larger picture.

Saturday, September 15 (Moon in Scorpio)   Head to the gym or to an aerobics class. Do something to strengthen and tone your body and start to do it regularly. The issues that the solar eclipse raised are evident in your home life. Deal with them.

Sunday, September 16 (Moon in Scorpio)   Chill, Gemini. In the long run, keeping to yourself and completing work from home will benefit you. Take at least an hour to follow your regular exercise routine.

Monday, September 17 (Moon in Scorpio to Sagittarius 8:21 a.m.)   Make your decision about last week's trouble at work. You and your partner reach an agreement. You may sign up for a workshop or seminar on some aspect of the legal system.

Tuesday, September 18 (Moon in Sagittarius)   If you're in contract negotiations, you may sign on the dotted lines. Discuss things first with your partner or significant other.

Wednesday, September 19 (Moon in Sagittarius to Capricorn 7:52 p.m.)   The convergence of energies focuses on your finances—not just what you earn and spend, but on the financial resources you share with others. A spouse or business partner has financial advice you should listen to.

Thursday, September 20 (Moon in Capricorn)   Gather your information, and then lay down your strategy or plan. Be detailed, but not so detailed that there's no room for change. You're a mutable sign, which means that flexibility and adaptability are your greatest survival tools.

Friday, September 21 (Moon in Capricorn)   You may feel somewhat down in the dumps. Try to roll with the mood, Gemini, and know that by tomorrow, when the moon moves into a more compatible sign, your disposition will be much improved.

Saturday, September 22 (Moon in Capricorn to Aquarius 4:18 a.m.)   The moon joins Neptune in Aquarius in your solar ninth house. This combination of planets softens your mood and adds a spiritual flavor to whatever you do. You're aware of synchronicities and the hidden order of things.

Sunday, September 23 (Moon in Aquarius)   Friends figure prominently in events. This could spell involvement in a political group, a film group, or even an educational group. Whatever your involvement, you bring your knowledge and expertise to the group.

Monday, September 24 (Moon in Aquarius to Pisces 8:56 a.m.)   It's a career day that presents some intriguing challenges. Your best bet is to deal with each challenge as it surfaces and then to move on. Use your imagination to find creative solutions to problems.

Tuesday, September 25 (Moon in Pisces) Your imagination and intuition work in tandem, leading you toward a new way to do your job. If you've been bored with your career, spice it up.

Wednesday, September 26 (Moon in Pisces to Aries 10:23 a.m.) Mars won't be in your sign for much longer. Make the most of the planet's energy to complete long-standing projects or to tackle things on which you have procrastinated.

Thursday, September 27 (Moon in Aries) Mercury moves into Scorpio and your solar sixth house. This transit deepens your intuition and your investigative and research abilities. You come across with a certain intensity that makes whatever you say or write convincing.

Friday, September 28 (Moon in Aries to Taurus 10:18 a.m.) Mars moves into Cancer and your second house. Fasten your seat belt. Until the end of the year, a lot of your energy goes into earning money; you may even take a second job. And new financial opportunities may come your way.

Saturday, September 29 (Moon in Taurus) Your second job or your new job could be something you do from your home. You benefit from solitude and reflection.

Sunday, September 30 (Moon in Taurus to Gemini 10:35 a.m.) Lucky you! The month ends with the moon in your sign, and you're in a social mood. You reconnect with friends through e-mail; you may accept an invitation for dinner or drinks.

OCTOBER 2007

Monday, October 1 (Moon in Gemini) Your sex appeal, self-confidence, and general mood are great. Launch any work projects now. By the time Mercury turns retrograde on October 11, you'll be in the right frame of mind to revise and rewrite.

Tuesday, October 2 (Moon in Gemini to Cancer 12:58 p.m.)   As the moon moves into your solar second house, it's money issues again! This time, the news should be in your favor. You also take a deep inner look at whether you actually walk your talk.

Wednesday, October 3 (Moon in Cancer)   A family discussion highlights your deepest values. Have you been as compassionate as possible? Have you done at least one nice thing for someone else?

Thursday, October 4 (Moon in Cancer to Leo 6:28 p.m.)   Divination tools are on your mind. You have some burning question that needs an answer or, at the very least, additional insight. Try the tarot or even astrology! There are also oracles on the Web.

Friday, October 5 (Moon in Leo)   You usually love the Leo moon. It gives you an opportunity to shine. If you feel a bit down, look within for the answer. It may date back to when the moon was in Scorpio or Pisces.

Saturday, October 6 (Moon in Leo)   Get moving on your manuscript, Gemini. The lunar energies favor writing and communications. Keep a notebook handy to jot down ideas. You could get additional input from relatives.

Sunday, October 7 (Moon in Leo to Virgo 3:04 a.m.) With Saturn in Virgo, the Virgo moon adds pressure on you to tend to details. You become finicky about your home and family. Resist the temptation to become obsessive!

Monday, October 8 (Moon in Virgo)   Along comes Venus in Virgo to place pressure on you to be a perfectionist. This transit certainly favors romance and smooth sailing at home. You may be fastidious about how your home looks or how you organize your home office.

Tuesday, October 9 (Moon in Virgo to Libra 1:58 p.m.)   If you awaken frustrated and small things immediately start going wrong, you probably feel the effects of the Mercury retrograde a bit early. It happens sometimes. But when it happens to you, it could mean that the retrograde period will be filled with challenges.

Wednesday, October 10 (Moon in Libra)   Your artistic sensibilities may accelerate to the point where you keep working until you're finished. Starting tomorrow, when Mercury turns retrograde, revise what you've worked on.

Thursday, October 11 (Moon in Libra)   Mercury turns retrograde in Scorpio and your solar sixth house. This movement impacts your daily work routine and health. One of the most constructive ways to use the energy is to continue your regular exercise routine.

Friday, October 12 (Moon in Libra to Scorpio 2:14 a.m.)   With Mars and the moon forming harmonious angles to each other, your intuition and imagination zip along. You're able to bypass your left brain and dive straight into the heart of whatever you need.

Saturday, October 13 (Moon in Scorpio)   Stay on track. Don't allow coworkers or anyone else at work to distract you from what's important. You know the score.

Sunday, October 14 (Moon in Scorpio to Sagittarius 2:58 p.m.)   With the moon in optimistic Sagittarius, conjuncting expansive Jupiter, you're in fine shape. Even though this moon is opposed to your sun, the fire element is compatible with your sun's element. Enjoy yourself!

Monday, October 15 (Moon in Sagittarius)   You and your partner grasp the big picture of your relationship. The understanding may not come all at once, but you each have a clearer understanding of your individual needs.

Tuesday, October 16 (Moon in Sagittarius)   Don't sign the contract just yet. Don't negotiate either if you can help it. Wait until Mercury turns direct on November 1. If you must sign, do so with the understanding that you will have to revisit the contract at some point.

Wednesday, October 17 (Moon in Sagittarius to Capricorn 3:04 a.m.)   Venus and Saturn in Virgo and Mars in Cancer form harmonious angles to this transiting moon, but not to your sun sign. The combination favors a more grounded and realistic approach to the financial obligations that you and your partner share. Maybe it's time to set aside money for a child's college education.

Thursday, October 18 (Moon in Capricorn)   You help out an elderly relative or someone else who needs financial or emotional support. You have a need to balance the various parts of your life; the Capricorn moon may help you to do exactly that.

Friday, October 19 (Moon in Capricorn to Aquarius 12:52 p.m.)   You chafe at the restrictions that Saturn in your solar fourth house is imposing on you. The Aquarius moon provides the opportunity to break free of the status quo for a few days. Let the cosmos shake up your world. Embrace chaos.

Saturday, October 20 (Moon in Aquarius)   If a special Libra in your life celebrates a birthday, go all out to make the occasion memorable for that person. Life, after all, isn't just about you.

Sunday, October 21 (Moon in Aquarius to Pisces 7:03 p.m.)   Once again, the moon joins Uranus in Pisces in your solar tenth house. These transits may not be especially comfortable for you, but they definitely get your imagination moving in the right direction. Use your imagination to approach your career in a new way.

Monday, October 22 (Moon in Pisces)   You're deep in Mercury-retrograde country. If you have to travel, be sure to check your schedule because things may change without warning. Also, check on e-mails and letters you have sent to be sure the other person has received them.

Tuesday, October 23 (Moon in Pisces to Aries 9:25 p.m.)   Finally, a lunar transit that energizes you. This is a wonderful time for publicity and promotion. You have your finger on the public pulse, and it comes through in your public speaking. Get together with friends and celebrate autumn!

Wednesday, October 24 (Moon in Aries)   Celebration, daring, risk, courage—all these attributes come into play, but in an inner, emotional sense. You fully grasp the concept that you write the script of your life from the inside out. Be careful what you wish for. You might just get it!

Thursday, October 25 (Moon in Aries to Taurus 9:08 p.m.)   This lunar transit provides the perfect excuse to take a long weekend, kick back, and relax. You've earned the time off. Never forget to nurture yourself.

Friday, October 26 (Moon in Taurus)   You participate in an outdoor activity that takes you deep into the heart of nature. Finally, you can hear yourself think and let your feelings flow through you.

Saturday, October 27 (Moon in Taurus to Gemini 8:12 p.m.)   You're free to do pretty much whatever you want. You won't have a list; you'll be spontaneous and go wherever your spirit leads you. Synchronicities may signal the path to follow!

Sunday, October 28 (Moon in Gemini)   Your head and heart are in complete agreement over a personal issue. You're firm about the course you would like to follow, yet you're not so firm that you lose your flexibility.

Monday, October 29 (Moon in Gemini to Cancer 8:50 p.m.)   As the moon moves into nurturing Cancer and your solar second house, you feel the need to protect your

241

assets in some way. It could be as simple as taking out more insurance coverage on your home.

Tuesday, October 30 (Moon in Cancer)   Your mom or another nurturing female relates a dream or intuitive hunch; you are compelled to listen because the message is for you. Whether you heed it or not is entirely up to you. Free will is always the bottom line.

Wednesday, October 31 (Moon in Cancer)   Happy Halloween! Even though the moon doesn't move into flamboyant Leo until after midnight, dress and go trick or treating with your kids. If you don't have children, don a costume in which you can greet trick or treaters.

NOVEMBER 2007

Thursday, November 1 (Moon in Cancer to Leo 12:48 a.m.) Mercury turns direct. Travel, sign contracts, and communicate to your heart's content. The Leo moon galvanizes you to connect with neighbors and relatives.

Friday, November 2 (Moon in Leo)   Time to dust off that manuscript or screenplay. The lunar energy favors writers and writing. Your creativity puts you on center stage.

Saturday, November 3 (Moon in Leo to Virgo 8:45 a.m.) With the moon joining both Saturn and Venus in your solar fourth house, the heat is on to get your home in order. This could entail any number of things from a simple cleaning of your house to improvements and new furniture. But first and foremost, it concerns your family.

Sunday, November 4—Daylight Saving Time Ends (Moon in Virgo)   You and your loved ones stick close to home. You may invite neighbors and relatives over, your kids may have friends over, and generally, the atmosphere is festive. Think of this as a precursor to the Thanksgiving holidays.

Monday, November 5 (Moon in Virgo to Libra 6:47 p.m.) This evening, you steal away for a while to dive into your creative projects. Your challenge will be to focus on one thing and pour your energies into that. Friends may help you define the project.

Tuesday, November 6 (Moon in Libra) In two days, Venus moves into Libra. Get ready for this one by putting your creative priorities in order. The Venus transit, which will last until early December, will bring in new creative opportunities.

Wednesday, November 7 (Moon in Libra) Uranus turns direct in your solar tenth house on November 24. Prepare by applying your creative drive to your career so that when Uranus changes directions, you begin to see results.

Thursday, November 8 (Moon in Libra to Scorpio 7:19 a.m.) Venus moves into Libra and remains there until December 5. This period should be incredibly romantic for you, as long as you aren't looking for commitment in a new relationship. It's also a deeply creative time for you.

Friday, November 9 (Moon in Scorpio) The moon forms a harmonious angle with Mars in Cancer in your second house. This combination could help you grasp the bottom line on an investment opportunity or on some issue at work. Your energy is fluid and intuitive. Use it to your advantage.

Saturday, November 10 (Moon in Scorpio to Sagittarius 7:59 p.m.) The moon joins Jupiter in your solar seventh house. This combination should create an intriguing day with your personal or professional partner. You're able to see the larger scope of your relationship and to make decisions accordingly.

Sunday, November 11 (Moon in Sagittarius) You and a partner attend a seminar or workshop. In some way, you'll gain insights about yourselves and your relationship that may not even be related to the topic. Use these insights to improve your communications with each other.

Monday, November 12 (Moon in Sagittarius) With Mercury moving direct, you should proceed with contract negotiations. With Venus in Libra, the sign of justice and balance, don't hesitate to request everything that you want in the contract. Be fair to yourself!

Tuesday, November 13 (Moon in Sagittarius to Capricorn 8:01 a.m.) Mars and the moon form a harmonious angle to each other, but not to your sun sign. Still, you can use this energy to focus on areas of your life that need attention. Some of these areas might be finances, shared resources, insurance and taxes, and your fundamental values.

Wednesday, November 14 (Moon in Capricorn) Your thoughts turn toward cosmic questions. What happens when we die? Is the soul reborn? What is karma? Try to recall your dreams tonight. Answers may come to you through them.

Thursday, November 15 (Moon in Capricorn to Aquarius 6:31 p.m.) Mars turns retrograde in Cancer and remains that way through the end of the year. This transit could delay any checks that you're expecting to arrive through the mail. Your physical energy may not be quite as robust as it usually is. Keep up your regular exercise routine.

Friday, November 16 (Moon in Aquarius) You and a group of friends could be planning an overseas trip. You may not be traveling for sheer pleasure. There's a deep meaning to the journey. It may be to study some aspect of a foreign culture or country.

Saturday, November 17 (Moon in Aquarius) On November 24, Uranus turns direct in Pisces and your solar tenth house. This is good news for your career. You can expect events to move forward smoothly. You can prepare for this movement by listing your priorities for November 24 or November 26.

Sunday, November 18 (Moon in Aquarius to Pisces 2:15 a.m.)   The moon moves into your solar tenth house, stimulating professional matters. You may feel somewhat vulnerable today with a colleague or a boss. Go with the flow of events; try not to get upset about things over which you have no control. Use your imagination and intuition to navigate events successfully.

Monday, November 19 (Moon in Pisces)   Be careful about an emotional display in public. It will come about suddenly, if it happens at all, and will catch you off guard. You may provide support and compassion for a colleague who is going through a rough time.

Tuesday, November 20 (Moon in Pisces to Aries 6:25 a.m.)   Here's that wonderful Aries moon you enjoy so much. Your friends are important to you. You may spend time connecting with them through e-mail, by phone, or in person.

Wednesday, November 21 (Moon in Aries)   Party time! The festivities are spontaneous, but enjoyable. You and someone you considered a friend may discover that you have more in common than you thought. Is this the beginning of a romance?

Thursday, November 22 (Moon in Aries to Taurus 7:19 a.m.)   Happy Thanksgiving! The company you keep will be more important than the location or even what you eat! Take a look at the faces around you. What kind of people are they? What do they reflect about you?

Friday, November 23 (Moon in Taurus)   Can you keep a secret? Well, you will. And it may not even be your secret, but one that someone else has entrusted to you. Follow your instincts; listen to your intuition.

Saturday, November 24 (Moon in Taurus to Gemini 6:29 a.m.)   Uranus turns direct in your solar tenth house and the moon moves into your sign! Events could be exciting in a strange way. You attract unusual, idiosyncratic people.

Sunday, November 25 (Moon in Gemini)   A positive and uplifting day overall. You're in the groove, and you're able to do just about everything quickly. Be careful that you don't move so fast that the day passes in a blur. Pause to enjoy the smaller things in life.

Monday, November 26 (Moon in Gemini to Cancer 6:07 a.m.)   Compared to yesterday, nothing seems to move quickly. It's as if you woke in a slow-motion dream. Don't resist. Move with it and see where this strange state takes you.

Tuesday, November 27 (Moon in Cancer)   You should have a pretty good idea how you experience this lunar transit. You're more sensitive than usual and maybe more concerned about emotional security issues. You could be nostalgic for some part of your past. One good way to use this energy is to create a collage from old photos.

Wednesday, November 28 (Moon in Cancer to Leo 8:23 a.m.)   Finally, another fire-sign moon! The Leo moon makes you flamboyant in some way. Perhaps you wear flashier clothes. Maybe you talk to strangers. Or it could be that you act like a political candidate on the campaign trail.

Thursday, November 29 (Moon in Leo)   You help out around your neighborhood or in your community. Stray animals could be included in what you're doing. Does this volunteer effort come from the heart?

Friday, November 30 (Moon in Leo to Virgo 2:45 p.m.)   The moon joins Saturn in Virgo and your solar fourth house. You may feel somewhat oppressed, particularly about a family issue. Bear with it; pretty soon, this feeling will pass.

DECEMBER 2007

Saturday, December 1 (Moon in Virgo)   Mercury moves into Sagittarius. This transit lasts until December 20 and should be a good one for communications with both personal and professional partners. However, the energy under this transit can be volatile at times, with each person eager to say what has to be said.

Sunday, December 2 (Moon in Virgo)   Things may feel surreal, with your mood lifting, then plunging. But you and a family member talk honestly about a particular issue. That's something to cheer about!

Monday, December 3 (Moon in Virgo to Libra 1:02 a.m.)   It's hard to miss the festive feel to the air. It's either the proximity of the holidays or a special look from someone you would like to get to know. You're in the sort of mood where you may even decide to write poetry this evening. Keep a journal of your musings for the next few days.

Tuesday, December 4 (Moon in Libra)   You find this journal business compelling and decide to keep making entries for the next six months. It's a good way to get in touch with your feelings, your deepest beliefs, your creative aspirations, and what you're looking for in a mate.

Wednesday, December 5 (Moon in Libra to Scorpio 1:32 p.m.)   Both the moon and Venus move into Scorpio. This double whammy is excellent for romance at work. But this romance, if it happens, will be intense. Until December 30, when Venus changes signs again, things at work should go smoothly for you. You receive help from women.

Thursday, December 6 (Moon in Scorpio)   Your emotions rush like a swollen river. You may be secretive about what you do (or whom you see); if you want to strike back at someone, don't. Wait until the moon has moved into Sagittarius.

Friday, December 7 (Moon in Scorpio)   You're on the prowl for information. You may research something—or someone—and pull out all the stops. Take notes on what you uncover. You're the consummate detective.

Saturday, December 8 (Moon in Scorpio to Sagittarius 2:12 a.m.)   Do you still feel like striking back or getting even with anyone involved in Thursday's events? If so, evaluate what your reaction might mean for your relationship with this person. Is it still worth having your say?

Sunday, December 9 (Moon in Sagittarius)   Your spiritual values come into play. You may try to integrate these values into your most intimate relationships. But you can't force this sort of integration. It has to happen on its own.

Monday, December 10 (Moon in Sagittarius to Capricorn 1:51 p.m.)   With Mars moving retrograde in Cancer and the moon in Capricorn, your day could be a bit weird. But you don't mind weird as long as it keeps life interesting. A few things to watch out for: financial advice from people whose personal finances are a mess and errors on your bank statement.

Tuesday, December 11 (Moon in Capricorn)   If you have your natal moon or ascendant in Capricorn, this may be a good day. You'll be emotionally strong and resilient; others won't mess with you. But if you don't have any natal planets in Capricorn, act like you know what you're doing so that no one questions your authority.

Wednesday, December 12 (Moon in Capricorn)   You know you don't have all the answers. You know you don't even have half the answers. But you have something else: adaptability and the ability to win over just about anyone who opposes you.

Thursday, December 13 (Moon in Capricorn to Aquarius 12:02 a.m.)   A friendly moon for you, Gemini. This moon usually gives you the opportunity to explore worlds beyond your own. Whether you travel to these worlds mentally or physically, the journey always expands your belief system.

Friday, December 14 (Moon in Aquarius) Take heed. On December 18, Jupiter moves into Capricorn for a transit that takes about a year. If you have natal planets in Capricorn or the other earth signs, this should be a very good time for you! Certain areas of your life will expand; new opportunities will pour in.

Saturday, December 15 (Moon in Aquarius to Pisces 8:15 a.m.) You and a colleague or friends are holiday shopping. Make a day of it and finish up if at all possible. One of your parents needs help getting out to shop. If you brought work home with you, put it off until tomorrow.

Sunday, December 16 (Moon in Pisces) You, like just about everyone else in your office, are in a festive mood. If you're quick and alert, you can take advantage of this goodwill by promoting a project that is near and dear to your heart. You may encounter some opposition, but you're able to overcome it.

Monday, December 17 (Moon in Pisces to Aries 1:53 p.m.) With the moon moving into fiery Aries, you could be somewhat edgy and temperamental. But overall, this lunar energy fits your lightning-quick mind. You're galvanized to rethink some of your goals and dreams.

Tuesday, December 18 (Moon in Aries) Jupiter moves into Capricorn. It spends about a year transiting this sign and expanding your interest in metaphysics. You also will have other people's resources at your disposal. A partner or spouse may get a substantial raise.

Wednesday, December 19 (Moon in Aries to Taurus 4:38 p.m.) Saturn turns retrograde in Virgo and your fourth house. This is hardly welcome news for the holidays. Try to use this energy to review and reevaluate your goals and dreams for yourself and your family.

Thursday, December 20 (Moon in Taurus)   Mercury joins Jupiter in Capricorn, pressuring you to become much more practical in terms of mortgages, loans, insurance, and taxes. Your conscious mind has a harder, more pragmatic edge.

Friday, December 21 (Moon in Taurus to Gemini 5:14 p.m.)   This lunar transit comes just in time for the holidays, buoying your spirits and mitigating some of the Capricorn influence you're experiencing. You head out to the mall or some great specialty shop to do some last-minute shopping.

Saturday, December 22 (Moon in Gemini)   If you have a moon rising or other planets in Capricorn, you may be reaping unexpected benefits from the Jupiter transit. If you don't have your natal chart, get yours online through one of the Web sites that offers free natal charts.

Sunday, December 23 (Moon in Gemini to Cancer 5:19 p.m.)   It's somehow appropriate that the moon moves into Cancer just as Christmas approaches. Home, hearth, and family are all accentuated. Nostalgia may be thick in the air as family and friends recall bygone days.

Monday, December 24 (Moon in Cancer)   Release old grudges, heartaches, and bitterness. Mend damaged relationships with relatives and friends. Then you'll be in great shape for the approaching new year.

Tuesday, December 25 (Moon in Cancer to Leo 6:53 p.m.)   Merry Christmas! Regardless of how you celebrate, you shine among your loved ones. Your generous spirit may put a dent in your pocketbook when the credit card bills come due, but it's only money.

Wednesday, December 26 (Moon in Leo)   The day after a major holiday is often a blue-funk day. But with a Leo moon in your court, your mood is optimistic and upbeat and infects everyone with whom you come into contact. It's hard to keep a Gemini down for too long!

Thursday, December 27 (Moon in Leo to Virgo 11:45 p.m.) By the time the moon moves into Virgo, try to be asleep. You'll save yourself worry and angst! If you're awake, make lists about new year's goals.

Friday, December 28 (Moon in Virgo) Fret to your heart's content. When you get tired of fretting, put this lunar energy to good use by exercising, perfecting, cleaning, and practicing feng shui on your home. In other words, get things in order.

Saturday, December 29 (Moon in Virgo) Get with the agenda. It's an organization day. Regardless of whether you have guests over to your place or you're going elsewhere to celebrate, have your priorities set. Line up a babysitter, a caterer, parking—whatever you need.

Sunday, December 30 (Moon in Virgo to Libra 8:38 a.m.) Venus moves into Sagittarius and your solar seventh house. Even though Venus is opposed to your sun, the most serious consequence is a tendency toward overindulgence. If you're in love, you and your partner go overboard. If you're looking for romance, you perhaps look too hard. Generally this transit favors a pleasant time with your partner.

Monday, December 31 (Moon in Libra) With Venus in Sagittarius and the moon in Libra, the entire day is made to order for your need for variety and versatility. There's an emphasis on romance, hope, and your creativity.

HAPPY NEW YEAR!

JANUARY 2008

Tuesday, January 1 (Moon in Libra to Scorpio 8:33 p.m.) It's a number 6 day. It's a new year and a new start. Dance to your own tune. A domestic change works out for the best. Be diplomatic, resourceful, and helpful, but avoid scattering your energies.

Wednesday, January 2 *(Moon in Scorpio)*   The moon is in your sixth house, Gemini. Like yesterday, the energy is oriented to helping others make adjustments. However, keep your resolutions about exercise and diet.

Thursday, January 3 *(Moon in Scorpio)*   Control issues could surface. Be aware of things happening in secret. Use your intuition; watch out for deception. But avoid going to extremes; forgive and forget. You'll do just fine in spite of everything.

Friday, January 4 *(Moon in Scorpio to Sagittarius 9:14 a.m.)*   It's a number 9 day. Let go of your preconceived notions about your life. Visualize for the future. Set your goals, and then get to work. Clear your desk as you prepare for a new challenge.

Saturday, January 5 *(Moon in Sagittarius)*   The moon is in your seventh house. It's a good day for partnerships and relations with your spouse. It could also involve matters related to an unknown person, a contract, or a lawsuit.

Sunday, January 6 *(Moon in Sagittarius to Capricorn 8:43 p.m.)*   It's a number 2 day. The energy related to partnerships that began yesterday continues to flow. Be cooperative and supportive, especially in dealing with your spouse or business partner. Family members play a major role.

Monday, January 7 *(Moon in Capricorn)*   Mercury moves into your ninth house. There's a lot of activity and talk related to higher education, long-distance travel, or matters of philosophy and worldviews. You're interested in ideas, and a foreign person or destination could play a role.

Tuesday, January 8 *(Moon in Capricorn)*   The moon is in your eighth house. You could deal with taxes, insurance, or investments. Your experiences are likely to be more intense than usual and could relate to belongings and things you possess or share with another person, such as your spouse.

Wednesday, January 9 (Moon in Capricorn to Aquarius 6:13 a.m.)   It's a number 5 day. It's all about freedom of thought and action. Consider a change of scenery, or a change in your perspective. Taking a risk could pay off in a big way.

Thursday, January 10 (Moon in Aquarius)   The moon moves into your ninth house. Like yesterday, you feel restless and want a change. Sign up for a workshop or seminar, or plan a long trip to a foreign country. Take time to research your destination.

Friday, January 11 (Moon in Aquarius to Pisces 1:44 p.m.)   It's a number 7 day. There's an air of mystery. You could be embarking on a journey into the unknown. Look beneath the surface of whatever holds your attention. See things as they are and not how you wish them to be.

Saturday, January 12 (Moon in Pisces)   The moon is in your tenth house. Professional concerns occupy your thoughts. You're more emotional and warm toward fellow workers, but avoid mixing your personal life with your professional world. Deal with the public.

Sunday, January 13 (Moon in Pisces to Aries 7:24 p.m.)   It's a number 9 day. Complete any projects that you've been working on. Make room for something new. Accept whatever comes your way. Use the day for reflection and expansion.

Monday, January 14 (Moon in Aries)   The moon is in your eleventh house. Friends play an important role. Start something new as a new cycle begins. Focus on your wishes and dreams. Make sure that your goals are an expression of who you really are. Take time to share your ideas with a group of friends or associates.

Tuesday, January 15 (Moon in Aries to Taurus 11:13 p.m.)   It's a number 2 day. Be supportive and patient with others. Partnerships are highlighted. Let things develop. Don't make waves. A new relationship could develop that will be very satisfying. Show your appreciation of others.

Wednesday, January 16 (Moon in Taurus)   The moon is in your twelfth house. You may feel a need to withdraw and work on your own. Unconscious thoughts and feelings that could relate to your past may arise. Relations with women can be difficult. Keep secrets to yourself.

Thursday, January 17 (Moon in Taurus)   You're feeling highly sensual and quite opinionated. Guard against being overstubborn. Physical activity and health issues are highlighted.

Friday, January 18 (Moon in Taurus to Gemini 1:30 a.m.)   It's a number 5 day. Get ready for change that could include a possible move or relocation. Variety is the spice of life. Let go of old structures; get a new point of view.

Saturday, January 19 (Moon in Gemini)   The moon is in your first house—your sun sign. You get recharged for the month ahead. Your vitality increases; you're more appealing to the public. You get your ideas across clearly. However, you could be extremely sensitive and concerned about what others think of you.

Sunday, January 20 (Moon in Gemini to Cancer 3:06 a.m.)   It's a number 7 day. Like yesterday, you're sensitive about what others think about you. Maintain your emotional balance. See things as they are, not as you wish them to be. Keep any secrets entrusted to you.

Monday, January 21 (Moon in Cancer)   The moon is in your second house. Financial matters are a priority. Plan ahead related to your income and spending. Put off big purchases for a few days. You tend to equate financial assets with security.

Tuesday, January 22 (Moon in Cancer to Leo 5:22 a.m.)   It's a number 9 day. Look beyond the immediate.

Plan a long trip to a foreign land. Strive for universal appeal. Let go of preconceived notions. Spiritual values surface.

Wednesday, January 23 (Moon in Leo)   The moon is in your third house. You could be taking a short trip that might involve relatives. Take what you know and share it with others. But stay in conscious control of your emotions. Matters from the past could arise.

Thursday, January 24 (Moon in Leo to Virgo 9:49 a.m.)   Venus moves into your eighth house. Your emotions are more intense than usual. Sexual issues arise and can relate to the way you feel about your shared belongings.

Friday, January 25 (Moon in Virgo)   Pluto moves into your eighth house and remains there until April when it goes retrograde. You can look forward to a transformation in your finances. Your spouse or partner may do very well, but watch for problems related to taxes, insurance, or investments.

Saturday, January 26 (Moon in Virgo to Libra 5:36 p.m.)   It's a number 4 day. Organizational skills are highlighted. You build foundations for the future. Persevere to get things done. Emphasize quality. You'll be finding outlets for your creativity.

Sunday, January 27 (Moon in Libra)   The moon is in your fifth house. Like yesterday, there's an emphasis on your creative life. Move beyond organizing and spend time pursuing your creative talents. You have the ability to tap deeply into the collective unconscious. In love, there's great emotional depth.

Monday, January 28 (Moon in Libra)   Mercury goes retrograde and stays that way for three weeks. You can expect some disruption of plans during this time. Communications can be difficult. Group activities can be particularly challenging. If you sign any contracts, make sure you read the fine print.

Tuesday, January 29 (Moon in Libra to Scorpio 4:35 a.m.) It's a number 7 day. Gather information, but don't make any absolute decisions until tomorrow. You could find that others delay making commitments or living up to them. Maintain emotional balance; avoid confusion and conflict.

Wednesday, January 30 (Moon in Scorpio) Mars goes direct in your second house. You experience a jolt of energy related to your finances. Decide what your priorities are in handling your finances. Even if you experience a sudden increase of income, put off any big purchases for a few days.

Thursday, January 31 (Moon in Scorpio to Sagittarius 5:08 p.m.) It's a number 9 day. Finish what you've started. Complete projects and make room for the new, but don't take on anything new. Visualize your future. Set your goals and get to work.

FEBRUARY 2008

Friday, February 1 (Moon in Sagittarius) The moon is in your seventh house and it's a number 7 day. A mystery could be unfolding right in front of you. Look beneath the surface for clues. Follow your intuition. Knowledge is essential for success. A partnership plays an important role.

Saturday, February 2 (Moon in Sagittarius) Keep your good humor, and look for the big picture. What are you doing and where are you going? Matters involving travel, publishing, and the law could be involved.

Sunday, February 3 (Moon in Sagittarius to Capricorn 4:52 a.m.) It's a number 9 day. Complete whatever you've been working on, whether it's a home-repair project or a business-related matter. Get ready for something new, but don't start on it. Plan your future. Discover how you can expand your horizons.

Monday, February 4 (Moon in Capricorn)   The moon is in your eighth house. You may attract power people to you. An interest in metaphysics is highlighted. Your energy is intense. Matters related to sex, death, and rebirth could play a role.

Tuesday, February 5 (Moon in Capricorn to Aquarius 2:10 p.m.)   It's a number 2 day. Don't make waves. The emphasis is on cooperation. Even though your mind is racing ahead, Gemini, let things develop. Learn the power of patience. Family members or business partners play a role.

Wednesday, February 6 (Moon in Aquarius)   There's a solar eclipse in your ninth house. Take a break from your regular routine. Matters involving your beliefs, higher education, and long-distance travel become clearer. But with the moon also in your ninth house, you may find yourself reacting emotionally to whatever you realize.

Thursday, February 7 (Moon in Aquarius to Pisces 8:47 p.m.)   It's a number 4 day. Persevere to get things done. Tear down in order to rebuild, but don't get sloppy. Fulfill your obligations and focus on building an outlet for your creativity.

Friday, February 8 (Moon in Pisces)   The moon is in your tenth house. Professional matters take precedence. You're responsive to the needs and moods of fellow workers. It's a good day for sales and dealing with the public.

Saturday, February 9 (Moon in Pisces)   Your imagination is highlighted. Watch for synchronicities. Use them as guideposts. Pay attention to your dreams. But don't fall into the trap of self-deception.

Sunday, February 10 (Moon in Pisces to Aries 1:18 a.m.)   It's a number 7 day. Spirituality is emphasized. Discuss and defend your beliefs. Knowledge is essential to

257

success. Keep any secrets entrusted to you. Go with the flow.

Monday, February 11 (Moon in Aries)   The moon is in your eleventh house. Friends play an important role. You could be joining a group of like-minded people. Focus on your wishes and dreams. Examine your overall goals; make sure they are an expression of who you really are.

Tuesday, February 12 (Moon in Aries to Taurus 4:35 a.m.)   It's a number 9 day. Clean your desk and get ready for the new cycle. Look beyond the immediate. Focus on promotion and expansion. Nurture your intuition.

Wednesday, February 13 (Moon in Taurus)   The moon is in your twelfth house. Work behind the scenes, especially on a new project. Use your intuition. Keep your ideas to yourself, or only discuss them with a trusted confidant.

Thursday, February 14 (Moon in Taurus to Gemini 7:20 a.m.)   It's a number 2 day. A new relationship could start. Help comes through friends. Show your appreciation. You also may be involved in soul-searching related to a current relationship.

Friday, February 15 (Moon in Gemini)   The moon is in your first house, which means the emotional self takes precedence. You're particularly sensitive to other people's feelings. Your moods shift from being happy one moment to being withdrawn the next. However, your feelings and your thoughts are aligned.

Saturday, February 16 (Moon in Gemini to Cancer 10:30 a.m.)   It's a number 4 day. Be methodical and thorough in whatever you're working on. You're in the right place at the right time. You can overcome any bureaucratic red tape.

Sunday, February 17 (Moon in Cancer)   Venus moves into your ninth house. You could feel restless and lovelorn. You could fall in love while on a long-distance journey or fall for a foreign-born person. Alternately, you could feel emotional ties to a particular institution of higher learning.

Monday, February 18 (Moon in Cancer to Leo 1:52 p.m.)   Mercury goes direct. Your communication with others, both individuals and groups, will go more smoothly than it has over the past three weeks. You get your point across. Misunderstandings are resolved.

Tuesday, February 19 (Moon in Leo)   Gather information as part of your daily activities, but don't make any absolute decisions until tomorrow. Secrets, mystery, intrigue, and confidential information play a role. Maintain your emotional balance, especially when dealing with relatives and neighbors.

Wednesday, February 20 (Moon in Leo to Virgo 7:07 p.m.)   There's a lunar eclipse in your fourth house. Emotional issues arise related to your home and family. You could feel emotionally possessive of loved ones. Don't buy real estate unless you feel intuitively certain about it.

Thursday, February 21 (Moon in Virgo)   With the moon in your fourth house, retreat to a private place for meditation. Like yesterday, you should make an effort to spend more time at home with loved ones. Beautify your surroundings with a home-repair or redecoration project.

Friday, February 22 (Moon in Virgo)   Look after health matters and tend to details. Stop worrying and fretting. Dig deep for information. Watch your diet and exercise, but also take time to relax.

Saturday, February 23 (Moon in Virgo to Libra 2:45 a.m.)   It's a number 2 day. Don't make waves. Let things develop on their own. Your marriage or business partnership plays a significant role. Be kind and understanding. Don't rush about or show resentment.

Sunday, February 24 (Moon in Libra)   The moon is in your fifth house. Be emotionally honest. There's great emotional depth in a relationship. Pursue a creative project or spend time with children.

Monday, February 25 (Moon in Libra to Scorpio 1:06 a.m.)   It's a number 4 day. Stay focused on your work. You build new foundations that will serve as a basis for your creative efforts. Control your impulses to meander. Emphasize quality.

Tuesday, February 26 (Moon in Scorpio)   The moon is in your sixth house. It's a service-oriented day. Go out of your way to help others. You may feel somewhat emotionally repressed. Keep your resolutions about diet and exercise.

Wednesday, February 27 (Moon in Scorpio)   Your experiences are likely to be intense. You could be investigating something that involves secrecy, but avoid going to extremes. Be aware of possible deception. Avoid making any large purchases.

Thursday, February 28 (Moon in Scorpio to Sagittarius 1:23 a.m.)   It's a number 7 day. Yesterday's endeavors related to investigating secret or confidential matters continue. Go with the flow. Gather information, but don't make any absolute decisions. Keep any secrets entrusted to you.

Friday, February 29 (Moon in Sagittarius)   The moon is in your seventh house. The highlight is on partnerships. Focus on personal relationships. Loved ones and partners play a major role. Be aware that any conflicts will be emotional. You could have a difficult time remaining detached and objective.

MARCH 2008

Saturday, March 1 (Moon in Sagittarius to Capricorn 1:33 p.m.)   It's a number 8 day, and your power day. Unexpected money comes your way. If you're going to win the lottery, today's the day! You have a chance to expand your horizons, to gain recognition, even fame and power.

Sunday, March 2 (Moon in Capricorn)   The moon is in your eighth house. You could be attracting powerful people to you. An interest in metaphysics plays a role. Be aware that your experiences may be intense.

Monday, March 3 (Moon in Capricorn to Aquarius 11:25 p.m.)   It's a number 1 day. You're at the top of your cycle. Initiate a new project. Get out and meet new people, have new experiences. You get a fresh start. Don't be afraid to turn in a new direction.

Tuesday, March 4 (Moon in Aquarius)   Mars moves into your second house. You get a surge of energy related to finances. There's a lot of focus on earning money. Whatever you value most is emphasized in your activities.

Wednesday, March 5 (Moon in Aquarius)   The moon is in your ninth house. Discuss matters related to college and higher education, either for you or someone close to you. Long-distance travel could be involved.

Thursday, March 6 (Moon in Aquarius to Pisces 5:54 a.m.)   It's a number 4 day. Your organizational skills are emphasized. Persevere to get things done. In romance, your persistence pays off. You're building a foundation for the future.

Friday, March 7 (Moon in Pisces)   The moon is in your tenth house. Profession and career take precedence. Deal with any matters related to fellow workers. You're warm and understanding. Others respond well to you, including bosses and CEOs. Avoid any emotional displays in public.

Saturday, March 8 (Moon in Pisces to Aries 9:24 a.m.)   It's a number 6 day. Be diplomatic. Help others where you can; do a good deed. Focus on making people happy, but dance to your own tune.

Sunday, March 9—Daylight Saving Time Begins (Moon in Aries) The moon is in your eleventh house. Friends play an important role. You could be gathering with a group of like-minded individuals. Spirituality is emphasized. You gain from your associations.

Monday, March 10 (Moon in Aries to Taurus 12:15 p.m.) It's a number 8 day. Play it your way. Expect a financial coup. Focus on a power play. Business dealings go well. Be courageous and persevere.

Tuesday, March 11 (Moon in Taurus) The moon is in your twelfth house. After your power day, step back and withdraw from the action. Keep your feelings secret. Relations with the opposite sex can be difficult. Work behind the scenes.

Wednesday, March 12 (Moon in Taurus to Gemini 1:55 p.m.) Venus moves into your tenth house. You could get romantically involved with someone from the workplace. You're more emotional and warm toward coworkers. But be careful about blurring the lines between your personal and business life.

Thursday, March 13 (Moon in Gemini) The moon is in your first house. It's all about self-awareness and appearance. Your moods may fluctuate from happy one moment to sad the next.

Friday, March 14 (Moon in Gemini to Cancer 4:38 p.m.) Mercury moves into your tenth house. Expect rapid communication regarding professional or career matters. Business dealings move quickly and smoothly. You're in the public eye; you communicate well with others.

Saturday, March 15 (Moon in Cancer) The moon is in your second house. You feel emotionally attached to your belongings. It's not the objects themselves but the memories attached to them that attracts you. Whatever you value plays an important role.

Sunday, March 16 (Moon in Cancer to Leo 9:04 p.m.) It's a number 5 day. Approach the day with an unconventional mind-set. Change your perspective. Experiment and let go of old structures. Get ready for change.

Monday, March 17 (Moon in Leo) The moon is in your third house. Take what you've learned recently, and let others know about it. Get your ideas across as you go about your everyday activities. You could have contact with neighbors or relatives. You tend to get emotional in your interactions.

Tuesday, March 18 (Moon in Leo) Yesterday's energy continues to flow. You feel particularly passionate about something or someone. You're impulsive and honest. Drama is highlighted. It's a good day for publicizing whatever you're doing. Showmanship is emphasized.

Wednesday, March 19 (Moon in Leo to Virgo 3:25 a.m.) It's a number 8 day. It's your power day. Expect a financial coup. In speculative matters, pay attention to the number 8. It's all about material success.

Thursday, March 20 (Moon in Virgo) The moon is in your fourth house today. Spend time at home with your family or working on a home-repair project. Take care of family matters, especially if you can bring an issue to an end.

Friday, March 21 (Moon in Virgo to Libra 11:45 a.m.) It's a number 1 day. You're at the top of your cycle. You get a fresh start. Be independent and creative. Stress originality. Trust your hunches. Make room for a new love.

Saturday, March 22 (Moon in Libra) The moon is in your fifth house. The energy related to the creative effort you began yesterday continues. You have the ability to tap deeply into the collective unconscious. Children and animals play roles.

263

Sunday, March 23 (Moon in Libra to Scorpio 10:07 p.m.)   It's a number 3 day. Your intuition is highlighted. Social activities and spiritual values are stressed. Ease up on your routines. Spread your good news and make time to listen to others.

Monday, March 24 (Moon in Scorpio)   The moon is in your sixth house. The emphasis turns to your daily work and service to others. Attend to all the details. Don't overlook any seemingly minor matters that could take on importance. Keep your resolutions about exercise and diet.

Tuesday, March 25 (Moon in Scorpio)   Dig deeply into secret or hidden matters. What you find in your investigation could create intense emotional reaction. Avoid going to extremes. Forgive and forget.

Wednesday, March 26 (Moon in Scorpio to Sagittarius 10:12 a.m.)   It's a number 6 day. Do a good deed for someone. Be diplomatic and understanding, generous and tolerant. Focus on making people happy.

Thursday, March 27 (Moon in Sagittarius)   The moon is in your seventh house. The focus turns to personal relationships. Loved ones and partners play an important role. You could deal with legal matters. Confrontations with the opposite sex are likely. Be careful that others don't manipulate your feelings.

Friday, March 28 (Moon in Sagittarius to Capricorn 10:44 p.m.)   It's a number 8 day. You're ending the workweek on a power day. Take a chance. Financial matters work to your favor. Expect a windfall!

Saturday, March 29 (Moon in Capricorn)   The moon is in your eighth house. It's a goal-oriented Saturday, and you may deal with money or possessions that you share with another person, a spouse, or a business partner. Take care of any matters related to taxes, insurance, or investments. Be aware that emotions can get intense.

Sunday, March 30 (Moon in Capricorn) Maintain your emotional equilibrium. Your ambition and drive are highlighted, but take time to exercise and relax. Be conservative. Don't speculate. Don't take a risk. Think structure and self-discipline.

Monday, March 31 (Moon in Capricorn to Aquarius 9:35 a.m.) It's a number 2 day. Partnerships are highlighted; don't make waves. Patience is called for. Be understanding, kind, and cooperative. Other people might nag, but avoid showing resentment.

APRIL 2008

Tuesday, April 1 (Moon in Aquarius) The moon is in your ninth house. Plan for a long trip or take an armchair journey to a distant land. Matters related to college or any type of higher education take on importance. In romance, you could be attracted to a foreign-born person.

Wednesday, April 2 (Moon in Aquarius to Pisces 4:56 a.m.) Mercury moves into your twelfth house, and Pluto goes retrograde in your seventh house. You could talk or write about matters related to your past or childhood. Exchange ideas about mystical or spiritual matters. You could rebuild an old friendship, but be aware of control issues.

Thursday, April 3 (Moon in Pisces) The moon is in your tenth house. Your focus turns to professional matters. You get along with others in a group and also with the public in general. But avoid getting overemotional about any matters, particularly if you're in the public eye.

Friday, April 4 (Moon in Pisces to Aries 8:28 p.m.) It's a number 3 day. Others see you as optimistic. Your charm and wit are appreciated. Remain flexible, open to change. Follow your intuition. Relax and enjoy yourself.

Saturday, April 5 (Moon in Aries)   The moon is in your eleventh house. Friends play an important role. You get along well with others, and they can provide you with unexpected help. Focus on your wishes and goals. Attend to an activity that benefits the greater good of all.

Sunday, April 6 (Moon in Aries to Taurus 9:20 p.m.)   Venus joins the moon in your eleventh house. Yesterday's energy continues with an emphasis on romance. Your wishes and dreams related to a special friend are realized. Just make sure that it's what you really want.

Monday, April 7 (Moon in Taurus)   The moon is in your twelfth house. Withdraw from public view. Work behind the scenes. Unconscious attitudes could be difficult. Relations with the opposite sex may be strained. Keep your feelings secret.

Tuesday, April 8 (Moon in Taurus to Gemini 9:27 p.m.)   It's a number 7 day. Look beneath the surface for the reasons others are delaying commitments or not living up to them. Express your concerns, but maintain your emotional balance. Avoid self-deception. Knowledge is essential to success.

Wednesday, April 9 (Moon in Gemini)   The moon is in your first house. You're recharged for the month ahead. You feel physically vital, and you're more appealing to the public. Relations with the opposite sex go well. Your thoughts and feelings are aligned.

Thursday, April 10 (Moon in Gemini to Cancer 10:43 p.m.)   It's a number 9 day. Finish up whatever you've been working on. Look beyond the immediate. Strive for universal appeal. Follow your intuition. Clear your desk of the old, but don't start anything new.

Friday, April 11 (Moon in Cancer)   The moon is in your second house. You identify emotionally with your possessions or whatever you value. It's not the objects themselves that are important, but the feelings you hold related to them. Take care of any payments and collect what's owed you.

Saturday, April 12 (Moon in Cancer)   Stick close to home and family. Tend to loved ones. Do something special with those close to you. Be aware that you may be particularly sensitive to the varying moods of others, but keep your criticisms to yourself.

Sunday, April 13 (Moon in Cancer to Leo 2:29 a.m.)   It's a number 3 day. Your attitude determines everything. Be happy, positive, upbeat. Expect an invitation from a friend or loved one. Have fun in preparation to tomorrow's discipline and focus.

Monday, April 14 (Moon in Leo)   The moon is in your third house. Write in a journal. You can go deep inside and gain a useful perspective. Keep conscious control of your emotions when dealing with others, especially relatives and neighbors.

Tuesday, April 15 (Moon in Leo to Virgo 9:07 a.m.)   It's a number 5 day. Get ready for change. Variety and freedom from restrictions are emphasized. Take a risk or experiment with a new idea. Approach the day with an unconventional mind-set.

Wednesday, April 16 (Moon in Virgo)   The moon is in your fourth house. Retreat to a private place and meditate. Attend to a home-repair project or buy something to beautify your house. Recall your dreams.

Thursday, April 17 (Moon in Virgo to Libra 6:11 p.m.)   It's a number 7 day. It's all about mystery and intrigue. Be aware of any confidential information or secret meetings. Gather information, but don't make any absolute decisions until tomorrow. Keep your eyes open, and go with the flow.

Friday, April 18 (Moon in Libra)   The moon is in your fifth house. Be emotionally honest and open. In love,

267

there's great emotional depth. You could have more involvement with children and animals. Pursue the creative part of your life.

Saturday, April 19 (Moon in Libra)   Romance and relationships are highlighted. Like yesterday, you could feel romantic and creative. Attend a concert or the theater, or visit a museum or an art gallery. You seek harmony and peace, and your personal magnetism attracts others to you.

Sunday, April 20 (Moon in Libra to Scorpio 5:02 a.m.)   It's a number 1 day. You're at the top of your cycle. Be independent and creative. Get out and meet new people. Do something that you've never done before. You get a fresh start. A flirtation could turn serious.

Monday, April 21 (Moon in Scorpio)   The moon is in your sixth house. Take care of details in your daily work and your personal life. Make doctor or dentist appointments. Help coworkers. Don't let your fears hold you back. Confront them.

Tuesday, April 22 (Moon in Scorpio to Sagittarius 5:08 p.m.)   It's a number 3 day. Your popularity is on the rise. Your vitality and natural ability to express yourself are noticed. Stay optimistic. Put your keen imagination to work. Remain flexible and open.

Wednesday, April 23 (Moon in Sagittarius)   The moon is in your seventh house. The focus turns to personal relationships. Loved ones and partners play an important role. Deal with contracts or other legal matters. Be careful that others don't manipulate your feelings.

Thursday, April 24 (Moon in Sagittarius)   Look to the big picture. Use your sense of humor when dealing with others. Be impulsive and inquisitive. Don't limit yourself. A publishing project could find acceptance.

Friday, April 25 (Moon in Sagittarius to Capricorn 5:48 p.m.)   It's a number 6 day. Diplomacy wins your way.

Be generous and tolerant. Help others, but avoid scattering your energies. Music plays a role. Find your rhythm.

Saturday, April 26 (Moon in Capricorn)   The moon is in your eighth house. Your experiences could be intense. You could deal with your feelings regarding shared resources. Also, inheritance, taxes, insurance, and investments could play a role.

Sunday, April 27 (Moon in Capricorn to Aquarius 5:28 p.m.)   It's a number 8 day. Play it your way. Open your mind to a new approach, which could bring in big bucks. You have a chance to gain recognition and a new sense of power.

Monday, April 28 (Moon in Aquarius)   The moon is in your ninth house. You could feel restless and look for something new. Plan a long trip or sign up for a workshop on a subject that interests you. You could renew an interest in philosophies, mythology, or worldviews. A foreign-born person could play a role.

Tuesday, April 29 (Moon in Aquarius)   Your visionary abilities are high. You can glimpse the future. Look beyond the immediate; play your hunches. Help others, but know when to say enough is enough.

Wednesday, April 30 (Moon in Aquarius to Pisces 2:11 a.m.)   Venus moves into your twelfth house. A secret love affair could blossom. Make sure that it's what you want. Perform dream work or meditate, or work on a creative project.

MAY 2008

Thursday, May 1 (Moon in Pisces)   The moon is in your tenth house. Focus on your professional concerns. You could deal with bosses and others in power. Your life is more public. You're more responsive to the needs and moods of a group and the public in general. An office romance could be dangerous.

Friday, May 2 (Moon in Pisces to Aries 6:51 a.m.)
Mercury goes direct in your first house. You'll talk a lot about yourself and your plans. You could also discuss a health matter.

Saturday, May 3 (Moon in Aries) The moon is in your eleventh house. You get along well with friends who are more helpful than you realized. You and friends might work together on a matter related to the greater good. It could fit well with your own wishes and dreams.

Sunday, May 4 (Moon in Aries to Taurus 7:58 a.m.) It's a number 4 day. Your organizational skills come into play. Clean up and get everything in order. You could find missing papers. Control your impulses to wander; fulfill your obligations. You're building a creative base.

Monday, May 5 (Moon in Taurus) Mars moves into your third house. There could be a lot of social activity going on related to relatives and neighbors. Be aware that you tend to be more aggressive. Control your temper on the road.

Tuesday, May 6 (Moon in Taurus to Gemini 7:18 a.m.) It's a number 6 day. Do a good deed for someone. Try to make other people happy. Be understanding, but avoid scattering your energies. Take time to dance to your own tune.

Wednesday, May 7 (Moon in Gemini) The moon is in your first house. Your feelings and thoughts are aligned. You get recharged for the month ahead. Your physical vitality is strong, and you're appealing to the public.

Thursday, May 8 (Moon in Gemini to Cancer 7:03 a.m.) It's a number 8 day. Focus on a power play. Business discussions go well. You attract financial success. But be careful not to hurt others.

Friday, May 9 (Moon in Cancer) Jupiter goes retrograde in your eighth house. Be aware that you could face some setbacks related to shared possessions. If you were planning to jointly buy a house or vehicle, things might not happen as fast as you would like. Any plans to expand a business could be delayed.

Saturday, May 10 (Moon in Cancer to Leo 9:11 a.m.) It's a number 1 day. You're at the top of your cycle. Stress originality; put your creativity to use. Explore, discover, and develop your ideas. Take the initiative and don't be afraid to turn in a new direction.

Sunday, May 11 (Moon in Leo) The moon is in your third house. You could look forward to a gathering of relatives, friends, and neighbors. You could be unduly influenced by matters from the past. A female relative could play a role. Keep conscious control of your emotions.

Monday, May 12 (Moon in Leo to Virgo 2:49 p.m.) It's a number 3 day. Your attitude determines everything. Stay positive and upbeat. Spread your good news. Diversify, and insist on getting all the information. Make time to listen to others.

Tuesday, May 13 (Moon in Virgo) The moon is in your fourth house. Retreat to the home front; spend time with your family. Recall your dreams, meditate, and handle home repairs.

Wednesday, May 14 (Moon in Virgo to Libra 11:48 p.m.) It's a number 5 day. Approach the day with an unconventional mind-set. Take a risk; experiment. Freedom of thought and action is highlighted. Prepare for change.

Thursday, May 15 (Moon in Libra) The moon is in your fifth house. Follow your heart on a creative project. You can tap deeply into the collective unconscious for inspiration. In love, there's great emotional depth. But you may feel overpossessive regarding a loved one.

271

Friday, May 16 (Moon in Libra)   The moon is in your fifth house. Your focus turns to a creative project. You can leap ahead as you tap deeply into the collective unconscious. In love, there's great depth in a relationship.

Saturday, May 17 (Moon in Libra to Scorpio 11:00 a.m.)   It's a number 8 day. Play it your way. If you play Lotto, buy an extra ticket. Expect a financial windfall. Open your mind to the possibilities.

Sunday, May 18 (Moon in Scorpio)   The moon is in your sixth house. Be of service to others. Visit someone who is ill or in need of help. Do a good deed. But know when enough is enough. Tend to your own health needs. Watch your diet and exercise.

Monday, May 19 (Moon in Scorpio to Sagittarius 11:20 p.m.)   It's a number 1 day. You're at the top of your cycle. You get a fresh start. Refuse to deal with people who have closed minds. Trust your hunches; follow your intuition. Stress originality. If you're ready, make room for a new love.

Tuesday, May 20 (Moon in Sagittarius)   The moon is in your seventh house. It's all about partnerships and working together. Loved ones or partners play a major role. Any conflicts can be emotional, especially when dealing with the opposite sex. Don't let others manipulate your feelings.

Wednesday, May 21 (Moon in Sagittarius)   You get a sense of the big picture. It could involve publishing or the law, courts, and justice system. In romance, there's strong passion. You're impulsive and inquisitive. Don't limit yourself.

Thursday, May 22 (Moon in Sagittarius to Capricorn 11:56 a.m.)   It's a number 4 day. Revise and rewrite. Tear down the old in order to rebuild. You develop a creative base for the future. Avoid scattering your energies. You can overcome any obstacles. You're in the right place at the right time.

Friday, May 23 (Moon in Capricorn)   The moon is in your eighth house. You could deal with inherited money, or taxes and investments. Whatever it is affects your feelings about shared income or possessions. Control your emotions. You could deal with powerful people.

Saturday, May 24 (Moon in Capricorn to Aquarius 11:52 p.m.)   Venus is in your first house. You feel particularly romantic. You're physically vital and recharged for the month ahead. Relations with the opposite sex go well. Your thoughts and feelings are aligned.

Sunday, May 25 (Moon in Aquarius)   The moon is in your ninth house. You feel a need to get away from the routine. Plan a long trip or find a workshop or class you'd like to take. A foreign country or foreign-born person could play a role. You take a greater interest in worldviews.

Monday, May 26 (Moon in Aquarius)   Mercury goes retrograde, and so does Neptune. With Mercury turning retrograde, expect some delays and glitches in communication and travel plans over the next three weeks. It could affect computers and other machinery. Neptune also goes retrograde in your ninth house. That means you tend to turn inward and spend time reviewing your beliefs and philosophies.

Tuesday, May 27 (Moon in Aquarius to Pisces 9:39 a.m.)   It's a number 9 day. Finish up whatever you've been working on. Get ready for a new project, but don't start anything just yet. Take time to reflect and consider how to expand your horizons.

Wednesday, May 28 (Moon in Pisces)   The moon is in your tenth house. The emphasis is on your profession or career. You work well with others. You're more in the public view. Avoid making any emotional displays, especially in dealings with bosses, and be careful about crossing the line between your professional and personal lives.

Thursday, May 29 (Moon in Pisces to Aries 3:53 p.m.)   It's a number 2 day. Cooperation is highlighted. Your spouse or partner plays a major role. Don't make waves or show resentment, but take time to consider the direction you're headed and your motivation for continuing on this path.

Friday, May 30 (Moon in Aries)   The moon is in your eleventh house. While yesterday's focus was on partnership, today you're dealing with friends and group associations. You get along well with others, and things go smoothly in a group setting. Friends come to your aid. Make sure that your wishes and goals are an expression of who you really are.

Saturday, May 31 (Moon in Aries to Taurus 6:19 p.m.)   It's a number 4 day. Get organized. Clean your room or office. Get your papers in order. Persevere to get things done. Don't get sloppy; control your impulses to wander off in another direction. Clear out the old so there's room for the new.

JUNE 2008

Sunday, June 1 (Moon in Taurus)   The moon is in your twelfth house. You could have some dealings with government offices, hospitals, or other institutions. For the most part, it's a good day for solitary pursuits or dealing with secrets.

Monday, June 2 (Moon in Taurus to Gemini 6:07 p.m.)   It's a number 3 day. Stay optimistic. Your attitude determines everything. Be happy and positive. Spread your good news. Diversify wherever you can. Insist on all the information you need.

Tuesday, June 3 (Moon in Gemini)   The moon is in your first house. You could be somewhat moody. You deal with your self-awareness and appearance. You get recharged for the month ahead.

Wednesday, June 4 (Moon in Gemini to Cancer 5:17 p.m.)   It's a number 5 day. The emphasis is on freedom of thought and action. Get ready for change and variety. Be careful since you'll be in a hurry all day and could be accident prone.

Thursday, June 5 (Moon in Cancer)   The moon is in your second house. Deal with finances. Make sure you know what your priorities are in handling your income. Your possessions as well as your values give you comfort.

Friday, June 6 (Moon in Cancer to Leo 6:01 p.m.)   It's a number 7 day. You could deal with confidential information and intrigue. Express your desires, but avoid self-deception. See things as they are and not how you wish them to be.

Saturday, June 7 (Moon in Leo)   The moon is in your third house. You could move about on short trips. Take what you know and share it with others. You could receive an invitation for a social gathering.

Sunday, June 8 (Moon in Leo to Virgo 10:02 p.m.)   It's a number 9 day. Clear up odds and ends. Finish up on a project. Visualize for the future. Set your goals, and then get to work. Strive for universal appeal. You're up to the challenge.

Monday, June 9 (Moon in Virgo)   The moon is in your fourth house. You get a fresh start, especially concerning your home and family. Take time to retreat to a private place for meditation. Let go of a bad habit.

Tuesday, June 10 (Moon in Virgo)   Tend to details. Make those appointments you've been putting off. Clear your desk of old papers. Pay the bills. Attend to health matters. Exercise and watch your diet.

Wednesday, June 11 (Moon in Virgo to Libra 5:56 a.m.)   It's a number 3 day. Make time to listen to others.

Ease up on your routines. Enjoy casual conversation. Relax and enjoy yourself. Foster generosity.

Thursday, June 12 (Moon in Libra)   The moon is in your fifth house. You get a spark of creativity that thrusts you ahead in a project. You could take a chance. It's a good day for speculation, love, and sex for pleasure. You're also more possessive of loved ones.

Friday, June 13 (Moon in Libra to Scorpio 4:54 p.m.)   It's a number 5 day. Get ready for change. Experiment. Get a new perspective. Approach the day with an unconventional mind-set.

Saturday, June 14 (Moon in Scorpio)   The moon is in your sixth house. You could feel somewhat burdened and emotionally repressed. Don't let your fears hold you back. Confront them. Be of service to others.

Sunday, June 15 (Moon in Scorpio)   Expect intense emotional experiences. Your sexuality is heightened, so is your intuition. Avoid going to extremes. Control issues might surface. Watch for possible deception, but forgive and forget.

Monday, June 16 (Moon in Scorpio to Sagittarius 5:20 a.m.)   It's a number 8 day. It's your power day. Material success is at hand. You attract financial success. This week you can expand your horizons and gain recognition and power.

Tuesday, June 17 (Moon in Sagittarius)   The moon is in your seventh house. The focus turns to relationships, especially partners, either personal or business. The opposite sex plays a prominent role. Any conflicts will be emotional.

Wednesday, June 18 (Moon in Sagittarius to Capricorn 5:52 p.m.)   Venus moves into your second house. It's a good day for money, and especially favorable for speculative ventures and investments. You could be attracted to someone through money dealings.

Thursday, June 19 (Moon in Capricorn)   Mercury goes direct. Things start to move smoothly. All the confusion, miscommunication, and delays recede into the past. You get your message across. Everything works better, including computers and other machinery. Misunderstandings are resolved.

Friday, June 20 (Moon in Capricorn)   The moon is in your eighth house. Your experiences are intense. Matters of sex, death, and rebirth play a role. An inheritance could come your way and affect your feelings about shared possessions.

Saturday, June 21 (Moon in Capricorn to Aquarius 5:34 a.m.)   It's a number 4 day. Spend time on getting organized. Take care of your obligations and control your impulse to wander off. Persevere to get things done. You're building a foundation for the future.

Sunday, June 22 (Moon in Aquarius)   The moon is in your ninth house. You take an interest in philosophy, religion, or mythology. You reflect on your worldviews. Plan a long trip or make plans to attend a workshop or seminar.

Monday, June 23 (Moon in Aquarius to Pisces 3:33 p.m.)   It's a number 6 day. It's all about service to others. Do a good deed for someone. Visit a sick family member. Focus on making people happy. A domestic adjustment works out for the best. Avoid scattering your energies.

Tuesday, June 24 (Moon in Pisces)   The moon is in your tenth house. The emphasis is on career or professional matters. You get along well with fellow workers, but be aware that they could be changing positions. Avoid any emotional displays in public.

Wednesday, June 25 (Moon in Pisces to Aries 10:50 p.m.)   It's a number 8 day. Play it your way. Open your mind to a new approach that could bring in big bucks. You attract financial success. Be aware that you're playing with power. Don't hurt others.

Thursday, June 26 (Moon in Aries)   Uranus goes retrograde in your tenth house. You could start to experience some upheavals in your career and professional life. The upheavals could be related to your plans for the future.

Friday, June 27 (Moon in Aries)   The moon is in your eleventh house. You have deep contact with friends, who play an important role. Focus on your wishes and dreams. Help comes from unexpected quarters.

Saturday, June 28 (Moon in Aries to Taurus 2:51 a.m.)   It's a number 2 day. Cooperation is highlighted. Be kind and understanding. Use your intuition to plan your day. There could be discussions about a marriage or partnership.

Sunday, June 29 (Moon in Taurus)   The moon is in your twelfth house. Withdraw from public view. Unconscious attitudes related to the past and your childhood can be difficult. Relate your deepest feelings to someone you trust.

Monday, June 30 (Moon in Taurus to Gemini 4:04 a.m.)   It's a number 4 day. Start off the workweek by getting organized. Tear down the old in order to rebuild. Revise and rewrite. Stay focused. You're building a creative base. Emphasize quality. You're in the right place at the right time.

JULY 2008

Tuesday, July 1 (Moon in Gemini)   Mars moves into your fourth house. There's a lot of activity in the home. Beautify your home. Take the family to a sporting event. You could be dealing with parents.

Wednesday, July 2 (Moon in Gemini to Cancer 3:54 a.m.)   It's a number 4 day. Get grounded and organized. Be methodical and thorough. Stick with it. Emphasize quality. You're building a base for a creative outlet.

Thursday, July 3 (Moon in Cancer)   The moon is in your second house. Deal with your finances. Investments, particularly in property, could pay off. Take care of your bills and collect what's owed to you. In whatever you are pursuing, make sure that your values remain intact.

Friday, July 4 (Moon in Cancer to Leo 4:16 a.m.)   It's a number 6 day. A change you make in your home works out for the best. Be of service to others; be diplomatic in your dealings. However, be aware of emotional outbursts and of others making unfair demands on your time. Dance to your own tune.

Saturday, July 5 (Moon in Leo)   The moon is in your third house. You'll probably take care of your everyday needs. Take your cell phone with you because you'll have things to talk about with others, including relatives or neighbors.

Sunday, July 6 (Moon in Leo to Virgo 7:04 a.m.)   It's a number 8 day. Play it your way. Open your mind to a new approach. It could bring in an unexpected windfall. Be careful not to hurt others.

Monday, July 7 (Moon in Virgo)   The moon is in your fourth house. Take care of issues at home. Tend to an important family matter. You may feel emotionally possessive. Bring an end to something unresolved. Take time to retreat to a private place to meditate.

Tuesday, July 8 (Moon in Virgo to Libra 1:32 p.m.)   It's a number 1 day. Be independent and creative. You get a fresh start. Stress originality, new ideas. Take the initiative; don't be afraid to turn in a new direction.

Wednesday, July 9 (Moon in Libra)   The moon is in your fifth house. Your creative energy expands. You could deal with children. You're protective and nurturing. Animals play a large role. In love, there's great depth.

Thursday, July 10 (Moon in Libra to Scorpio 11:35 p.m.)   Mercury moves into your second house. There's a lot of activity related to financial matters. Make sure you know what your priorities are regarding your income. Look to the future and prepare for it.

Friday, July 11 (Moon in Scorpio)   The moon is in your sixth house. Attend to daily details and be of service. Help your coworkers, but don't overlook your own needs. Make appointments that you've been putting off.

Saturday, July 12 (Moon in Scorpio)   Venus moves into your third house. You feel affection toward relatives. You could get together for a family gathering. Alternately, you could embark on an affair with someone in your neighborhood. Consider the consequences before you act.

Sunday, July 13 (Moon in Scorpio to Sagittarius 11:50 a.m.)   It's a number 6 day. Do a good deed for someone. Visit an ailing friend or relative. Focus on making people happy. Be understanding, tolerant, and generous. Diplomacy wins the way.

Monday, July 14 (Moon in Sagittarius)   The moon is in your seventh house. Loved ones and partners play a major role. You could deal with legal matters related to a partnership. It's difficult to stay detached and objective. Be careful not to allow others to manipulate your feelings.

Tuesday, July 15 (Moon in Sagittarius)   It's a number 8 day. It's your power day. Be courageous. Appear successful even if you don't feel that way. Expect a financial coup. You're attracting a lucrative deal. Don't hurt anyone.

Wednesday, July 16 (Moon in Sagittarius to Capricorn 12:20 a.m.)   The moon is in your eighth house. You could deal with an inheritance or legacy. Something related to metaphysics comes up. Everything probably seems intense, especially if you're dealing with shared resources or belongings.

Thursday, July 17 (Moon in Capricorn)   It's a goal-oriented day. Stay focused. Your ambition and drive are highlighted. You gain new opportunities, but that means new responsibilities. You may feel stressed, so take time to exercise and relax.

Friday, July 18 (Moon in Capricorn to Aquarius 11:41 a.m.)   It's a number 2 day. The spotlight is on cooperative efforts and partnerships. Be kind and understanding. Let things develop. Don't make waves. Be supportive and patient.

Saturday, July 19 (Moon in Aquarius)   The moon is in your ninth house. The emphasis is on higher education, and it could involve travel or an exploration of worldviews or philosophies. You could be involved in or preparing for a ceremony or religious function.

Sunday, July 20 (Moon in Aquarius to Pisces 9:09 p.m.)   It's a number 4 day. Take care of your obligations. Examine your budget and watch your spending. Clean out the old so there's room for the new. Control your impulses. You're in the right place at the right time.

Monday, July 21 (Moon in Pisces)   The moon is in your tenth house. Business dealings are highlighted. It's a good day for sales and dealing with the public. You get along well with fellow workers. Avoid any emotional displays in public.

Tuesday, July 22 (Moon in Pisces)   Imagination is highlighted. You're particularly intuitive. Watch for psychic events or synchronicities. Don't fall into the trap of self-deception. Pay attention to your dreams. Seek universal knowledge or eternal truths.

Wednesday, July 23 (Moon in Pisces to Aries 4:23 a.m.)   It's a number 7 day. There's mystery in the air. Something hidden or secretive comes to your attention. Dig deep for information, but don't make any final decisions on what you uncover until tomorrow.

Thursday, July 24 (Moon in Aries)   The moon is in your eleventh house. Friends play a significant role. You get along well with others, particularly those in a group association. Examine your overall goals, and make sure that they're an expression of who you are.

Friday, July 25 (Moon in Aries to Taurus 9:15 a.m.)   It's a number 9 day. Look beyond the present. Plan a long journey. Complete projects and make room for the new. Strive for universal appeal. Spiritual values are emphasized.

Saturday, July 26 (Moon in Taurus)   Mercury is in your third house. Get your message across. Share what you know with others. You communicate well, especially if you maintain control of your emotions.

Sunday, July 27 (Moon in Taurus to Gemini 11:56 a.m.)   It's a number 2 day. Cooperation is highlighted. You could be involved in discussions related to a marriage or partnership. Don't rush or show resentment. Go with the flow. Use your intuition to get a sense of your day.

Monday, July 28 (Moon in Gemini)   The moon is in your first house. You get your batteries recharged for the month ahead. You're physically vital; you get along well with the opposite sex. Your feelings and thoughts are aligned.

Tuesday, July 29 (Moon in Gemini to Cancer 1:12 p.m.)   It's a number 4 day. Tear down in order to re-build. Revise and rewrite. Persevere to get things done. Emphasize quality. You're building a creative base for the future.

Wednesday, July 30 (Moon in Cancer)   The moon is in your second house. Deal with finances. You feel comfortable surrounded by your possessions. It's not the objects themselves, but the feelings you associate with the objects that's important to you.

Thursday, July 31 (Moon in Cancer to Leo 2:22 p.m.)   It's a number 6 day. It's a service day. Help others where you can. Focus on making people happy. Be diplomatic, generous, and tolerant. But know when to say enough is enough.

AUGUST 2008

Friday, August 1 (Moon in Leo)   There's a solar eclipse in your third house. Something will come to light about a relative or neighbor. Solar eclipses tend to trigger external events so you see people in a new light, and that affects how you communicate with them.

Saturday, August 2 (Moon in Leo to Virgo 4:59 p.m.)   It's a number 5 day. The emphasis is on freedom of thought and movement. Get ready for a change of scenery or a possible relocation. Variety is the spice of life. Experiment and find a new outlook.

Sunday, August 3 (Moon in Virgo)   The moon is in your fourth house. Work out of your home, or work on a home-repair project. Retreat to a private place to meditate. But spend time with your family.

Monday, August 4 (Moon in Virgo to Libra 10:28 p.m.)   It's a number 7 day. You could be launching a journey into the unknown. Look closely for the truth of whatever you're pursuing. Dig deep for information. Knowledge is essential for success. See things as they are, not how you'd like to see them.

Tuesday, August 5 (Moon in Libra)   Venus moves into your fourth house. Spend time with family and loved ones.

It's a great day for romantic love, especially in your home. You might feel emotionally possessive of those close to you. Beautify your home.

Wednesday, August 6 (Moon in Libra)   The moon is in your fifth house. Pursue a romance or dive into a creative project. There's great emotional depth in whatever you pursue. Be yourself; be emotionally honest.

Thursday, August 7 (Moon in Libra to Scorpio 7:27 a.m.)   It's a number 1 day. You get a new beginning. Your individuality is stressed. You take a leadership role. Don't be afraid to turn in a new direction. Take the initiative. Express your opinions dynamically.

Friday, August 8 (Moon in Scorpio)   The moon is in your sixth house. It's a service day. Help others where you can. Visit someone who is ill or in need of help. Don't forget about your own needs. Exercise, diet, and deal with health issues.

Saturday, August 9 (Moon in Scorpio to Sagittarius 7:11 p.m.)   It's a number 3 day. You feel vital and optimistic. You get your batteries recharged. Your attitude determines everything. Relax and enjoy yourself. Spread your good news and listen to others.

Sunday, August 10 (Moon in Sagittarius)   Mercury moves into your fourth house. There's a lot of activity at home, especially with young people. Expect a lot of conversation and other forms of communication, such as a flurry of e-mails from far-flung family members.

Monday, August 11 (Moon in Sagittarius)   The moon is in your seventh house. Partnerships take center stage, both personal and business-oriented. There could be discussions about marriage or other contracts and legal matters. The opposite sex plays a prominent role.

Tuesday, August 12 (Moon in Sagittarius to Capricorn 7:43 a.m.)   It's a number 6 day. Domestic purchases are highlighted. Some change or adjustment in the home scene works out for the best. Be generous and tolerant. Focus on making people happy, but avoid scattering your energies.

Wednesday, August 13 (Moon in Capricorn)   The moon is in your eighth house. You could attract the attention of powerful people. Your experiences could be intense. Matters related to shared belongings, investments, taxes, or insurance could play a role.

Thursday, August 14 (Moon in Capricorn to Aquarius 6:57 p.m.)   It's a number 8 day. Play it your way. If ever there's a good day to speculate on the Lotto, it's today. Expect a financial coup. Unexpected money comes your way.

Friday, August 15 (Moon in Aquarius)   The moon is in your ninth house. You could be involved in a religious ceremony or ritual. Look for the big picture. A long trip could be part of it.

Saturday, August 16 (Moon in Aquarius)   There's a lunar eclipse in your ninth house. You take a new interest in higher education or travel to a foreign land. It's something you're thinking a lot about and feel strongly about. Any communication with someone from a foreign country goes well.

Sunday, August 17 (Moon in Aquarius to Pisces 3:47 a.m.)   It's a number 2 day. Help comes through friends and loved ones or through a partner. Show your appreciation to others. Use your intuition regarding a new relationship or partnership. There could be some soul-searching related to a long-standing relationship.

Monday, August 18 (Moon in Pisces)   The moon is in your tenth house. You could deal with bosses. Business activities are highlighted. It's a good day for sales or dealing with the public. You're more emotional than usual toward fellow workers

Tuesday, August 19 (Moon in Pisces to Aries 10:11 a.m.)
Mars is in your fifth house. You can expect a lot of activity
and strong emotions, including possessiveness, related to
children and loved ones. Alternately, you feel extremely
passionate about a creative project.

Wednesday, August 20 (Moon in Aries) The moon is
in your eleventh house. You get along well with friends,
and you could meet them at a sporting event. Your friends
provide unexpected help related to your wishes and
dreams.

***Thursday, August 21 (Moon in Aries to Taurus 2:38
p.m.)*** It's a number 6 day. Do a good deed for someone. Be diplomatic in dealing with others. Keep the focus
on making people happy. Be understanding and generous,
but don't scatter your energies.

Friday, August 22 (Moon in Taurus) The moon is in
your twelfth house. Withdraw from the action. Work on
your own. Remain behind the scenes. A secret matter
should remain a secret. Be aware that issues from your
childhood could surface.

***Saturday, August 23 (Moon in Taurus to Gemini 5:49
p.m.)*** It's a number 8 day. You're being watched by
people in power. Be courageous. Expect a financial coup.
Focus on a power play. Business negotiations go well.

Sunday, August 24 (Moon in Gemini) The moon is in
your first house. The focus turns to your appearance and
self-awareness. You may feel moody one moment and
happy the next. Your feelings and thoughts are aligned.

***Monday, August 25 (Moon in Gemini to Cancer 8:19
p.m.)*** It's a number 1 day. You're at the top of your
cycle. You get a fresh start. Be independent and creative.
Don't follow others. Stress originality, new ideas. Trust
your hunches.

Tuesday, August 26 (Moon in Cancer)   The moon is in your second house. Money issues take center stage. Make financial decisions and decide your priorities for handling your money. You feel emotionally tied to whatever you value.

Wednesday, August 27 (Moon in Cancer to Leo 10:51 p.m.)   It's a number 3 day. Stay optimistic. Your attitude determines everything. Be happy, positive, and upbeat. Make time to listen to others. Relax and enjoy yourself.

Thursday, August 28 (Moon in Leo)   Mercury moves into your fifth house. You communicate well with children and loved ones. You act as a wise counselor. You get your ideas across related to a creative project. Take a chance; it'll pay off.

Friday, August 29 (Moon in Leo)   The moon is in your third house. Work on your journal. You write from a deep place. You could gather with relatives or neighbors. If so, try to keep conscious control of your emotions when talking with others.

Saturday, August 30 (Moon in Leo to Virgo 2:19 a.m.) Venus moves into your fifth house. Pursue creative projects, especially if you love what you're doing or you're working with someone you love. You could feel possessive toward loved ones.

Sunday, August 31 (Moon in Virgo)   The moon is in your fourth house. You deal with your foundations. Spend time at home with your family. Recall your dreams. Retreat to a private place to gather your wits. Attend to a home-repair project.

SEPTEMBER 2008

Monday, September 1 (Moon in Virgo to Libra 7:45 a.m.)   It's a number 5 day. Let go of old structures; get a new point of view. Approach the day in an unconventional way. Experiment, promote new ideas, and take chances. Get ready for change.

Tuesday, September 2 (Moon in Libra)   The moon is in your fifth house. Be yourself. Be emotionally honest. There's great emotional depth in a relationship. You could feel possessive of loved ones and children. Nurture a creative project.

Wednesday, September 3 (Moon in Libra to Scorpio 4:03 p.m.)   It's a number 7 day. A confidential matter that directly affects you comes to your attention. Dig deep for answers, but don't make any final decisions until tomorrow. Avoid confusion and conflicts.

Thursday, September 4 (Moon in Scorpio)   The moon is in your sixth house. You could feel somewhat emotionally repressed. Don't let your fears hold you back. Confront them. Attend to details and help others where you can, but know when to say enough is enough.

Friday, September 5 (Moon in Scorpio)   Your experiences could get intense and emotional. Control issues surface. Passions run high. You tend to go to extremes and deal with everything through your emotions if you don't check yourself.

Saturday, September 6 (Moon in Scorpio to Sagittarius 3:12 a.m.)   It's a number 1 day. After a few rough days, you get a fresh start. Launch new ideas. Get out and meet new people and have new experiences. In romance, make room for a new love.

Sunday, September 7 (Moon in Sagittarius)   Jupiter goes direct in your eighth house. You expand your horizons with the help of a loved one or partner. You see the big picture. You benefit through shared resources. An interest in metaphysics expands.

Monday, September 8 (Moon in Sagittarius to Capricorn 3:46 p.m.)   It's a number 3 day. Your popularity is on the rise. You express yourself well. Expect an invitation from a friend or loved one. Be happy, positive, and upbeat. Play your hunches. Your attitude determines everything.

Tuesday, September 9 (Moon in Capricorn)   The moon is in your fifth house. It's a good creative time. You have an ability to tap deeply into the collective unconscious. You're loving, protective, and nurturing with children. Animals play a role.

Wednesday, September 10 (Moon in Capricorn)   The moon is in your eighth house. The focus is dealing with your shared assets in any joint venture. It could relate to marriage or a business partnership. Sex issues may play a role. Alternately, you explore life's mysteries, including what happens at the end of life.

Thursday, September 11 (Moon in Capricorn to Aquarius 3:20 a.m.)   It's a number 6 day. It's a service day. Be diplomatic in dealing with others, including those who nag and complain. Be generous and understanding. Domestic purchases are highlighted.

Friday, September 12 (Moon in Aquarius)   The moon is in your ninth house. You could prepare for or plan a long trip to a foreign country. You take new interest in worldviews, ideas, philosophy, and mythology. Sign up for a workshop or seminar.

Saturday, September 13 (Moon in Aquarius to Pisces 12:05 p.m.)   It's a number 8 day. It's your power day. You attract financial success. You have opportunities to expand, to gain recognition, fame, and power.

Sunday, September 14 (Moon in Pisces)   The moon is in your tenth house. Matters related to your profession or career come into focus. You get along well with fellow workers. Help others where you can. You could deal with bosses. Make sure you control your emotions.

Monday, September 15 (Moon in Pisces to Aries 5:39 p.m.)
It's a number 1 day. You're at the top of your cycle. Stress individuality and originality. Get started on a new project, and don't be afraid to turn in a new direction. Creative people play a role.

Tuesday, September 16 (Moon in Aries) The moon is in your eleventh house. Focus on your wishes and dreams, Gemini. You may gather with a group of like-minded friends who can help you while you aid the group's goals. Relations with friends go well.

Wednesday, September 17 (Moon in Aries to Taurus 8:57 p.m.) It's a number 3 day. Your imagination is keen. Play your hunches. Stay optimistic. Your charm and wit are appreciated. Make time to listen to others.

Thursday, September 18 (Moon in Taurus) The moon is in your twelfth house. Withdraw from the action and take time to turn inward. It's a great day for intuitive placement or a spiritual discipline.

Friday, September 19 (Moon in Taurus to Gemini 11:17 p.m.) It's a number 5 day. Get ready for change. Release old structures. Find a new point of view. Be more careful since you'll be in a hurry and could be accident prone.

Saturday, September 20 (Moon in Gemini) The moon is in your first house. It's all about self-awareness. You're particularly sensitive to the moods of others, and your mood varies. Your feeling and thoughts are aligned.

Sunday, September 21 (Moon in Gemini) You're feeling creative, Gemini. It's a particularly good day for expressing yourself in writing. With the moon on the ascendant, your face is in front of the public. You feel vital, and relations with the opposite sex go well.

Monday, September 22 (Moon in Gemini to Cancer 1:49 a.m.) It's a number 8 day. It's your power day. Go for it. Expect a financial coup. Be courageous; and let go of any fears of failure. Business discussions go well.

Tuesday, September 23 (Moon in Cancer)   Venus moves into your sixth house. It's a good day for a romantic flirtation at work. You're concerned about your appearance. Your work and health issues are resolved. Everything goes easier for you.

Wednesday, September 24 (Moon in Cancer to Leo 5:14 a.m.)   Mercury goes retrograde in your fifth house. Communications can be difficult, especially with loved ones and children. They might misinterpret what you say, or you might misunderstand them. Creative projects could be delayed. Leave plenty of time for short journeys.

Thursday, September 25 (Moon in Leo)   The moon is in your third house. Your communications with others are subjective and could be misunderstood. A female relative plays a role. Keep conscious control of your emotions when communicating with others.

Friday, September 26 (Moon in Leo to Virgo 9:53 a.m.) It's a number 3 day. Your charm and wit are appreciated. Your popularity is on the rise. Expect an invitation from a friend. Stay positive and optimistic. Make time to listen to others, and spread your own good news.

Saturday, September 27 (Moon in Virgo)   The moon is in your fourth house. Work at home if you can arrange it. Retreat to a private place to spend some time in meditation. But come out and do something with family members. Plan or carry out a home-repair project.

Sunday, September 28 (Moon in Virgo to Libra 4:06 p.m.) It's a number 5 day. Freedom of thought and action is emphasized. Variety is the spice of life. You can overcome obstacles with ease. Experiment; take a risk. Change your perspective.

Monday, September 29 (Moon in Libra)   The moon is in your fifth house. It's a great day for romance, Gemini. Go out with that special person or plan a date. You're also involved with the creative facets of your life.

Tuesday, September 30 (Moon in Libra)   It's a number 7 day. There's an aura of mystery surrounding the day. You set off on an excursion into the unknown. Dig deep; investigate a secret matter. Look beneath the surface for answers or explanations. See things as they are, not how you would like them to be.

OCTOBER 2008

Wednesday, October 1 (Moon in Libra to Scorpio 12:27 a.m.)   The moon is in your sixth house. The month begins with a service day. Help others wherever you can. Stay in touch with someone who is ill. But don't spread yourself too thin. Watch your own health. Don't forget to exercise.

Thursday, October 2 (Moon in Scorpio)   You feel passionate about whatever you're investigating. Something is missing or out of focus, and you're going to find out what it is. You could deal with secrets.

Friday, October 3 (Moon in Scorpio to Sagittarius 11:15 a.m.)   Mars is in your sixth house. There are energy and activity related to physical activity, working out, and dealing with your health issues. Swimming would be a good activity. You look for the bottom line.

Saturday, October 4 (Moon in Sagittarius)   The moon is in your seventh house. You deal intensely with partnerships, either business or personal. Loved ones and partners play an important role. Be aware that any conflicts will be emotional.

Sunday, October 5 (Moon in Sagittarius to Capricorn 11:49 p.m.)   It's a number 1 day. You're at the top of your cycle. You get a fresh start. Be independent and creative. Refuse to be discouraged by naysayers. In romance, a flirtation turns more serious.

Monday, October 6 (Moon in Capricorn)   The moon is in your eighth house. Your experience might turn intense, especially if you're dealing with shared possessions. You could attract powerful people to you. An interest in metaphysics plays a role. Sex, death, and rebirth could be current themes.

Tuesday, October 7 (Moon in Capricorn)   You're goal oriented. You could deal with banks and financial institutions. Elderly people play a role. Your ambition and drive to succeed are highlighted.

Wednesday, October 8 (Moon in Capricorn to Aquarius 12:03 p.m.)   It's a number 4 day. Take care of your obligations. Persevere to get things done. Don't get sloppy in your work. You may need to tear down in order to rebuild. Revise and rewrite.

Thursday, October 9 (Moon in Aquarius)   The moon is in your ninth house. You probably feel restless and look beyond the everyday scope of your life. Ideas, philosophies, and worldviews catch your interest. You might plan or daydream about a long journey to a foreign land.

Friday, October 10 (Moon in Aquarius to Pisces 9:31 p.m.)   It's a number 6 day. The focus turns to helping others. Be understanding, generous, and tolerant. Diplomacy wins the way. An adjustment in your domestic scene may be needed.

Saturday, October 11 (Moon in Pisces)   The moon is in your tenth house. Your profession or career is highlighted. You communicate well with coworkers, Gemini. You're responsive to the needs of a group. It's a good day for sales and dealing with the public.

Sunday, October 12 (Moon in Pisces)   Your imagination is highlighted. Watch for psychic events and synchronicities. Pay attention to your dreams. Ideas bubble to the surface. Seek universal knowledge and eternal truths. Compassion is emphasized.

Monday, October 13 (Moon in Pisces to Aries 3:07 a.m.) It's a number 9 day. Strive for universal appeal. Look beyond the immediate. Discard preconceived notions. Visualize your future, set your goals, and then get to work. Your sex appeal is heightened.

Tuesday, October 14 (Moon in Aries) The moon is in your eleventh house. Initiate a new project. Friends play an important role, especially if you join together with a group of like-minded individuals. Focus on your wishes and dreams.

Wednesday, October 15 (Moon in Aries to Taurus 5:31 a.m.) Mercury goes direct. Confusion, miscommunication, and delays recede into the past. Things move smoothly. You get your message across. Everything works better, including computers and other electronic equipment.

Thursday, October 16 (Moon in Taurus) The moon is in your twelfth house. Withdraw from the action and keep to yourself. Work on a solo project. Keep your feelings secret. Relations with the opposite sex can be difficult. Things affecting you from the past could surface.

Friday, October 17 (Moon in Taurus to Gemini 6:26 a.m.) It's a number 4 day, and the moon enters your first house. You'll be concerned with your self-image and dealing with the person you are becoming. Don't obsess. Focus on getting organized, clearing out the old, and preparing for the new. You're building a creative base.

Saturday, October 18 (Moon in Gemini) Venus moves into your seventh house. Any type of creative partnership works well. You feel physically vital and get along well with the opposite sex. It's a great day for romance. You're sensitive to the feelings of others, particularly a partner.

Sunday, October 19 (Moon in Gemini to Cancer 7:41 a.m.)   It's a number 6 day. It's your service day. Do a good deed for someone. Try to make people happy. Domestic purchases are highlighted. Dance to your own tune.

Monday, October 20 (Moon in Cancer)   The moon is in your second house. Deal with finances. Take care of payments and collect what's owed to you. Consider your priorities for handling income. Put off big purchases for a few days.

Tuesday, October 21 (Moon in Cancer to Leo 10:36 a.m.)   It's a number 8 day. It's your money day. The financial picture brightens. Business dealings go well. You're watched by people in power. Be courageous.

Wednesday, October 22 (Moon in Leo)   You're on! Strut your stuff. Drama is highlighted. Promote whatever you're passionate about. You're impulsive and honest. Focus on advertising and self-promotion. Showmanship is the key word.

Thursday, October 23 (Moon in Leo to Virgo 3:41 p.m.)   It's a number 1 day. You get a fresh start. You're at the top of your cycle. Stress your individuality. Begin a new project; don't be afraid to turn in a new direction. Trust your hunches. Be ambitious and persistent.

Friday, October 24 (Moon in Virgo)   The moon is in your fourth house. Stick close to home. Spend time with loved ones, and work on a home-improvement project. Take time to retreat to a quiet place for meditation. You feel somewhat moody and sensitive to the feelings of others.

Saturday, October 25 (Moon in Virgo to Libra 10:48 p.m.)   It's a number 3 day. Be optimistic and fun loving. Approach the day with a positive attitude, and watch how things fall in place. Your wit and charm pay off. Stay flexible, and watch for opportunities.

Sunday, October 26 (Moon in Libra)   The moon is in your fifth house. Your creative juices flow. It's a great day for pursuing something innovative and original that inspires you. In love, there's great depth in romance. You feel particularly sensual.

Monday, October 27 (Moon in Libra)   Yesterday's energy continues to flow. Romance and relationships are highlighted. There's also an emphasis on creativity, personal grace, and magnetism.

Tuesday, October 28 (Moon in Libra to Scorpio 7:48 a.m.)   It's a number 6 day. Be understanding and helpful, even in the face of emotional outbursts. Diplomacy is called for. Make intelligent concessions to your family.

Wednesday, October 29 (Moon in Scorpio)   The moon is in your sixth house. You could feel put upon by others who make unfair demands. Offer help and encouragement, but know when to say enough is enough. Don't let your fears hold you back in your daily activities.

Thursday, October 30 (Moon in Scorpio to Sagittarius 6:41 p.m.)   It's a number 8 day. It's your power day. Stick with the number 8 in any speculation. Open your mind to a new approach that could result in big bucks. You attract financial success, but be careful not to hurt others. Remember that you're playing with power.

Friday, October 31 (Moon in Sagittarius)   The moon is in your seventh house. The emphasis is on partnerships. Don't make waves. Let things develop in their own time. Don't criticize, condemn, or complain. Be kind and understanding.

NOVEMBER 2008

Saturday, November 1 (Moon in Sagittarius)   Neptune goes direct in your ninth house. Things clear up related to plans for college. It could involve yourself, your child, or another relative. If traveling overseas, you'll have a great sense of compassion for those who are not as well off as you.

Sunday, November 2—Daylight Saving Time Ends (Moon in Sagittarius to Capricorn 6:13 a.m.) It's a number 8 day, your power day. Look for a financial windfall, an unexpected check. Business discussions work to your favor. People in power are watching you. Be courageous. Find a new approach that will bring in big money.

Monday, November 3 (Moon in Capricorn) The moon is in your eighth house. You deal with life's mysteries, including end-of-life issues. Your sexual energy is strong. You're also resourceful and able to develop new assets and abilities. That's especially true in dealing with projects involving a partner.

Tuesday, November 4 (Moon in Capricorn to Aquarius 7:02 p.m.) Mercury moves into your sixth house. There's a lot of activity and communication in your job and daily responsibilities. Your e-mail box is full! You could receive a message, letter, or call from someone in the military or hear something about that person.

Wednesday, November 5 (Moon in Aquarius) The moon is in your ninth house. Issues related to publishing, publicity, or advertising arise. Foreign travel could be included. Check on your father's health or his situation at work.

Thursday, November 6 (Moon in Aquarius) Group activities are highlighted. A social event brings you in contact with people who are supportive of your efforts. Look beyond the immediate. Play your hunches. Follow your wishes and dreams.

Friday, November 7 (Moon in Aquarius to Pisces 5:44 a.m.) It's a number 4 day. Take some time to get organized. Be methodical and thorough. Revise and rewrite.

Tear down the old in order to build the new. Emphasize quality.

Saturday, November 8 (Moon in Pisces)   The moon is in your tenth house. Your life is public. You gain an elevation in prestige related to your profession and career. You get along better with coworkers, but don't blur the boundaries between your professional and personal lives.

Sunday, November 9 (Moon in Pisces to Aries 12:27 p.m.)   It's a number 6 day. It's all about service to others. Be diplomatic in your dealings with others. Make concessions, but don't abandon your principles. Do a good deed for someone.

Monday, November 10 (Moon in Aries)   The moon is in your eleventh house. You get along well with friends. You could gather with a group of like-minded individuals. You assist the group's efforts, but in doing so, you gain support for your own goals. Make sure that your goals are an expression of who you really are.

Tuesday, November 11 (Moon in Aries to Taurus 3:06 p.m.)   It's a number 8 day. Play it your way. You have a chance to gain recognition, fame, and power. You attract financial success. But remember that you're playing with power. So be careful not to hurt others.

Wednesday, November 12 (Moon in Taurus)   Venus moves into your eighth house. You see through people's masks and have an ability to understand their motives. You might be feeling jealous or possessive in a romance. You gain financially through your marriage or partnership.

Thursday, November 13 (Moon in Taurus to Gemini 3:13 p.m.)   It's a number 1 day. You're at the top of your cycle. You get a fresh start on a new project. Explore and discover. Your creativity is highlighted. Stress originality. In romance, a flirtation could get out of hand!

Friday, November 14 (Moon in Gemini)   The moon is in your first house. You get your batteries recharged. You're appealing to the public. You feel physically vital; relations with the opposite sex go well.

Saturday, November 15 (Moon in Gemini to Cancer 2:53 p.m.)   It's a number 3 day. Your attitude determines everything. Be happy, positive, and upbeat. Spread your good news. Make time for conversation and listen to others.

Sunday, November 16 (Moon in Cancer)   Mars moves into your seventh house. There's a lot of energy moving into a relationship. Be aware that this hot energy can help promote the relationship or tear it apart. It all depends on your approach. Be careful not to let others manipulate your feelings.

Monday, November 17 (Moon in Cancer to Leo 4:08 p.m.)   It's a number 5 day. It's all about freedom from restrictions, freedom of thought and action. Get ready for change. Find a new perspective. You could be changing jobs or moving.

Tuesday, November 18 (Moon in Leo)   The moon is in your third house. Take what you know and share it with others in your everyday world. But stay in conscious control of your emotions when talking with others. Express your deepest feelings in a journal.

Wednesday, November 19 (Moon in Leo to Virgo 8:13 p.m.)   It's a number 7 day. You launch a voyage into the unknown. You pursue something mysterious. Knowledge is essential to your success. Dig deep for information, and then consider what it means. Don't make any decisions based on your research until tomorrow.

Thursday, November 20 (Moon in Virgo)   The moon is in your fourth house. Stay close to home. Spend time with your family and work on a home–repair project. You're somewhat moody today, and you're also sensitive to the moods of others. Go with the flow.

Friday, November 21 (Moon in Virgo) Attend to details. Stop worrying and fretting. Watch your diet and get some exercise. But also take time to relax. Stick close to home. It's a good day to express your thoughts in a journal.

Saturday, November 22 (Moon in Virgo to Libra 3:20 a.m.) It's a number 1 day. Get out and meet new people. Pick up new ideas and have new experiences. Take the initiative to turn in a new direction. Originality is highlighted. In romance, you get a fresh start.

Sunday, November 23 (Moon in Libra) Mercury joins Mars in your seventh house. There's a lot of activity related to partnerships, either personal or business. You could be talking at length with a partner and signing contracts. It's a great time for getting married. Keep in mind it's a difficult time to remain detached and objective. You tend to express your opinions with emotion.

Monday, November 24 (Moon in Libra to Scorpio 12:54 p.m.) It's a number 3 day. Your popularity is on the rise. Your charm and wit are appreciated. Trust your intuition in dealing with others. Remain positive, upbeat, and flexible to changing circumstances. Ease up on your routines; take time to listen to others.

Tuesday, November 25 (Moon in Scorpio) The moon is in your sixth house. It's a service day. Do a good deed. Be diplomatic with someone who is nagging. A necessary adjustment in the domestic scene works to your advantage. Make an effort to beautify your home.

Wednesday, November 26 (Moon in Scorpio) Pluto returns to your eighth house after several months retrograde in your seventh house. Issues related to your finances arise again. The transformation that began early in the year but slowed down picks up. Be aware that an increase in your spouse's or partner's income could adversely affect matters related to taxes. Be careful with investments and insurance.

Thursday, November 27 (Moon in Scorpio to Sagittarius 12:14 a.m.)   Uranus goes direct in your tenth house. There could be a sudden and unexpected change in your workplace related to your profession or career. It could be a promotion, a change of job description, or a move to another company. You might even decide to start your own company.

Friday, November 28 (Moon in Sagittarius)   The moon is in your seventh house of partnerships. The focus is on personal or business relationships. You could sign legal papers. Be aware that any conflict will be emotional. Look to the big picture. Don't limit yourself.

Saturday, November 29 (Moon in Sagittarius to Capricorn 12:48 p.m.)   It's a number 8 day. Focus on a power play. It's all about material success. You attract great financial rewards. Remain goal oriented, but be careful not to hurt others as you gain power and recognition.

Sunday, November 30 (Moon in Capricorn)   The moon is in your eighth house. Your energy and experiences, especially related to sex, are intense. Matters related to death and rebirth also could play a role. An interest in metaphysical subjects comes into play.

DECEMBER 2008

Monday, December 1 (Moon in Capricorn)   The moon is in your eighth house. Your sexual energy is strong, your experiences intense. You could be possessive about belongings, especially those that you share. A project that has died or been put on hold could be revived.

Tuesday, December 2 (Moon in Capricorn to Aquarius 1:45 a.m.)   It's a number 9 day. Finish whatever you've been working on, and get ready for something new. But don't start a new project.

Wednesday, December 3 (Moon in Aquarius) The moon is in your ninth house. A publishing project could take a big step forward. Promote or publicize yourself or your activities. Get away from your usual routines. Find time to pursue a philosophy or worldview that interests you.

Thursday, December 4 (Moon in Aquarius to Pisces 1:24 p.m.) It's a number 2 day. The emphasis is on cooperation. Be kind and understanding. Let things develop with a partner. Don't make waves, rush about, or show resentment. Go with the flow.

Friday, December 5 (Moon in Pisces) The moon is in your tenth house. You're responsive to the needs and moods of a group or the public in general. People in powerful positions are watching. You get an elevation in prestige related to your profession.

Saturday, December 6 (Moon in Pisces to Aries 9:45 p.m.) It's a number 4 day. Emphasize quality in whatever you're working on. Be practical with money. You're in the right place at the right time. Within 24 hours, an object you lost or misplaced is found.

Sunday, December 7 (Moon in Aries) Venus moves into your ninth house. A love affair could ignite with a foreign-born person. Or you might fall in love with a foreign land and its people. You probably feel romantic and restless, ready to get away from the usual routines.

Monday, December 8 (Moon in Aries) The moon is in your eleventh house. You have deep contact with friends. Focus on your wishes and dreams. You could get help in realizing them by joining a group of like-minded individuals.

Tuesday, December 9 (Moon in Aries to Taurus 1:53 a.m.) It's a number 7 day. Secrets, mystery, and intrigue play a tantalizing role. You could launch an investigation concerning the unknown. Search beneath the surface for truth. See things as they are, not as you wish them to be.

Wednesday, December 10 (Moon in Taurus) The moon is in your twelfth house. Work at home. Remain behind the scenes and out of public view. Keep your thoughts and feelings secret. Use your intuition in making any decisions. Unconscious attitudes and matters from the past can be difficult.

Thursday, December 11 (Moon in Taurus to Gemini 2:34 a.m.) It's a number 9 day. Look beyond the immediate. Nurture your intuition. Visualize for the future, set your goals, and then get to work. Be confident, not obsequious.

Friday, December 12 (Moon in Gemini) Mercury moves into your eighth house. You communicate your ideas about life and death. There's interest in metaphysical subjects and the connection between science and spirit. You can gain considerable knowledge through your intuition rather than through books.

Saturday, December 13 (Moon in Gemini to Cancer 1:41 a.m.) It's a number 2 day. Use your intuition. The spotlight is on cooperation. Marriage is particularly important to you. Be kind and understanding. Don't make waves or take on any major projects.

Sunday, December 14 (Moon in Cancer) The moon is in your second house. You seek financial and domestic security. It's a good day for investments, but be practical. You feel your best surrounded by familiar objects. It's not the objects that are important but the feelings you associate with them.

Monday, December 15 (Moon in Cancer to Leo 1:23 a.m.) It's a number 4 day. Control your impulses. Examine your budget. Persevere to get things done. Clean out the old to make room for the new. Revise, rewrite. Don't get sloppy. You're building foundations for the future.

Tuesday, December 16 (Moon in Leo)   The moon is in your third house. Your communications with others in your everyday world are subjective. You need to keep conscious control of your emotions while communicating with others, especially relatives or neighbors.

Wednesday, December 17 (Moon in Leo to Virgo 3:36 a.m.)   It's a number 6 day. Diplomacy wins the day. Do a good deed for someone. Visit a sick family member or friend. Focus on making other people happy. Avoid scattering your energies.

Thursday, December 18 (Moon in Virgo)   The moon is in your fourth house. Retreat to a private place. You're dealing with the foundations of who you are. Meditate and keep track of your dreams. Spend time at home with your family and loved ones. You may feel emotionally possessive.

Friday, December 19 (Moon in Virgo to Libra 9:23 a.m.)   It's a number 8 day. Play it your way. You have an opportunity to gain recognition, fame, and power. Open your mind to a new approach that could lead to big bucks. Avoid doing anything that would hurt others.

Saturday, December 20 (Moon in Libra)   The moon is in your fifth house. Be open and honest. In love, there's great emotional depth. It's a great creative time. You have the ability to tap deeply into the collective unconscious.

Sunday, December 21 (Moon in Libra to Scorpio 6:37 p.m.)   It's a number 1 day. You're at the top of your cycle—time for a new beginning. You play a leadership role. Be independent and creative. Refuse to be discouraged by naysayers. A flirtation could get out of hand.

Monday, December 22 (Moon in Scorpio)   The moon is in your sixth house. Attend to health matters. Make doctor or dentist appointments. Exercise and watch your diet. You could be sensitive to the moods of others. You feel an emotional security related to your daily work.

Tuesday, December 23 (Moon in Scorpio)   Your emotions could flare up. You may have a tendency to go to extremes. Look into a matter that's taking place behind closed doors. Control issues could surface. Forgive and forget.

Wednesday, December 24 (Moon in Scorpio to Sagittarius 6:14 a.m.)   It's a number 4 day. Your organizational skills pay off. You build a solid base for your creative efforts. Persevere to get things done before the holidays begin. Don't get sloppy in your work. Control your impulse to wander off. Be methodical and thorough.

Thursday, December 25 (Moon in Sagittarius)   The moon is in your seventh house. Cooperation, partnership, and teamwork play roles. Loved ones are important. Be aware that any conflicts will be emotional. Merry Christmas.

Friday, December 26 (Moon in Sagittarius to Capricorn 6:57 p.m.)   It's a number 6 day. Focus on making people happy. Domestic purchases are highlighted. Beautify your home. Be generous and tolerant. Do a good deed for someone.

Saturday, December 27 (Moon in Capricorn)   Mars moves into your eighth house. You have an ability to dig deeply into secret matters. You also cut to the heart of a matter regarding finances. Your sex drive is strong; so is a desire for leadership. Your intuition is strong regarding a potential partner.

Sunday, December 28 (Moon in Capricorn)   The moon, as well as Mars, is in your eighth house. Yesterday's energy expands. There's an intense emotional involvement with someone. You enjoy the good things in life together. Your psychic abilities are also aroused, and you could pursue an interest in life-after-death questions.

Monday, December 29 (Moon in Capricorn to Aquarius 7:44 a.m.)   It's a number 9 day. Accept whatever comes your way, but don't start anything new until tomorrow. Use the day for reflection, expansion, and concluding projects. Visualize for the future, set your goals, and then get to work.

Tuesday, December 30 (Moon in Aquarius)   The moon is in your ninth house. You need to get away from the usual routine. You wish to expand your life in the coming year through travel and study, especially related to philosophy and metaphysics. Much of what you learn could come through dreams and meditation.

Wednesday, December 31 (Moon in Aquarius)   Saturn goes retrograde. It's not the greatest way to end the year, with a major planet turning retrograde. However, remember that Saturn has its place in the grand scheme of things. Without it, the physical universe wouldn't hold together very well!

HAPPY NEW YEAR!

SYDNEY OMARR

Born on August 5, 1926, in Philadelphia, Pennsylvania, Sydney Omarr was the only person ever given full-time duty in the U.S. Army as an astrologer. He is regarded as the most erudite astrologer of our time and the best known, through his syndicated column and his radio and television programs (he was Merv Griffin's "resident astrologer"). Omarr has been called the most "knowledgeable astrologer since Evangeline Adams." His forecasts of Nixon's downfall, the end of World War II in mid-August of 1945, the assassination of John F. Kennedy, Roosevelt's election to a fourth term and his death in office . . . these and many others are on the record and quoted enough to be considered "legendary."

ABOUT THE SERIES

This is one of a series of twelve *Sydney Omarr® Day-by-Day Astrological Guides* for the signs of 2008. For questions and comments about the book, contact the author at www.tjmacgregor.com.